ASP.NET Core 5 Secure Coding Cookbook

Practical recipes for tackling vulnerabilities in your ASP.NET web applications

Roman Canlas

BIRMINGHAM—MUMBAI

ASP.NET Core 5 Secure Coding Cookbook

Copyright © 2021 Packt Publishing

Group Product Manager: Aaron Lazar

Publishing Product Manager: Richa Tripathi

Senior Editor: Ruvika Rao

Content Development Editor: Vaishali Ramkumar

Technical Editor: Karan Solanki

Copy Editor: Safis Editing

Project Coordinator: Deeksha Thakkar

Proofreader: Safis Editing

Indexer: Manju Arasan

Production Designer: Nilesh Mohite

First published: June 2021

Production reference: 3040821

Published by Packt Publishing Ltd.

Livery Place

35 Livery Street

Birmingham

B3 2PB, UK.

ISBN 978-1-80107-156-7

www.packt.com

To the reader, I hope I have piqued your interest in writing secure code and you'll learn as much as I have in writing this book.

– Roman Canlas

Foreword

When tackling the topic of security, we should ask ourselves why we make technology and tools in the first place. Do we create for security or for a specific application? Afterall, there is a reason why we call software *applications*. We are applying purposes to our software. For this wisdom, we look to a woman who knew a lot about software, hardware, and big boats:

"A ship in port is safe, but that's not what ships are built for."

- Grace Hopper

Similarly, your application is built for a reason. But, as Grace implies, security must be achieved, even if it isn't our primary purpose.

In *ASP.NET Core 5 Secure Coding Cookbook*, author *Roman Canlas* has set a precedent by writing a book with a title that you have to think about for a few seconds, before you can fully grok its purpose. Much like the title, you'll find yourself pondering and contemplating over the content of this book, finding new ways to apply this wisdom. You'll find practical solutions and detailed explanations, from security coding fundamentals, to fixing issues in injection, authentication, exposed data, and more.

One of the backbones of ASP.NET Core 5 is to provide an application development framework that champions and enables secure coding. It is no accident that Microsoft has provided these tools.

"Security is... our top priority - if we don't solve these security problems, then people will hold back."

- Bill Gates

As Bill Gates once said, there is nothing more important than security. If your code isn't secure, then, as a developer, you will not build a robust application; it will be limited. Likewise, your users will also hold back and will be hesitant to how they might use and trust your application. It's critical that the framework allows secure coding capabilities, and it's equally important that you take this book to heart and implement these patterns, processes, and practices.

Take this book with you in your career, and then refer back to these recipes as often as you can. Just like chefs should review their recipes before they cook their culinary creations, you also should review these recipes before you serve your customers with a masterpiece of your own.

Ed Price
Senior Program Manager of Architectural Publishing
Microsoft | Azure Architecture Center (`http://aka.ms/Architecture`)
Co-Author of 5 Books, including *The Azure Cloud Native Architecture Mapbook* and *ASP.NET Core 5 for Beginners* (both from **Packt**)

Contributors

About the author

Roman Canlas is a senior application security engineer working at a Fortune 500 company where he successfully established its global application security program from the ground up. His years of experience as a developer have led to him being an expert in secure code reviews and static application security testing, focusing on web technologies.

Roman holds multiple certifications: the GIAC Web Application Penetration Tester (GWAPT), ISC2's Certified Secure Software Lifecycle Professional (CSSLP), and EC-Council's Certified Application Security Engineer in .NET (CASE.NET).

Roman also has a master's degree in information systems and a bachelor's in computer science.

To Doug, Tim, and Chuck, thanks for believing in me and supporting my personal endeavor. To Richa, for believing in the book's topic and giving me the opportunity to write for Packt. To Vaishali, Ruvika, Karan, Nithya, Deeksha, and the rest of the Packt team, I thank you all for your tireless efforts. To Allan Mangune and Hemant Shah, both great technical reviewers, I am grateful for your comments and feedback.

About the reviewers

Hemant Shah is a strong advocate of shift left in the industry. His software developer training and background allow him to speak the developer's language in managing AppSec programs and helps the development team understand the value and impact of delivering secure software. He is a cloud and application security professional with a bachelor's degree in information technology with around 15 years of experience in designing, troubleshooting, and securing large-scale applications with sound exposure to OWASP. Secure coding reviews, risk assessment procedures, authentication technologies, policy formation, threat modeling, and design reviews are the key areas he is focused on.

Allan SP Mangune is a certified public accountant and holds a post-graduate degree of Master of Science in computer information systems from the University of Phoenix. He has been writing software since 2000 and practicing secure coding since he gained, in 2008, his Certified Ethical Hacker v5 credential. He has helped clients with their digital transformation journey and digital security. He has delivered Agile project management workshops to large organizations for more than a decade. He is a certified ScrumMaster and holds a Prince2 Agile Foundation certificate. For 10 years, he was awarded Microsoft MVP for ASP.NET and Development Technologies. He used to be a Microsoft Certified Trainer. He builds his own drones during his free time.

Table of Contents

Preface

1

Secure Coding Fundamentals

2

Injection Flaws

3

Broken Authentication

4

Sensitive Data Exposure

5

XML External Entities

8

Cross-Site Scripting

9

Insecure Deserialization

10

Using Components with Known Vulnerabilities

13

Best Practices

Other Books You May Enjoy

Index

Preface

ASP.NET Core is fast becoming the web application framework of choice for developers and is now in the top ranks of platform popularity. ASP.NET Core web applications are also no exception when it comes to being targets for malicious attacks. As more and more web developers write code to create these ASP.NET Core web applications, the need to educate developers on writing secure code also increases.

An ASP.NET Core application developed with secure code can withstand attacks and help reduce its risk of exploitation. With proper guidance on fixing security flaws in code, ASP.NET Core web applications can prevent or stop security problems.

This book covers code examples written in C# with steps on remediating various ASP.NET Core web application vulnerabilities discovered by a secure code review or security test. You'll find practical examples and different ways to solve the security bugs introduced by insecure code in a recipe-style format.

This book begins with a chapter on the fundamentals of secure coding, but the succeeding content is patterned using the OWASP Top 10 (2017 version). The OWASP Top 10 is the de facto standard documentation for the most common risks to web applications.

Each chapter in this book (starting with Chapter 2, Injection Flaws) represents problem-solution content for each type of risk. Chapter 12, Miscellaneous Vulnerabilities focuses on various other vulnerabilities that were previously in the OWASP Top 10 for additional coverage. The last chapter discusses secure coding best practices.

By the end of this book, you will be able to identify the different types of vulnerabilities in ASP.NET Core web applications and will have the know-how to remediate them in code.

Who this book is for

This book is intended for developers and software engineers who use the ASP.NET Core framework to develop web applications. Ideal for both the beginner and the experienced, this book will guide the novice on learning the necessary foundations of writing secure code, and the seasoned to use it as a quick source for step-by-step ASP.NET Core secure coding recipes.

This book is also excellent for application security engineers who want to know more about the details of securing ASP.NET Core applications through code and will help them understand how to fix issues identified by the security tests that they perform daily.

What this book covers

Chapter 1, *Securing Coding Fundamentals*, is about basic secure coding patterns that every ASP.NET Core developer must know.

Chapter 2, *Injection Flaws*, explores recipes for various injection flaws, such as SQL injection, NoSQL injection, command injection, LDAP injection, and XPath injection.

Chapter 3, *Broken Authentication*, covers recipes for vulnerabilities that focus on insufficiently protected credentials, user enumeration, weak password requirements, and insufficient session expiration.

Chapter 4, *Sensitive Data Exposure*, shows how to implement HTTPS in our ASP.NET Core web applications, enable HSTS, ensure that the latest version of TLS is applied, and secure the cryptographic keys to prevent data leakage

Chapter 5, *XML External Entities*, covers recipes for remediating malicious XML External Entities. This chapter explains a sample insecure code snippet on XXE injection. An explanation of how to fix XXE injection will be discussed.

Chapter 6, *Broken Access Control*, explores recipes that use the built-in authorization mechanism in ASP.NET Core and the steps to implement role-based authorization to prevent unauthorized access to resources in your web application.

Chapter 7, *Security Misconfiguration*, discusses recipes to prevent security misconfiguration by turning debugging off in code, adding security features, and stopping unwanted information leaks to prying attackers with proper application settings.

Chapter 8, *Cross-Site Scripting*, covers recipes for remediating different types of XSS. This chapter explains insecure code for Reflected, Stored, and DOM XSS. This chapter also explains how to fix these cross-site scripting vulnerabilities in code.

Chapter 9, *Insecure Deserialization*, covers recipes on how to safely deserialize input using properly configured libraries, mitigate risks that an obsolete .NET class brings in your ASP.NET Core web application, and use a better deserializer alternative to securely deserialize data streams.

Chapter 10, *Using Components with Known Vulnerabilities*, discusses recipes for fixing ASP.NET Core web applications that use components with known vulnerabilities.

Chapter 11, Insufficient Logging and Monitoring, explores recipes for fixing insufficient logging and monitoring in ASP.NET Core web applications and explains how the lack of these features puts web applications at risk.

Chapter 12, Miscellaneous Vulnerabilities, discusses recipes for fixing vulnerabilities that are no longer in the OWASP Top 10 list and various ASP.NET Core web application vulnerabilities.

Chapter 13, Best Practices, covers best practice recipes with proven patterns that enable ASP.NET Core security features.

To get the most out of this book

Follow along the recipes using the sample Online Banking web application found in this book's GitHub repository. Each recipe has a `before` and `after` folder. You will begin with each recipe using the `before` folder with an initial version of the sample Online Banking web application as a starting point. The `after` folder will serve as a reference to validate whether all steps are executed correctly.

.NET 5	Windows
Visual Studio Code	
DB Browser for SQLite	
Git	
MongoDB 3.4	
ApacheDS	
DevSkim	
Retire.js	

All the recipes in this book were tested using Windows. Most of the recipes should also work in Linux and macOS (with ASP.NET Core being a cross-platform web framework) except for recipes that require software and plugins that only run in Windows.

If you are using the digital version of this book, we advise you to type the code yourself or access the code via the GitHub repository (link available in the next section). Doing so will help you avoid any potential errors related to the copying and pasting of code.

You may benefit from following the author on Twitter (https://twitter.com/ securecodeninja) **or adding them as a connection in LinkedIn** (https://www. linkedin.com/in/romancanlas)

Download the example code files

You can download the example code files for this book from GitHub at https://
github.com/PacktPublishing/ASP.NET-Core-Secure-Coding-Cookbook.
If there's an update to the code, it will be updated on the existing GitHub repository.

We also have other code bundles from our rich catalog of books and videos available at
https://github.com/PacktPublishing/. Check them out!

Download the color images

We also provide a PDF file that has color images of the screenshots/diagrams used
in this book. You can download it here: https://static.packt-cdn.com/
downloads/9781801071567_ColorImages.pdf.

Conventions used

There are a number of text conventions used throughout this book.

Code in text: Indicates code words in text, database table names, folder names,
filenames, file extensions, pathnames, dummy URLs, user input, and Twitter handles.
Here is an example: "The AddTransient method allows our custom validator
CustomerValidator to be discoverable by ASP.NET Core."

A block of code is set as follows:

```
if (result.Succeeded)
{
    _logger.LogInformation("User logged in.");
    return LocalRedirect(returnUrl);
}
```

When we wish to draw your attention to a particular part of a code block, the relevant
lines or items are set in bold:

```
var result = await
_signInManager.PasswordSignInAsync(Input.Email, Input.Password,
  Input.RememberMe, lockoutOnFailure: true);
```

Any command-line input or output is written as follows:

```
git clone https://github.com/PacktPublishing/ASP.NET-Core-
Secure-Coding-Cookbook.git
```

1. **Bold**: Indicates a new term, an important word, or words that you see onscreen. For example, words in menus or dialog boxes appear in the text like this. Here is an example: "Select one record and click its **Edit** link."

> **Tips or important notes**
> Appear like this.

Sections

In this book, you will find several headings that appear frequently (*Getting ready*, *How to do it...*, *How it works...*, *There's more...*, and *See also*).

To give clear instructions on how to complete a recipe, use these sections as follows:

Getting ready

This section tells you what to expect in the recipe and describes how to set up any software or any preliminary settings required for the recipe.

How to do it...

This section contains the steps required to follow the recipe.

How it works...

This section usually consists of a detailed explanation of what happened in the previous section.

There's more...

This section consists of additional information about the recipe in order to make you more knowledgeable about the recipe.

See also

This section provides helpful links to other useful information for the recipe.

Get in touch

Feedback from our readers is always welcome.

General feedback: If you have questions about any aspect of this book, mention the book title in the subject of your message and email us at customercare@packtpub.com.

Errata: Although we have taken every care to ensure the accuracy of our content, mistakes do happen. If you have found a mistake in this book, we would be grateful if you would report this to us. Please visit www.packtpub.com/support/errata, selecting your book, clicking on the Errata Submission Form link, and entering the details.

Piracy: If you come across any illegal copies of our works in any form on the internet, we would be grateful if you would provide us with the location address or website name. Please contact us at copyright@packt.com with a link to the material.

If you are interested in becoming an author: If there is a topic that you have expertise in and you are interested in either writing or contributing to a book, please visit authors.packtpub.com.

Share Your Thoughts

Once you've read *ASP.NET Core 5 Secure Coding Cookbook*, we'd love to hear your thoughts! Scan the QR code below to go straight to the Amazon review page for this book and share your feedback.

https://packt.link/r/180107156X

Your review is important to us and the tech community and will help us make sure we're delivering excellent quality content.

1
Secure Coding Fundamentals

Understanding secure coding principles is one of the foundations of being a security minded ASP.NET Core developer. Applying these concepts in practice by writing secure code will help your web applications improve their security posture.

This introductory chapter is all about basic secure coding patterns that every ASP.NET Core developer must know. Learning about these defensive techniques will help you mitigate security vulnerabilities in code, and with these recipes, you will be able to understand how to implement proper **input validation** by using **whitelisting**, perform **input sanitization**, and how to **escape output** and **protect data**.

In this chapter, we're going to cover the following recipes:

- Enabling whitelist input validation using validation attributes
- Whitelist validation using the `FluentValidation` library
- Syntactic and semantic validation
- Input sanitizing
- Input sanitization using the `HTMLSanitizer` library
- Output encoding using `HtmlEncoder`
- Output encoding using `UrlEncoder`
- Output encoding using `JavascriptEncoder`
- Protecting sensitive data using the Data Protection API

Technical requirements

This book was written and designed to be used with Visual Studio Code, Git, and .NET 5.0. The code examples in these recipes will be presented in ASP.NET Core Razor pages. The sample solution also uses SQLite as the database engine for a more simplified setup. You can find the code for this chapter at `https://github.com/PacktPublishing/ASP.NET-Core-Secure-Coding-Cookbook/tree/main/Chapter01`.

Input validation

One of the most effective ways to defend your application against injection attacks is *writing proper input validation*. This defensive programming technique verifies if the input conforms to an expected data format, such as data type, length, or range (to name a few). The input can be from an untrusted source, and without validation, a bad actor can feed malicious data to the ASP.NET Core web application, potentially exploiting a vulnerability. This process could affect the application and could lead it to perform unintended actions.

There are two ways to validate input:

- Blacklisting
- Whitelisting

With the blacklisting validation strategy, known bad input is defined in a list. The data is then verified against this list to decide if the input should be accepted or rejected. However, this approach is flawed as you can only define so much bad input, and it would not be a comprehensive list. An attacker can simply bypass this validation by constructing payloads that are not on the blacklist. Here's an example of blacklisting presented in pseudocode:

```
when receiving a string input
    for each character in string input
        if character is in blacklist
            reject string input
        return error
```

Whitelisting validation is the opposite, but it's the preferred tactic. Here's its equivalent in pseudocode:

```
when receiving a string input
    for each character in string input
        if character is not in whitelist
            reject string input
        return error
```

Here, known-good input is listed, where data is allowed into the system if it exists in the list and denied if not.

> **Note**
>
> The majority of this chapter focuses on input validation because I cannot emphasize enough how important it is to validate input. Proper input validation is perhaps the single most critical fundamental secure coding practice, and it will make your ASP.NET Core web application significantly improve its application security.

Enabling whitelist validation using validation attributes

Web developers can take advantage of the built-in validation framework that ASP.NET Core provides. The intrinsic **Data Annotation Attribute (DAA)** allows you to validate values that are bound to model properties. Validating against a matching pattern enables us to filter input, and we can specify the regular expression as our whitelist. If the model's value does not resemble a regular expression, it will be considered bad input.

There are plenty of validation attributes that you can use to build business rules around your model, but for us to implement whitelist validation, the `RegularExpression` attribute must come into play.

In this recipe, we will use the `RegularExpression` attribute to define a pattern for our model properties to whitelist characters.

Getting ready

Open the command shell and download the sample Online Banking app by cloning the ASP.NET Secure Coding Cookbook repository:

```
git clone https://github.com/PacktPublishing/ASP.NET-Core-
Secure-Coding-Cookbook.git
```

Run the sample app to verify that there are no build or compile errors. In your command shell, navigate to the sample app folder at `\Chapter01\input-validation\ before\OnlineBankingApp` and run the following command:

```
dotnet build
```

The `dotnet build` command will build our sample OnlineBankingApp project and its dependencies.

How to do it...

Let's take a look at the steps for this recipe:

1. From the starting exercise folder, launch Visual Studio Code by typing the following command:

    ```
    code .
    ```

2. Open the `Models/Customer.cs` file and add a
   `[RegularExpressionAttribute]` validation attribute on top of the
   `FirstName`, `MiddleName`, and `LastName` model properties, as highlighted in
   the following code. Include the `^[A-Z]+[a-zA-Z]*$` expression as well:

```
[RegularExpression(@"^[A-Z]+[a-zA-Z]*$",
    ErrorMessage = "First Name must contain only
        letters")]
[Display(Name = "First Name")]
[StringLength(60, MinimumLength = 3)]
[Required]
public string FirstName { get; set; }


[RegularExpression(@"^[A-Z]+[a-zA-Z]*$",
    ErrorMessage = "Middle Name must contain only
        letters")]
[Display(Name = "Middle Name")]
[StringLength(60, MinimumLength = 3)]
[Required]
public string MiddleName { get; set; }


[RegularExpression(@"^[A-Z]+[a-zA-Z]*$",
    ErrorMessage = "Last Name must contain only
        letters")]
[Display(Name = "Last Name")]
[StringLength(60, MinimumLength = 3)]
[Required]
public string LastName { get; set; }
```

3. Navigate to **Terminal** | **New Terminal** in the menu or simply press *Ctrl* + *Shift* + *'* in
   Visual Studio Code.

4. Type the following command in the Terminal to build and run the sample app:

```
dotnet run
```

5. Open a browser and go to `http://localhost:5000/Customers/Create`.

6.   The browser will display the web page for creating new customers, as shown in the following screenshot:

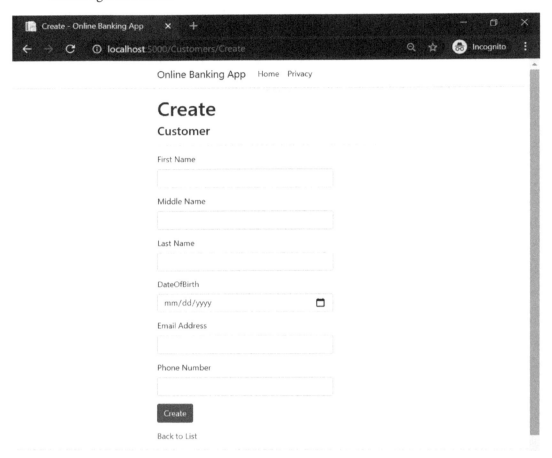

Figure 1.1 – Create Customer page

7.   In the **First Name** text box, enter an input that contains numbers and press *Tab* to shift the focus to a different input element.

8.   The validation will kick in and an error message will appear:

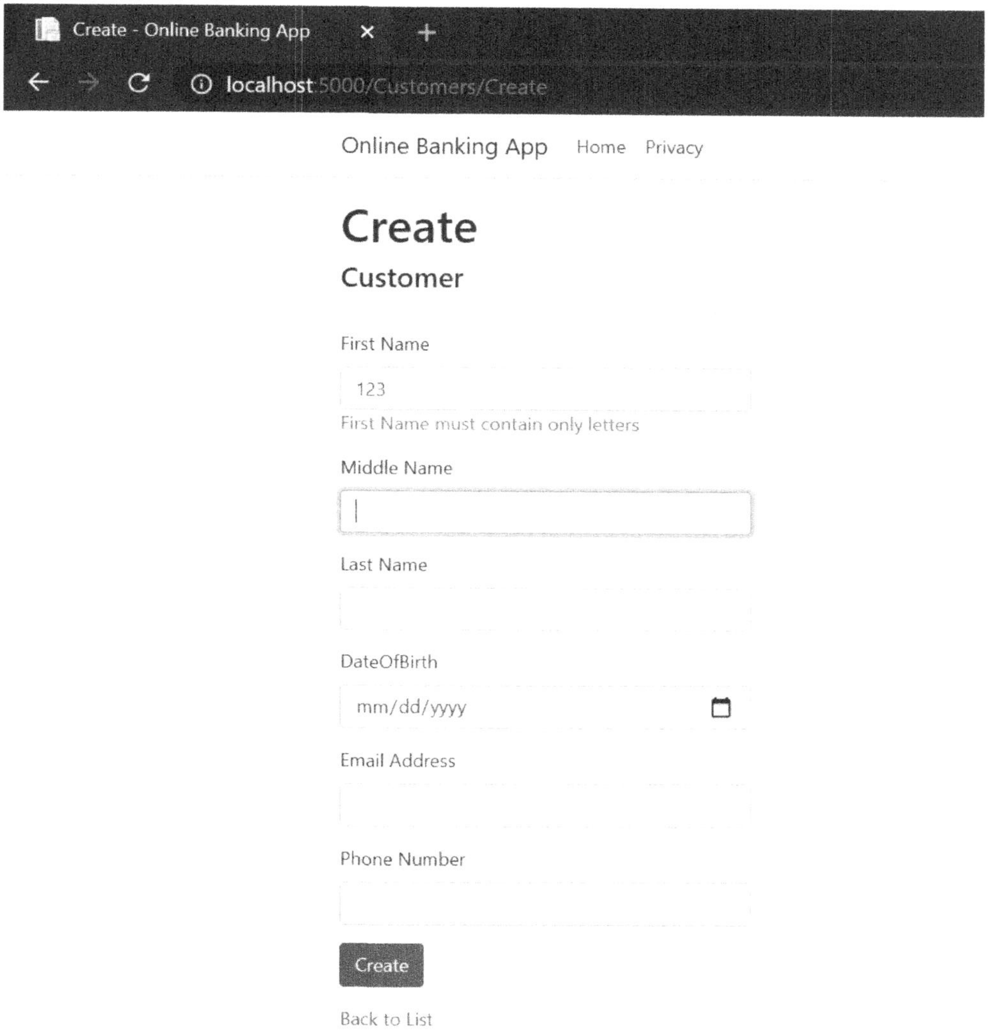

Figure 1.2 – First Name attribute validation

By using [RegularExpression] attribute validation, the validation rule was applied to the FirstName property model, thereby limiting the characters that are allowed in the **First Name** field.

How it works...

The `FirstName`, `MiddleName`, and `LastName` properties of the `Customer` class are annotated with the `[RegularExpression]` validation attributes so that these model property values are checked against a pattern.

The `^[A-Z]+[a-zA-Z]*$` regular expression pattern specifies that letters are only allowed in these fields and that the first letter should be in uppercase format. This whitelisting technique prevents a bad actor from injecting malicious input and only permits known-good characters for customer names.

By implementing validation in the model, we avoid unnecessary code repetition, thus making our code more maintainable and reducing the chances of introducing security bugs. This model validation is performed automatically and fails securely if the input is invalid.

> **Note**
>
> Regular expressions are a complex topic and are beyond the scope of this cookbook. To learn more about regular expressions, see *.NET Regular Expressions* on the official Microsoft documentation site: `https://docs.microsoft.com/en-us/dotnet/standard/base-types/regular-expressions`.

Whitelist validation using the FluentValidation library

Most web developers may want to decouple the validation rules from their models and prefer the solution to be written in a unit test-friendly way. You may wish to create your own library that performs whitelisting validation or opt to use a popular and easy-to-use third-party library such as `FluentValidation`, which has excellent validation features.

Getting ready

Using Visual Studio Code, open the sample Online Banking app folder at `\Chapter01\input-validation-fluentvalidation\before\OnlineBankingApp`.

How to do it...

Let's take a look at the steps for this recipe:

1. Launch Visual Studio Code and open the starting exercise folder by typing the following command:

```
code .
```

2. Navigate to **Terminal | New Terminal** in the menu or simply press *Ctrl + Shift + '* in Visual Studio Code.

3. Type the following command to install the FluentValidation package in your project:

```
dotnet add package FluentValidation
```

4. Open the Startup.cs file and add a reference to the following namespaces. This will provide access to the FluentValidation classes and methods:

```
using FluentValidation;
using FluentValidation.AspNetCore;
```

5. Add a reference to the OnlineBankingApp.Models namespace:

```
using OnlineBankingApp.Models;
```

6. In the ConfigureServices method, add calls to the AddFluentValidation and AddTransient methods to configure FluentValidation and add the custom validator service, which we will create in the next step:

```
public void ConfigureServices(IserviceCollection
    services)
{
    services.AddRazorPages().AddFluentValidation();
    services.AddTransient<IValidator<Customer>,
        CustomerValidator>();
//code removed for brevity
```

7. In the Models folder, create a new file for our custom validator and name it CustomValidator.cs.

8. Add the following code to `CustomValidator.cs`:

```
using FluentValidation;

namespace OnlineBankingApp.Models
{
    public class CustomerValidator :
        AbstractValidator<Customer> {
        public CustomerValidator() {
            RuleFor(x => x.FirstName)
                .Matches(@"^[A-Z]+[a-zA-Z]*$");
            RuleFor(x => x.MiddleName)
                .Matches(@"^[A-Z]+[a-zA-Z]*$");
            RuleFor(x => x.LastName)
                .Matches(@"^[A-Z]+[a-zA-Z]*$");
        }
    }
}
```

9. Navigate to **Terminal | New Terminal** in the menu or simply press *Ctrl + Shift + '* in Visual Studio Code.

10. Type the following command in the Terminal to build and run the sample app:

```
dotnet run
```

11. Open a browser and go to `http://localhost:5000/Customers/Create`.

12. The browser will display the web page for creating new customers, as shown in *Figure 1.1*.

13. In the **First Name** text box, enter an input that contains numbers and press *Tab* to shift the focus to a different input element.

14. The validation will kick in and an error message will appear (see *Figure 1.2*).

How it works...

`FluentValidation` is a server-side validation framework that allows developers to define validation rules using lambda expressions. To integrate this library into our sample Online Banking web app, we installed the `FluentValidation` package and added it as a reference to our solution:

```
using FluentValidation.AspNetCore;
```

The call to the `AddFluentValidation` extension method allows the model binding feature of the ASP.NET Core framework to use this library's validation features:

```
services.AddRazorPages().AddFluentValidation();
```

> **Note**
> You can still use ASP.NET Core's built-in validator implementation and validation attributes, and then combine them with the `FluentValidations` package.

Then, we derived our own `CustomerValidator` class from `AbstractValidator` so that we have a class to set our validation rules in. Inside this validator class, there are calls to the `FluentValidation` package's regular expression, which has a built-in validator to check if any of the name properties contain letters as defined in the matching pattern:

```
RuleFor(x => x.FirstName).Matches(@"^[A-Z]+[a-zA-Z]*$");
RuleFor(x => x.MiddleName).Matches(@"^[A-Z]+[a-zA-Z]*$");
RuleFor(x => x.LastName).Matches(@"^[A-Z]+[a-zA-Z]*$");
```

We also made a call to the `AddTransient` method to add the custom validator to the collection service:

```
services.AddTransient<IValidator<Customer>,
CustomerValidator>();
```

The `AddTransient` method allows `CustomerValidator` to be discovered by ASP.NET Core.

There's more...

The two previous recipes are both examples of *server-side validation*. This type of validation performed by code running on the web server. With ASP.NET Core web applications (or any web app in general), there's another way of performing validation, and it is executed in the user-agent (typically, a web browser). Web developers can write *client-side validation* using either HTML5 form validation or by writing custom JavaScript code.

When scaffolding ASP.NET Core web application projects, templates make it easy to implement client-side validation easy by having *unobtrusive jQuery libraries* instantly added as references to `Pages\Shared\_ValidationScriptsPartial.cshtml`:

```
<script src="~/lib/jquery-validation/dist/jquery.validate.min.
js"></script>
<script src="~/lib/jquery-validation-unobtrusive/jquery.
validate.unobtrusive.min.js"></script>
```

The input tag helpers that we place in our Razor pages render *HTML5 data-* attributes* that our unobtrusive JavaScript library will then read and validate from the client-side, before the browser sends any request to a web server. This setup simplifies the process of adding client-side validation to our ASP.NET Core web application.

> **Tip**
> *Do not* rely entirely upon client-side validation and *do not* trust input coming from the client. A user can disable JavaScript via their browser's settings, which will prevent the client-side validation code from executing.

See also...

If you're interested in learning more about the FluentValidation library, see the *ASP.NET Core* section of the official FluentValidation library: `https://docs.fluentvalidation.net/en/latest/aspnet.html`.

Syntactic and semantic validation

The preceding recipe is one form of **syntactic validation**, where we validate the correctness of the field's structure (in this case, the names should only contain alphabetical characters).

Another type of validation is based on **semantics**, where the validity of the input relies on a specific business context.

Creating a custom validation attribute to implement semantic validation

In semantic validation, a context check is done to ensure that the data conforms to a business rule. Using our Online Banking app as an example, we can define a business rule, stating that a customer must have a reputable email address before a record can be created.

In this recipe, you will learn how to perform semantic validation using custom validation attributes.

Getting ready

Request a free API key at `https://emailrep.io/key`. **EmailRep** is a simple public API for checking an email's reputation. Once your request has been approved, you will receive an email from `EmailRep.io` that contains your API key. Use this API key when consuming the `EmailRep.io` web API.

Enable secrets storage for safekeeping our EmailRep API key. Open a Terminal and run the following command:

```
dotnet user-secrets init
```

Then, run the following command:

```
dotnet user-secrets set "EmailRepApiKey" "key=place-your-api-key-here"
```

Using Visual Studio Code, open the sample Online Banking app folder at `\Chapter01\input-validation\before\OnlineBankingApp`.

How to do it...

Let's take a look at the steps for this recipe:

1. Launch Visual Studio Code and open the starting exercise folder by typing the following command:

   ```
   code .
   ```

2. In the `Services` folder, create a new file and name it `EmailReputation.cs`. Inside it, add references to the following namespaces:

   ```
   using System.Net;
   using System.IO;
   ```

```
using System.Text.Json;
using Microsoft.Extensions.Configuration;
using OnlineBankingApp.Models;
```

3. Declare an IEmailReputation interface:

```
namespace OnlineBankingApp.Services
{
    public interface IEmailReputation
    {
        bool IsRisky(string input);
    }
}
```

4. Within the same OnlineBankingApp.Services namespace, declare a
    EmailReputation class that inherits from the IEmailReputation interface.
    Inject the IConfiguration service into its constructor:

```
public class EmailReputation : IEmailReputation
{
    private readonly IConfiguration Configuration;
    public EmailReputation(IConfiguration config)
    {
        Configuration = config;
    }
}
```

5. Implement the IsRisky method in EmailReputation:

```
public bool IsRisky(string email)
{
    var emailRepApiKey =
        Configuration["EmailRepApiKey"];
    HttpWebRequest repEmailRequest =
        (HttpWebRequest)WebRequest.Create
            ($"https://emailrep.io/{email}");
    repEmailRequest.Headers.Add("Cookie",
        $"{emailRepApiKey}");
```

```
repEmailRequest.Headers.Add("User-Agent",
    "MyAppName");
HttpWebResponse repEmailResponse =
    (HttpWebResponse) repEmailRequest.GetResponse();
Stream newStream =
    repEmailResponse.GetResponseStream();
var repEmail = new
    StreamReader(newStream).ReadToEnd();
var reputation =
    JsonSerializer.Deserialize<Reputation>
        (repEmail);
if (reputation.suspicious ||
  reputation.details.blacklisted ||
  reputation.details.spam ||
  reputation.details.malicious_activity ||
  reputation.details.malicious_activity_recent)
    return true;
return false;
}
```

Here, we made a call to the EmailRep query API and sent the API key and the name of the app as part of the request headers; that is, Cookie and User-Agent. The response is in JSON format. We can deserialize this to retrieve the reputation information.

> **Tip**
>
> Secrets such as API keys *shouldn't be hardcoded* in code or configuration files. A compromised account with access to the code repository is all it takes to leak these sensitive pieces of information. Developers should store passwords and credentials in a safer environment, such as Azure Key Vault or AWS Key Management Service.
>
> In this recipe, we're using the *secret manager tool* to safekeep our EmailRep API key during development. To learn more about the secret manager tool and how to store your secrets, see the *Safe storage of app secrets in development in ASP.NET Core* section of the Microsoft documentation: https://docs.microsoft.com/en-us/aspnet/core/security/app-secrets?view=aspnetcore-5.0&tabs=windows.

6. Navigate to the `Model` folder of the `OnlineBankingApp` project and create a new file called `ReputableEmailAttribute.cs` to begin creating a custom validation attribute.

7. Add the following namespace references to the `ReputableEmailAttribute.cs` file:

```
using System.ComponentModel.DataAnnotations;
using System.Net;
using System.IO;
using System.Text.Json;
```

8. Declare a `Reputation` and a `Details` class:

```
public class Details
{
    public bool blacklisted { get; set; }
    public bool malicious_activity { get; set; }
    public bool malicious_activity_recent { get; set;}
    public bool spam { get; set; }
    public bool suspicious_tld { get; set; }
}
public class Reputation
{
    public Details { get; set; }
    public string email { get; set; }
    public string reputation { get; set; }
    public bool suspicious { get; set; }
}
```

Both classes will hold the deserialized information from the response we receive from the `EmailRep.io` API.

> **Note**
>
> The `EmailRep.io` API's response contains more information than the properties we define in the `Reputation` and `Details` classes. We've used what's most essential for this recipe, but you're free to include more if you desire.

9. Declare another class named ReputableEmailAttribute in
    the OnlineBankingApp.Models namespace that inherits from
    ValidationAttribute and defines the GetErrorMessage property:

```
namespace OnlineBankingApp.Models
{
    public class ReputableEmailAttribute :
        ValidationAttribute
    {
        public string GetErrorMessage() =>
            "Email address is rejected because of its
                reputation";
    }
}
```

10. Override the IsValid method of ValidationAttribute with the
    following code:

```
protected override ValidationResult IsValid(object
  value,ValidationContext validationContext)
{
    string email = value.ToString();
    var service = (IEmailReputation)
        validationContext.GetService
            (typeof(IEmailReputation));
    if (service.IsRisky(email))
        return new ValidationResult(GetErrorMessage());

    return ValidationResult.Success;
}
```

11. Modify the Models/Customer.cs file and annotate the Email property with
    the new custom [ReputableEmail] validation attribute:

```
[ReputableEmail]
[Display(Name = "Email Address")]
[Required]
[EmailAddress]
public string Email { get; set; }
```

12. Navigate to **Terminal | New Terminal** in the menu or simply press *Ctrl + Shift + ʹ* in Visual Studio Code.

13. Type the following commands in the Terminal to build and run the sample app:

```
dotnet run
```

14. Open a browser and go to `http://localhost:5000/Customers`.

15. The browser will display a list of customers that have been generated by the seeded data.

16. Select one record and click its **Edit** link:

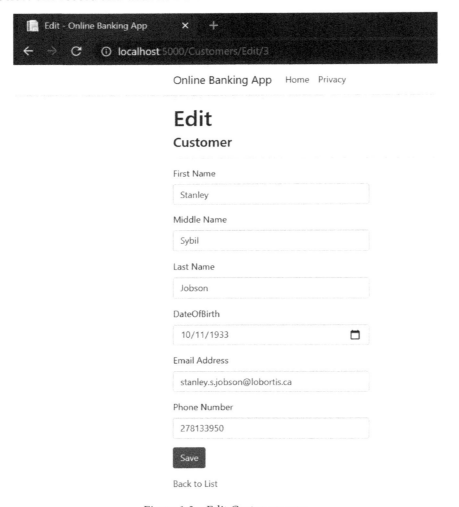

Figure 1.3 – Edit Customer page

17. You will be redirected to the **Edit** page, where you will be able to modify the details of a **Customer**.

18. Change the current **Email Address** field and give it a value of `email@test.xyz`.

19. Click **Save**. Notice the error message that appears, indicating that the email has been rejected:

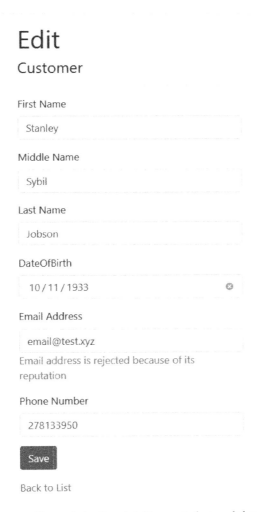

Figure 1.4 – Email Address attribute validation

By creating our custom validation attribute and annotating the email address, we can now execute semantic validation within the Customer model. Writing proper custom model validators is recommended because it provides more control and flexibility when creating validation rules.

How it works...

We created a new class that inherits from `ValidateAttribute` and override its `IsValid` method. To enforce semantic validation, we created a service that our custom attribute will use to make a call to the **EmailRep Query API** and determine if its `EmailAddress` is associated with any known malicious activity, marked as spam, suspicious, or blacklisted:

```
if (reputation.suspicious ||
    reputation.details.blacklisted ||
    reputation.details.spam ||
    reputation.details.malicious_activity ||
    reputation.details.malicious_activity_recent)
    return new ValidationResult(GetErrorMessage());
return ValidationResult.Success;
```

This type of validation, where an email address is rejected based on its reputation, might be familiar to you. This validation is called blacklisting. **Blacklisting validation** is one of the validation strategies that you can use in your ASP.NET Core web application.

Poor validation can expose your ASP.NET Core web application to unnecessary security risks. It is critical to implement sufficient validation strategies in your application to cover both the syntax and semantical rules, thus reducing the chances of injection and logic vulnerabilities. Using built-in validation frameworks or trusted third-party validation libraries such as FluentValidation are good countermeasures.

> **Note**
>
> Many other companies offer the same email reputation service, which provides a score and assesses the risk of an email address. Utilize a reliable API service based on your requirements and needs to check an email address's integrity before saving the record on your database.

Input sanitization

Another complementing strategy that a developer can implement in processing input is to remove or replace unwanted characters from the data. Your application might expect some free-form text or HTML formatted input, and to avoid attacks that will take advantage of this vector, you must perform **sanitization**.

You can write your own methods for sanitizing and, similar to input validation, implement either a whitelisting or blacklisting approach for modifying input.

In this recipe, you will learn how to write your own code for sanitizing input.

Getting ready

Using Visual Studio Code, open the sample Online Banking app folder at `\Chapter01\ input-sanitization\before\OnlineBankingApp`.

How to do it...

Let's take a look at the steps for this recipe:

1. Launch Visual Studio Code and open the starting exercise folder by typing the following command:

    ```
    code .
    ```

2. Open the `Models/FundTransfer.cs` file and add a reference to the `System. Text.RegularExpressions` namespace:

    ```
    using System.Text.RegularExpressions;
    ```

3. Modify the code in the `Note` model property:

    ```
    [StringLength(60)]
    [DataType(DataType.MultilineText)]

    public string Note {
        get => note;

        set => note = Regex.Replace(value,
            @"[\!\@\$\%\^\&\<\>\?\|\;\[\]\{\~]+"
                , string.Empty);

    }
    ```

4. Navigate to **Terminal | New Terminal** in the menu or simply press *Ctrl + Shift + '* in Visual Studio Code.

5. In the Visual Studio Code Terminal, type the following command to build and run the sample app:

```
dotnet run
```

6. Open a browser and go to `http://localhost:5000/FundTransfers/Create`.

7. Select an account to transfer from and to via the drop-down list.

8. Enter an **Amount** to transfer.

9. In the **Notes** multi-text field, attempt to exploit the app by entering a malicious script tag (that is, `<script>alert()</script>`), as shown in the following screenshot:

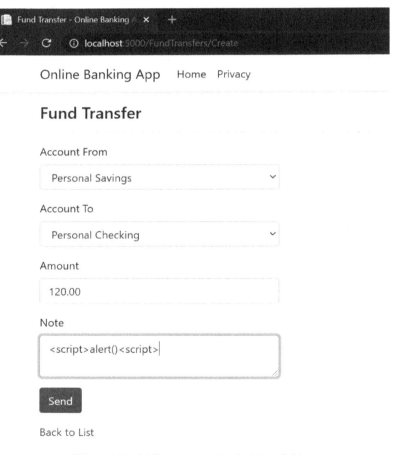

Figure 1.5 – Malicious input in the Note field

10. Click **Send**.

11. The sample app will redirect you to the **Fund Transfers** page, where you will see the recently created fund transfer record.

12. Notice that the less than and greater than characters were removed from the **Note** section and have now been sanitized:

Figure 1.6 – Sanitized Note value

We can pass the `[\!\@\$\%\^\&\<\>\?\|\;\[\]\{\~]` + regular expression as one of the `Regex.Replace` method parameters, specifying that we want to remove unwanted characters matching this pattern. This method changes the **Note** input value from `<script>alert()</script>` to `scriptalert()/script`, making the rendered output safer.

How it works...

Our sample Online Banking app has a **Fund Transfer** page that allows users to transfer money between accounts. One of its form fields is **Notes**, which lets a user enter freeform text formatted with HTML tags.

We modified the **Note** model property's set assessor to sanitize the value being assigned to it to prevent unwanted characters or markup, such as the `<script>` tag.

We added a reference to the `System.Text.RegularExpressions` namespace so that we can use the `Regex.Replace` method to sanitize input. Using the `Regex.Replace` method, we specified a regular expression pattern to look out for in the value; we replace it with an empty string if a match is found.

Input sanitization using the HTMLSanitizer library

There are other open source libraries out there that do a good job of sanitizing input, and one of them is HTMLSanitizer.

In this recipe, you will learn how to sanitize input using the HTMLSanitizer third-party library.

Getting ready

Using Visual Studio Code, open the sample Online Banking app folder at \Chapter01\ input-sanitization-htmlsanitizer\before\OnlineBankingApp.

How to do it...

Let's take a look at the steps for this recipe:

1. Launch Visual Studio Code and open the starting exercise folder by typing the following command:

   ```
   code .
   ```

2. Navigate to **Terminal | New Terminal** in the menu or simply press *Ctrl* + *Shift* + ' in Visual Studio Code.

3. Type the following command to install the HtmlSanitizer package in your project:

   ```
   dotnet add package HtmlSanitizer
   ```

4. Open the Models/FundTransfer.cs file and add a reference to Ganss.XSS, which is the HtmlSanitizer namespace:

   ```
   using Ganss.XSS;
   ```

5. Modify the code in the Note model property setter:

   ```
   [StringLength(60)]
   [DataType(DataType.MultilineText)]
   public string Note {
       get => note;
       set => note = new HtmlSanitizer().Sanitize(value);
   }
   ```

6. In the Visual Studio Code Terminal, type the following command to build and run the sample app:

```
dotnet run
```

7. Open a browser and go to http://localhost:5000/FundTransfers/Create.

8. Select an account to transfer from and to via the drop-down list.

9. Enter an **Amount** to transfer.

10. In the **Notes** multi-text field, enter <b>Contingency Fund<b> <script>alert()</script>. This is a string that's formatted with a bold tag that has a malicious script tag next to it, as shown in the following screenshot:

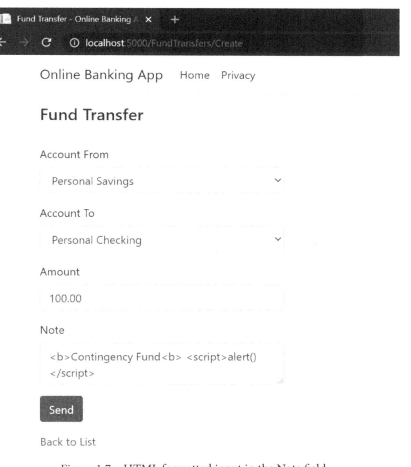

Figure 1.7 – HTML formatted input in the Note field

11. Click **Send**.

12. The sample app will redirect you to the **Fund Transfers** page, where you will see the recently created fund transfer record.

13. Notice that the **Contingency Fund** string is bold formatted but with the script tag completely removed:

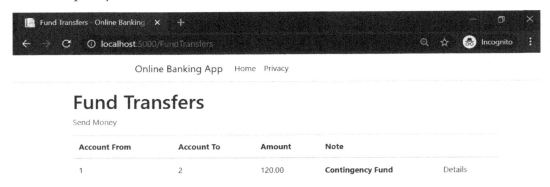

Figure 1.8 – Formatted and sanitized Note value

Using the `HtmlSanitizer` NuGet package, we can sanitize the user-controlled input and prevent our sample solution from having **XSS** vulnerabilities.

How it works...

To allow safe HTML formatting for our **Notes** in our sample Online Banking app, we must clean the input so that it doesn't contain any harmful tags and attributes. `HTMLSanitizer` helps us with this task, and with its built-in **whitelisting mechanism**, it will only allow specific HTML or CSS tags and attributes.

The preceding code shows that the `Sanitize` method strips the rest of the tags or attributes from the input string that are not in the whitelist.

By default, `HTMLSanitizer` already provides a list of safe tags. You can create your own whitelist, but for our example, we do not need to set the `AllowTags` or `AllowAttribute` properties of the `Sanitizer` instance; just call the `Sanitize` method and pass the value.

Output encoding

Output encoding or **escaping** is yet another defensive technique that helps neutralize injection attacks. This process replaces the characters in the untrusted data, which allows the application to display the output safely in its proper context.

In an ASP.NET Core web application, there's different contextual output that a developer should know about to understand the right encoder to use in a given context. These are **HTML, HTML attribute context, CSS context**, and **JavaScript context**.

By default, the Razor engine in ASP.NET Core automatically escapes output, apart from a few exceptions, where a method will disable such encoding. ASP.NET Core also provides a variety of encoders that we can use to explicitly implement proper contextual output.

In the next few recipes, we will learn how to perform output encoding with `HtmlEncoder`, `UrlEncoder`, and `JavascriptEncoder`.

Output encoding using HtmlEncoder

HTML encoding converts special characters so that the browser will interpret the text correctly and not render it as HTML. For instance, a string may contain a less than character <, and in HTML standards, this is an HTML entity being used to open and close tags. This needs to be escaped into `&lt;` to preserve the meaning of the text.

The protection that escaping output provides lies in preventing the attacker from changing the intent or the input's purpose when it is parsed by the interpreter. This stops the malicious actor from trying to execute scripts within the HTML context.

The following table displays the most common HTML entities and their encoded counterparts. This is by no means a complete list:

Character	HTML Entity	Description
<	`&lt;`	Less than
>	`&gt;`	Greater than
	` `	Non-breaking space
"	`&quot;`	Quotation mark
'	`&apos;`	Apostrophe
&	`&amp;`	Ampersand

Table 1.1 – HTML entities

In this recipe, you will learn how to use `HtmlEncoder` to escape output in HTML.

Getting ready

Using Visual Studio Code, open the sample Online Banking app folder at `\Chapter01\output-encoding-html\before\OnlineBankingApp`.

How to do it...

Let's take a look at the steps for this recipe:

1. Launch Visual Studio Code and open the starting exercise folder by typing the following command:

```
code .
```

2. Open the `Pages\FundTransfers\Index.cshtml` file and add an `@inject` directive to the Razor page to inject the `HtmlEncoder` service:

```
@inject System.Text.Encodings.Web.HtmlEncoder htmlEncoder
```

3. Replace the markup inside the `Note` table data cell with the following code:

```
@if (item.Note is not null) {
    @(new Microsoft.AspNetCore.Html.HtmlString
        (htmlEncoder.Encode(item.Note)))
}
```

4. Navigate to **Terminal | New Terminal** in the menu or simply press *Ctrl* + *Shift* + ' in Visual Studio Code.

5. In the Visual Studio Terminal, type the following command to build and run the sample app:

```
dotnet run
```

6. Open a browser and go to `http://localhost:5000/FundTransfers`.

7. View the rendered HTML by right-clicking anywhere in the page and selecting **View page source** from the browser's context menu.

8. Notice the markup where **Notes** with the script tag has been HTML encoded:

```
<td>Contingency Fund &lt;script&gt;alert()&lt;/script&gt;
</td>
```

How it works...

The `System.Text.Encodings.Web` namespace brings in a wealth of character encoders that a developer can use to escape output. One of them is `HtmlEncoder`, which will help us HTML-encode our data.

Through dependency injection, we can add the `HtmlEncoder` object using the `@inject` directive:

```
@inject System.Text.Encodings.Web.HtmlEncoder htmlEncoder
```

The `htmlEncoder` variable will hold an instance of the `HtmlEncoder` object, and with its `Encode` method, we can pass in the value of the `Note` property from the `FundTransfer` object for escaping:

```
htmlEncoder.Encode(item.Note)
```

The `Encode` method transforms the value of `item.Note` and will now be an encoded string.

Output encoding using UrlEncoder

URL encoding converts characters in the output into ASCII format. It also replaces unsafe characters with a % character as a prefix and then adds two hexadecimal digits.

Here's a partial list of characters and their URL-encoded equivalents:

Character	Percent Encoded
<	%3c
=	%3d
>	%3e
?	%3f
*	%2a
+	%2b
,	%2c
–	%2d
.	%2e
/	%2f
line feed	%0a
	%0b
	%0c
carriage return	%0d
	%0e
	%0f

Table 1.2 – Percent encoded characters and their equivalents

In this recipe, you will learn how to use `UrlEncoder` to escape URLs.

Getting ready

Using Visual Studio Code, open the sample Online Banking app folder at `\Chapter01\ output-encoding-url\before\OnlineBankingApp`.

How to do it...

Let's take a look at the steps for this recipe:

1. Launch Visual Studio Code and open the starting exercise folder by typing the following command:

   ```
   code .
   ```

2. Open the `Pages\FundTransfers\Index.cshtml` file and add an `@inject` directive to the Razor page to inject the `UrlEncoder` service:

   ```
   @inject System.Text.Encodings.Web.UrlEncoder urlEncoder
   ```

3. Replace the markup inside the `Note` table data cell with the following code:

   ```
   <td>
   <a asp-page="./Create" asp-route-id="@item.ID"
   asp-fragment="@(item.Note is null ? string.Empty :
   urlEncoder.Encode(item.Note))" >Send Again</a>
   </td>
   ```

4. Navigate to **Terminal | New Terminal** in the menu or simply press *Ctrl + Shift + '* in Visual Studio Code.

5. In the Visual Studio Terminal, type the following command to build and run the sample app:

   ```
   dotnet run
   ```

6. Open a browser and go to `http://localhost:5000/FundTransfers`.

7. View the rendered HTML by right-clicking anywhere in the page and selecting **View page source** from the browser's context menu.

8. Notice the markup where the hyperlink for `Send Again`, along with its script tag, has been URL encoded:

```
<td>
<a href="/FundTransfers/Create?id=1#Contingency%20
Fund%20%3Cscript%3Ealert()%3C%2Fscript%3E">
Send Again</a>
</td>
```

The text in the fragment is now percent-encoded, thus replacing the potentially malicious characters such as < and > with %3C and %3E.

How it works...

The `asp-fragment` attribute gets assigned the `Note` model property value to be sent as a piece of persisting information to the **Create New Fund Transfer** page:

```
asp-fragment="@(item.Note is null ? string.Empty : item.Note)
```

Without encoding the `item.Note` URL fragment, the code that processes this data in the destination page could pick this value and parse it as-is in its literal form. The risk of processing unescaped data is that the interpreter may take this as code and execute it based on the wrong context.

We can use the `Encode` method of the `UrlEncoder` object to escape the `Note` model property value to prevent this from happening.

Output encoding using JavascriptEncoder

Web development wouldn't be complete without JavaScript. It has always been the de facto scripting language for developing web applications, and it is used for multiple purposes, from animation to validating input from the client side. There will be instances where developers will mix JavaScript code blocks with C# code or the Razor syntax within ASP.NET Core pages. This approach makes escaping outp`ut alongside JavaScript necessary, and it also prevents JavaScript code from being injected with malicious functions.

In this recipe, you will learn how to use `JavascriptEncoder` to escape output in JavaScript.

Getting ready

Using Visual Studio Code, open the sample Online Banking app folder at `\Chapter01\ output-encoding-js\before\OnlineBankingApp`.

How to do it...

Let's take a look at the steps for this recipe:

1. Launch Visual Studio Code and open the starting exercise folder by typing the following command:

    ```
    code .
    ```

2. Open the `Pages\Customers\Index.cshtml` file and add an `@inject` directive to the Razor page to inject the `JavascriptEncoder` service:

    ```
    @inject System.Text.Encodings.Web.JavaScriptEncoder
    jsEncoder
    ```

3. Replace `@section Scripts` with the following code:

    ```
    @section Scripts {
        <script type="text/javascript">

            $(document).ready(function() {
                @foreach (var item in Model.Customer) {
                    <text>
                        var $tr = $('<tr>').append
                            ($('<td>').text("@jsEncoder
                            .Encode(item.FirstName)"));
                        $tr.append($('<td>').text
                            ("@jsEncoder.Encode(item
                            .MiddleName)"));
                        $tr.append($('<td>').text
                            ("@jsEncoder.Encode
                                (item.LastName)"));
                        $tr.append($('<td>')
                            .text("@jsEncoder.Encode
                                (item.DateOfBirth.ToString
                                    ("d"))"));
    ```

```
                        $tr.append($('<td>').text
                            ("@jsEncoder.Encode
                            (item.Email)"));
                        $tr.append($('<td>').text
                            ("@jsEncoder.Encode
                            (item.Phone)"));
                        $tr.appendTo('#table');
                    </text>
                }
            });

        </script>
    }
```

4. Navigate to **Terminal | New Terminal** in the menu or simply press *Ctrl + Shift + '* in Visual Studio Code.

5. In the Visual Studio Terminal, type the following command to build and run the sample app:

```
dotnet run
```

6. Open a browser and go to `http://localhost:5000/Customers`.

7. View the rendered HTML by right-clicking anywhere in the page and selecting **View page source** in the browser's context menu.

8. Notice the markup where the hyperlink for **View Details**, along with its script tag, has been URL encoded:

```
var $tr = $('<tr>').append($('<td>').text("Dylan \u003C/
script\u003E\u003Cscript\u003Ealert()\u003C/script\
u003E"));
```

The characters in the model property values are now JavaScript encoded, thus preventing bad actors from exploiting the output and injecting arbitrary JavaScript code.

How it works...

Inside the `script` section, we have jQuery code that generates the content of an HTML table on the fly. A loop goes through each item of the `Customer` collection and renders it to each table's cell:

```
$(document).ready(function() {
    @foreach (var item in Model.Customer) {
        <text>
        ...code removed for brevity
        </text>
    }
});

</script>
}
```

Within the JavaScript context, we are using the `JavascriptEncoder` object and calling the `Encode` method to encode all the data in the model.

Protecting sensitive data using the Data Protection API

There is no question that part of the ASP.NET Core secure coding technique should involve protecting your application's sensitive data at rest. **Personally identifiable information** (**PII**), data classified as confidential, and enumerable keys and IDs should be encrypted. ASP.NET Core made it easy for developers to achieve this by developing a data protection stack in its framework that provides a simplified API.

In this recipe, you will learn how to use the **Data Protection API** (**DPAPI**) to protect parts of your ASP.NET Core web application that expose sensitive data.

Getting ready

Using Visual Studio Code, open the sample Online Banking app folder at `\Chapter01\ data-protection\before\OnlineBankingApp`.

How to do it...

Let's take a look at the steps for this recipe:

1. Launch Visual Studio Code and open the starting exercise folder by typing the following command:

    ```
    code .
    ```

2. Open the Pages\Customers\Index.cshtml.cs file and add a reference to the Microsoft.AspNetCore.DataProtection namespace:

    ```
    using Microsoft.AspNetCore.DataProtection;
    ```

3. Add the Data Protector interface as a private member:

    ```
    private readonly IDataProtector _dataProtector;
    ```

4. Modify the IndexModel page model so that it includes an additional parameter for the constructor:

    ```
    public IndexModel(OnlineBankingApp.Data
      .OnlineBankingAppContext context,
        IDataProtectionProvider dataProtector)
    {
        _context = context;
        _dataProtector = dataProtector.CreateProtector
            ("OnlineBankingApp.Pages.Customers");
    }
    ```

5. Add a new EncCustomerID property to the Customer class:

    ```
    [NotMapped]
    public string EncCustomerID { get; set; }
    ```

6. Encrypt the ID property of the Customer class using the Protect method:

    ```
    public async Task OnGetAsync()
    {
        foreach (var cust in _context.Customer)
        {
            cust.EncCustomerID =
                _dataProtector.Protect(cust.ID.ToString());
    ```

```
        }

        Customer = await _context.Customer.ToListAsync();
}
```

7. Change the line where the anchor tag is dynamically generated by the jQuery code:

```
$tr.append($('<td>').append("<a href='/Customers/
Details?id=@item.EncCustomerID'>See Details</a>"));
```

8. Open the `Pages\Customers\Details.cshtml.cs` file and add a reference to the `Microsoft.AspNetCore.DataProtection` namespace:

```
using Microsoft.AspNetCore.DataProtection;
```

9. Add the Data Protector interface as a private member:

```
private readonly IDataProtector _dataProtector;
```

10. Modify the `DetailsModel` page model so that it includes an additional parameter for the constructor:

```
public DetailsModel
    (OnlineBankingApp.Data.OnlineBankingAppContext
        context, IDataProtectionProvider dataProtector)
{
    _context = context;
    _dataProtector = dataProtector.CreateProtector
        ("OnlineBankingApp.Pages.Customers");
}
```

11. Change the `OnGetAsync` method:

```
public async Task<IActionResult> OnGetAsync(string id)
{
    if (id == null)
    {
        return NotFound();
    }
```

```
var decID =
    Int32.Parse(_dataProtector.Unprotect(id));


Customer = await _context.Customer
    .FirstOrDefaultAsync(m => m.ID == decID);
```

12. Open a browser and go to `http://localhost:5000/Customers`.

13. View the rendered HTML by right-clicking anywhere in the page and selecting **View page source** from the browser's context menu.

14. Notice the two lines of jQuery code where the hyperlink to the **Details** page is no longer exposing the actual **Customer ID** in the query string parameter:

```
$tr.append($('<td>').append("<a href='/Customers/Details?
id=CfDJ8CsNdycKdZtHo72FYN-pXqvrK1k8Z-c4FPe7huOeyCazSmmHbF
8fUaQAbio0JpDxOcg9J4-voevmBcHwpBsJWx77ZG5vhpzkLnGB8m13uBo
5BLiIdsl2Epk9kj97d5PRJw'>See Details</a>"));

. . .

$tr.append($('<td>').append("<a href='/Customers/Deta
ils?id=CfDJ8CsNdycKdZtHo72FYN-pXquGL7YVUQfASM5cVvyol-
OK-xQyErXGit9Kdgs6YyBBdEcNtoqq9c7kqr1J7EzkI0zszL-
700OTcVgXvqY4wdyseN-2uESydCdv-KOqOXboLg'>See Details</
a>"));
```

The `href` attribute has now been replaced with a URL that's been appended with a different value for the `id` query string parameter. This parameter now has the Customer ID in its encrypted form.

How it works...

Our **Customer ID** is initially exposed as a query string parameter value in the anchor tags and can be easily viewed using the browser developer tools. This makes the application vulnerable to enumeration-based types of attacks, so we need to protect this data from prying eyes:

```
<a href="/Customers/Details?id=1">See Details</a>
```

> **Note**
>
> Typically, numeric types as primary keys are a thing of the past now, and enterprise database design steers away from having numeric IDs and instead uses **Global Unique Identifiers** (**GUIDs**). But for simplification purposes, we can use integers to understand the risk of using guessable keys.

We can utilize the data protection services from the **DPAPI** and **encrypt** this information before rendering the link on the page.

Start by adding a reference to `Microsoft.AspNetCore.DataProtection` and utilizing `IDataProtectionProvider` by injecting this service into our `pagemodel`:

```
DetailsModel(OnlineBankingApp.Data.OnlineBankingAppContext
context, IDataProtectionProvider dataProtector)
```

Adding this interface to the constructor allows us to call the `CreateProtector` method so that we can create an instance of the `IDataProtector` object. One of the arguments required by `IDataProtector` is a unique *purpose string*, which we can use to encrypt and decrypt payloads:

```
_dataProtector = dataProtector.CreateProtector
("OnlineBankingApp.Pages.Customers");
```

We will use `OnlineBankingApp.Pages.Customers` as our purpose string for both the `Index` and `Detail` models to decipher the Customer ID, which is the information we are trying to protect. The *purpose string* creates isolation, which prevents consumers other than `DetailsModel` and `IndexModel` from decrypting the protected data.

We need to add a new property that will hold the encrypted Customer ID, so we must define `EncCustomerID` as a string data type. We will annotate it with `[NotMapped]` to prevent Entity Framework from creating a column for this new property:

```
[NotMapped]
public string EncCustomerID { get; set; }
```

Lastly, we must iterate through all the customers, protect their Customer IDs, and assign them to the `EncCustomerID` property:

```
foreach (var cust in _context.Customer)
{
    cust.EncCustomerID =
        _dataProtector.Protect(cust.ID.ToString());
}
```

Add `UnProtect` when needed from `DetailsModel`. Here, we must decrypt the protected data to pull the information from the database:

```
var decID = Int32.Parse(_dataProtector.Unprotect(id));
```

If `_dataProtector` was instantiated with a different **purpose string**, a `CryptographicException` will be thrown; otherwise, the ciphertext's decryption will be successful.

See also

The preceding recipe is a simple example of how to quickly implement **DPAPI** and protect your data in your ASP.NET Core web applications. To understand the philosophy behind the DPAPI, and to get a deeper understanding of the APIs, see *ASP.NET Core Data Protection* in the Microsoft official documentation at `https://docs.microsoft.com/en-us/aspnet/core/security/data-protection/introduction?view=aspnetcore-5.0`.

2
Injection Flaws

Injection flaws in code can have the most devastating effects on ASP.NET Core web applications. The lack of validation and sanitization of untrusted input allows this vulnerability to be exploited, leading to the execution of arbitrary OS commands, authentication bypass, unexpected data manipulation, and content. At worse, it can disclose sensitive information and lead to an eventual data breach.

This chapter introduces you to various injection flaws and explains how you can remediate this security defect in code.

In this chapter, we're going to cover the following recipes:

- Fixing SQL injection with Entity Framework
- Fixing SQL injection in ADO.NET
- Fixing NoSQL injection
- Fixing command injection
- Fixing LDAP injection
- Fixing XPath injection

By the end of this chapter, you will learn how to properly write secure code and remove security bugs that will prevent injection attacks.

Technical requirements

This book was written and designed to use with Visual Studio Code, Git, and .NET 5.0. Code examples in recipes are presented in ASP.NET Core Razor pages. The code exercises have been tested in a Windows environment but should work in Linux-based operating systems with some minor differences. The sample solution also uses SQLite as the database engine for a more simplified setup. MongoDB is required to be able to test the recipes for NoSQL injection. A tool that can open and browse SQLite databases such as the DB Browser for SQLite is also required. You can find the code for this chapter at `https://github.com/PacktPublishing/ASP.NET-Core-Secure-Coding-Cookbook/tree/main/Chapter02`.

What is SQL injection?

ASP.NET Core web applications interact with databases to store data and records. We use **Standard Query Language (SQL)** to communicate with a **Database Management System (DBMS)** to access and manage data. These queries are composed utilizing the programming language, platform, or library of choice, but the code to generate these queries can be written insecurely.

A developer can write code that produces a dynamic SQL by concatenating strings along with untrusted user input. Without proper countermeasures, a malicious actor can inject suspicious commands into the input string, thereby changing the query's intent, or execute an arbitrary SQL. Identified as **SQL Injection**, this vulnerability in code still prevails in web applications today.

Fixing SQL injection with Entity Framework

Entity Framework Core (EF Core) is a popular **Object-Relational Mapping (ORM)** framework of choice for ASP.NET Core developers. This framework is cross-platform, and its ease of use allows developers to instantly model and query data into objects. Nevertheless, ORM frameworks such as EF Core can still be misused.

In this recipe, we will execute a simple SQL injection to exploit the vulnerability, locate the security bug, and remediate the risk by rewriting a more secure version of the code.

Getting ready

Using Visual Studio Code, open the sample Online Banking app folder at `\Chapter02\sql-injection\razor\ef\before\OnlineBankingApp\`.

Testing a SQL injection

Here are the steps:

1. Navigate to **Terminal | New Terminal** in the menu or simply press *Ctrl* + *Shift* + ' in Visual Studio Code.

2. Type the following command in the terminal to build and run the sample app:

```
dotnet run
```

3. Open a browser and go to http://localhost:5000/FundTransfers.

4. The browser will display the web page for searching fund transfers using keywords in the **Filter By Notes** field, as shown in the following screenshot:

Figure 2.1 – Fund Transfers page

5. In the **Filter By Notes** textbox, type C and then hit the **Search** button.

6. The web page will now return one entry finding one match for the **Contingency Fund** note:

Figure 2.2 – Fund Transfers search result

7. Now try entering the SQL injection payload: `%';create table tbl1(one varchar(10), two smallint);Select * from Customers where id like '1`.

8. Notice that no error was thrown on the web page:

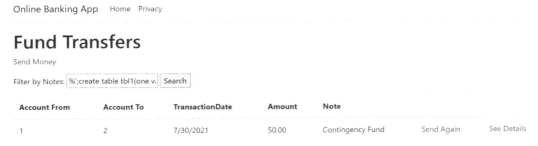

Figure 2.3 – Successful SQL injection

9. To confirm that the SQL injection payload was executed successfully, open the `\Chapter02\sql-injection\razor\ef\before\OnlineBankingApp\OnlineBank.db` SQLite database using the **DB Browser for SQLite** tool:

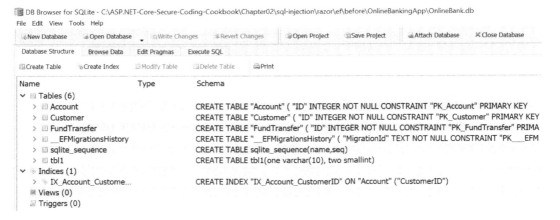

Figure 2.4 – OnlineBank.db in DB Browser for SQLite

Notice the newly created **tbl1** SQLite table

Now, let's see how to identify the SQL injection vulnerability in code that uses EF and mitigate the preceding issue by fixing this security flaw and applying a countermeasure.

How to do it...

Let's take a look at the steps for this recipe:

1. Launch Visual Studio Code and open the starting exercise folder by typing the following command:

    ```
    code .
    ```

2. Navigate to **Terminal | New Terminal** in the menu or simply press *Ctrl* + *Shift* + ' in Visual Studio Code.

3. Type the following command in the terminal to build the sample app to confirm that there are no compilation errors:

    ```
    dotnet build
    ```

4. Open the `Pages/FundTransfers/Index.cshtml.cs` file and locate the vulnerable part of the `OnGetAsync` method, where a dynamic query is composed:

    ```
    public async Task OnGetAsync()
    {
        var fundtransfer = from f in _context.FundTransfer
            select f;

        if (!string.IsNullOrEmpty(SearchString))
        {
            fundtransfer = _context.FundTransfer.
                FromSqlRaw("Select * from FundTransfer
                    Where Note Like'%" + SearchString +
                        "%'");
        }

        FundTransfer = await fundtransfer.ToListAsync();
    }
    ```

5. To remediate the SQL injection vulnerability, let's start by adding a reference to `System`.

6. Next, change the preceding highlighted code into the following by using the `FromSqlInterpolated` method:

```
fundtransfer = _context.FundTransfer.
FromSqlInterpolated($"Select * from FundTransfer Where
Note Like {"%" + SearchString + "%"}");
```

7. The `FromSqlInterpolated` method will create a LINQ query from the *interpolated string* supplied.

The interpolated parameter, `SearchString`, will then be converted into a `DbParameter` object, making the code safe from SQL injection.

How it works...

The **Entity Framework** allows you to execute raw SQL queries using the `FromSQLRaw` method. However, this method is dangerous as you can supply the argument with concatenated strings with the user input, `SearchString`:

```
_context.FundTransfer.FromSqlRaw("Select * from FundTransfer
Where Note Like'%" + SearchString + "%'");
```

Using the payload used in the SQL injection test, imagine replacing the `SearchString` value with the malicious string `%';create table tbl1(one varchar(10), two smallint);Select * from Customers where id like '1`.

With `FromSqlRaw` blindly concatenating the injected input, the SQL statement now reads as follows:

```
Select * from FundTransfer Where Note Like'%%';create table
tbl1(one varchar(10), two smallint);Select * from Customers
where id like '1 %'
```

This is a perfectly valid series of SQL statements, except that it has a dangerous command that creates a new table or, in other cases or DBMS, could turn into a remote code execution by spawning a shell.

This way of forming SQL statements is regarded as bad coding practice. To write better and secure code, use methods such as `FromSqlInterpolated` to help compose harmless SQL statements with parameterized values.

There's more...

Parameterization is a proven secure coding practice that will prevent SQL injection. Another way to rewrite the code in this recipe is to use the DbParameter classes.

Introduce an instance of SqLiteParameter (which is derived from DbParameter) into the code as follows:

```
var searchParameter =
    new SqliteParameter("searchString", SearchString);
fundtransfer = _context.FundTransfer
    .FromSqlRaw("Select * from FundTransfer
        Where Note Like'%@searchString%'",searchParameter);
```

Whitelisting is also a useful technique as a means to filter user input. You will have already seen this approach discussed in detail in *Chapter 1*, *Secure Coding Fundamentals*. Whitelisting will cause ASP.NET Core web applications to only process data that is in an expected format, but this technique is not as effective as using prepared statements or parameterized queries.

Fixing SQL injection in ADO.NET

ADO.NET is a data provider platform that is integral to the .NET Framework. Since the advent of the .NET Framework, ADO.NET has been the component used to query and manipulate data in the database. ADO.NET can be used in developing data-driven ASP. NET Core web applications, but similar to any data providers, developers may write insecure code when using any of the System.Data.* or Microsoft.Data.* classes.

In this recipe, we will identify the SQL injection vulnerability in the code when using the ADO.NET and mitigate the issue by fixing this security flaw and applying a countermeasure.

Getting ready

Using Visual Studio Code, open the sample Online Banking app folder at \Chapter02\ sql-injection\razor\ado.net\before\OnlineBankingApp\.

How to do it...

Let's take a look at the steps for this recipe:

1. Launch Visual Studio Code and open the starting exercise folder by typing the following command:

```
code .
```

2. Navigate to **Terminal | New Terminal** in the menu or simply press *Ctrl + Shift + '* in Visual Studio Code.

3. Type the following command in the terminal to build the sample app to confirm that there are no compilation errors:

```
dotnet build
```

4. Open the `Data/FundTransferDAL.cs` file, which is the class that represents the data access layer of the sample application and locate the vulnerable part of the `GetFundTransfers` method where the user-controlled input is passed into the search parameter:

```
public IEnumerable<FundTransfer> GetFundTransfers(string
    search)
{
    List<FundTransfer> fundTransfers =
        new List<FundTransfer>();

    using (SqliteConnection con =
        new SqliteConnection(connectionString))
    {
        SqliteCommand cmd =
            new SqliteCommand("Select *
                fromFundTransfer where Note like '%"
                    + search + "%'", con);
        cmd.CommandType = CommandType.Text;

        con.Open();
        SqliteDataReader rdr = cmd.ExecuteReader();
```

5. The preceding highlighted code is where the query is composed, and the search concatenated to form a SQL query.

6. To remediate the SQL injection vulnerability, change the preceding highlighted code:

```
public IEnumerable<FundTransfer> GetFundTransfers(string
    search)
{
    List<FundTransfer> fundTransfers =
        new List<FundTransfer>();

    using (SqliteConnection con =
        new SqliteConnection(connectionString))
    {
        SqliteCommand cmd =
            new SqliteCommand("Select * from
                FundTransfer where Note like '%" +
                    @search + "%'", con);
        cmd.CommandType = CommandType.Text;

        cmd.Parameters.AddWithValue("@search",search);

        con.Open();
        SqliteDataReader rdr = cmd.ExecuteReader();
```

Using the parameterization approach, we have converted the search string into a SQL parameter and passed the value into `SqlLiteParameterCollection`.

How it works...

The `SqlLiteCommand` instance is blindly passed with a raw SQL concatenated user input. This supplied string is a source for a SQL injection. The input string search is not validated and unsanitized, letting an adversary insert an arbitrary SQL command or modify the query's intention:

```
SqliteCommand cmd = new SqliteCommand("Select * from
FundTransfer where Note like '%" + search + "%'", con);
```

You can rewrite the vulnerable ADO.NET code and make it secure by using query parameters. The `AddWithValue` method from `SqliteParametersCollection` of the `SQliteCommand` object allows you to add query parameters and safely pass values into the query:

```
cmd.Parameters.AddWithValue("@search", search);
```

Changing the search string into a placeholder makes the query parameterized:

```
SqliteCommand cmd = new SqliteCommand("Select * from
FundTransfer where Note like '%" + @search + "%'", con);
```

When your ASP.NET Core web application executes the preceding lines of code, the query is now parameterized, safely passing the search value, and preventing malicious actors from altering the SQL.

There's more...

This recipe uses **SQLite** as the DBMS for the sample solution, but if you were to use **Microsoft SQL Server**, another option is to convert the query into a stored procedure and use it with DB parameters. You would then have to utilize the `SQLCommand` object and set the `CommandType` property to `System.Data.CommandType.StoredProcedure`, allowing the execution of parameterized stored procedures from code. These classes are available under the `System.Data.SqlClient` namespace and in the new `Microsoft.Data.SqlClient` package.

Here's a sample code snippet:

```
SqlCommand cmd = new
    SqlCommand("sp_SearchFundTransfer",con);
cmd.CommandType = CommandType.StoredProcedure;
cmd.Parameters.AddWithValue("@search", search);
```

To write better and secure code, use the built-in support for database features such as prepared statements or parameterized queries made possible by its data provider frameworks.

Fixing NoSQL injection

NoSQL databases are a different type of database in which non-relational and semi-structured data is stored. There are many kinds of NoSQL databases to name, such as Cassandra, Redis, DynamoDB, and MongoDB, each with its own query language. Although distinct from one another, these queries are also prone to injection attacks.

In this recipe, we will identify the **NoSQL injection** vulnerability in code that is using MongoDB as the backend and fix the problem by applying several countermeasures.

Getting ready

Using Visual Studio Code, open the sample Online Banking app folder at `Chapter02\nosql-injection\before\OnlineBankingApp`.

How to do it...

Let's take a look at the steps for this recipe:

1. Launch Visual Studio Code and open the starting exercise folder by typing the following command:

   ```
   code .
   ```

2. Navigate to **Terminal | New Terminal** in the menu or simply press *Ctrl* + *Shift* + *'* in Visual Studio Code.

3. Type the following command in the terminal to build the sample app to confirm that there are no compilation errors:

   ```
   dotnet build
   ```

4. Open the `Services/PayeeService.cs` file and locate the vulnerable part of the code in the `Get(string name)` method:

   ```
   public List<Payee> Get(string name) {
       var filter = "{$where: \"function()
           {return this.Name == '" + name + "'}\"}";
       return payees.Find(filter).ToList();
   }
   ```

5. To remediate the NoSQL injection vulnerability, change the preceding highlighted code:

```
public List<Payee> Get(string name) {
    return payees.Find(payee => payee.Name ==
        name).ToList();
}
```

The filter passed into the `Find` method is now replaced with a **Lambda** expression, a much more secure way of searching for a payee by name.

How it works...

The `Get` method has a string parameter that can be supplied with a non-sanitized or validated value. This value can alter the **MongoDB** filter composed with it, making the NoSQL database perform an unintended behavior.

The `name` parameter can be appended with an expression that would evaluate the query into a logical result different from what the query was expected to perform. A JavaScript clause can also be inserted into a query that can terminate the statement and add a new block of arbitrary code.

By way of some general advice, avoid using the `$where` operator. Simply apply a C# Lambda expression as a filter to prevent any injectable JSON or JavaScript expression.

There's more...

Suppose the preceding options are not possible and it is necessary to use the `$where` clause, you must then JavaScript-encode the input. Use the `JavaScriptEncoder` class from the `System.Text.Encodings.Web` namespace to *encode* the value being passed into the parameter:

1. First, modify the `PayeeService.cs` file to add a reference to the `Encoder` namespace:

```
using System.Text.Encodings.Web;
```

2. Next, define a property for `JavaScriptEncoder`:

```
private readonly JavaScriptEncoder _jsEncoder;
```

3. Change the `PayeeService` constructor and add a new parameter to inject
    `JavaScriptEncoder`:

    ```
    public PayeeService(IOnlineBankDatabaseSettings
    settings,JavaScriptEncoder jsEncoder)
    ```

4. Lastly, encode the `name` parameter using the `Encode` function of
    `JavaScriptEncoder`:

    ```
    var filter = "{$where: \"function() {return this.Name ==
    '" + _jsEncoder.Encode(name) + "'}\"}";
    ```

If a malicious input was passed into the `name` parameter and was escaped by the `Encode`
method, the C# MongoDB driver will throw an exception if the escaped value could not
be interpreted as a valid JavaScript expression.

To prevent **NoSQL injections**, developers must *avoid building dynamic queries using string
concatenation*. NoSQL databases offer ways to query and process data, but you must be
aware of potential security implications a feature might bring into the ASP.NET Core web
application.

Fixing command injection

Web applications such as the ones developed with ASP.NET Core have a plethora of
components and libraries that enable them to execute OS commands in the host. If not
written securely, the code that composes and runs these commands can likely expose the
ASP.NET Core web application to command injection exploitation. Shell commands can
be executed unexpectedly if this security flaw in code is not prevented.

In this recipe, we will identify the **command injection** vulnerability in code and fix the
security vulnerability.

Getting ready

Using Visual Studio Code, open the sample Online Banking app folder at `Chapter02\`
`command-injection\before\OnlineBankingApp`.

Testing command injection

Here are the steps:

1. Navigate to **Terminal** | **New Terminal** in the menu or simply press *Ctrl* + *Shift* + ' in Visual Studio Code.

2. Type the following command in the terminal to build and run the sample app:

```
dotnet run
```

3. Open a browser and go to `http://localhost:5000/Backups/Create`.

4. The browser will display the web page for initiating database backup, as shown in the following screenshot:

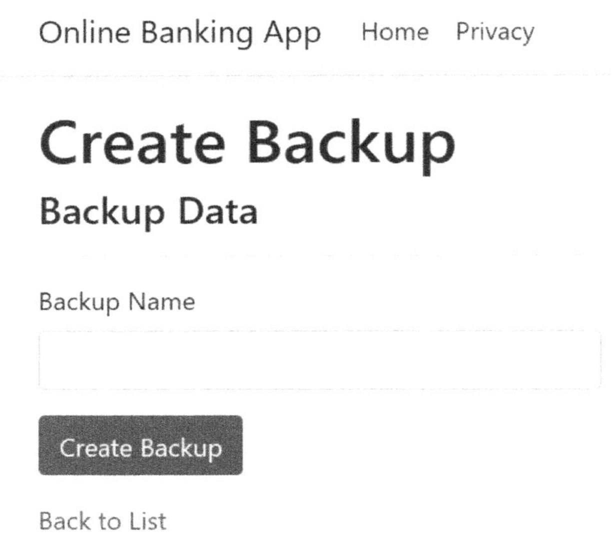

Online Banking App   Home   Privacy

Create Backup

Backup Data

Backup Name

Create Backup

Back to List

Figure 2.5 – Backup page

5. Enter this command injection payload, `backup & calc`, in the **Backup Name** field, and hit the **Create** button.

6. Notice that the page redirected to the list of backup pages and the backup was created. However, the calculator app has appeared:

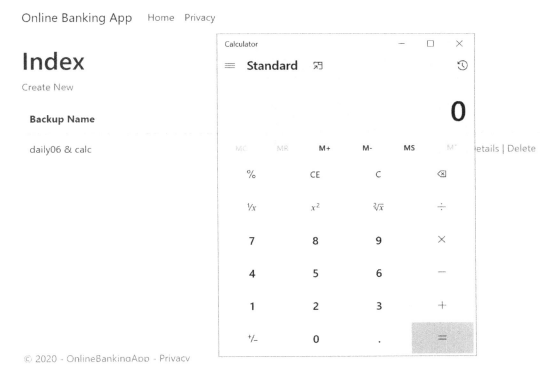

Figure 2.6 – Successful command injection

If this security bug is not handled, this problem could also expose the underlying hosts to **Remote Code Execution (RCE)**.

How to do it...

Let's take a look at the steps for this recipe:

1. Launch Visual Studio Code and open the starting exercise folder by typing the following command:

    ```
    code .
    ```

2. Navigate to **Terminal | New Terminal** in the menu or simply press *Ctrl + Shift + '* in Visual Studio Code.

3. Type the following command in the terminal to build the sample app to confirm that there are no compilation errors:

```
dotnet build
```

4. Open the `Services/BackupService.cs` file and locate the vulnerable part of the code in the `BackupDB(string backupname)` method:

```
public async Task BackupDB(string backupname)
{
    using (Process p = new Process())
    {
        string source =
            Environment.CurrentDirectory +
                "\\OnlineBank.db";
        string destination =
            Environment.CurrentDirectory +
                "\\backups\\" + backupname;
        p.StartInfo.Arguments =
            " /c copy " + source + " " + destination;
        p.StartInfo.FileName = "cmd";
        p.StartInfo.CreateNoWindow = true;

...code removed for brevity
```

5. To remediate the command injection vulnerability, add a new method that utilizes the built-in file copying function:

```
public async Task FileCopyAsync(string sourceFileName,
    string destinationFileName,
    int bufferSize = 0x1000,
    CancellationToken cancellationToken =
        default(CancellationToken))
{
    using (var sourceFile =
        File.OpenRead(sourceFileName))
    {
        using (var destinationFile =
            File.OpenWrite(destinationFileName))
        {
```

```
                    await
                    sourceFile.CopyToAsync(destinationFile,
                        bufferSize, cancellationToken);
            }
        }
    }
```

6. Rewrite the entire body of the `BackupDB` method and use the newly created method:

```
public async Task BackupDB(string backupname)
{
    string source =
        Environment.CurrentDirectory +
            "\\OnlineBank.db";
    string destination =
        Environment.CurrentDirectory + "\\backups\\"
            + backupname;
    await FileCopyAsync(source, destination);
}
```

We have refactored the `BackUpDB` method to use the `FileCopyAsync` method to limit your code to just perform file copying tasks, thereby preventing the execution of unwanted shell commands.

How it works...

In our sample solution, administrators are allowed to provide a name to create a database backup. The `BackUpDB` method accepts a user-controlled input parameter of the `string` type. The input string is used to form a command that will initiate a command shell to have files copied from the source to the destination.

The added input string is expected to have the destination filename, but this can be manipulated to include commands that are more than just a value for an argument. Without validation or sanitization, this could cause the application to execute unwanted shell commands under the web application's identity and authorization.

There's more...

One option of stopping OS command injection is to implement proper validation through the *whitelisting technique*. This technique can be achieved by using *regular expressions* (see the *Input validation* recipe in *Chapter 1, Secure Coding Fundamentals*):

1. Add a reference to the `System.Text.RegularExpressions` namespace:

    ```
    using System.Text.RegularExpressions;
    ```

2. Then, use the `RegEx` class and its `IsMatch` method to validate the input against a pattern to only accept valid characters:

    ```
    public async Task BackupDB(string backupname)
    {
        var regex = new Regex(@"^[a-zA-Z0-9]+$");
        if (!regex.IsMatch(backupname)) return;

        using (Process p = new Process())
        {
            string source =
                Environment.CurrentDirectory +
                    "\\OnlineBank.db";
            string destination =
                Environment.CurrentDirectory +
                    "\\backups\\" + backupname;
            p.StartInfo.Arguments = " /c copy " + source +
                " " + destination;
            p.StartInfo.FileName = "cmd";
            p.StartInfo.CreateNoWindow = true;
    // code removed for brevity
    ```

We have now added a whitelisting validation with the use of the `IsMatch` method. The `IsMatch` method prevents non-alphanumeric characters and input from being processed in the succeeding lines of code, mitigating the risk of command injection.

Fixing LDAP injection

The **Light Directory Access Protocol (LDAP)** is a standard protocol used to access directory services such as Microsoft's Active Directory and Apache Directory. Web applications use LDAP to search the directory server to get users and group information, which also serves as a means of authentication. This retrieval of data from the web application to the LDAP directory server is possible because of the LDAP query language and its filters. Developers write code to compose these queries. Like any other dynamic query construction, this method can open the code to injection, particularly **LDAP injection**, when the concatenated user-controlled input is not validated or sanitized.

In this recipe, we will identify the **LDAP injection** vulnerability in code and fix the security vulnerability.

Getting ready

Using Visual Studio Code, open the sample Online Banking app folder at `\Chapter02\ldap-injection\before\OnlineBankingApp\`.

How to do it...

Let's take a look at the steps for this recipe:

1. Launch Visual Studio Code and open the starting exercise folder by typing the following command:

```
code .
```

2. Navigate to **Terminal | New Terminal** in the menu or simply press *Ctrl + Shift + '* in Visual Studio Code.

3. Type the following command in the terminal to build the sample app to confirm that there are no compilation errors:

```
dotnet build
```

4. Open the `Services/LdapDirectoryService.cs` file and locate the vulnerable part of the code in the `Search(string userName)` method:

```
public User Search(string userName)
{
    using (DirectoryEntry entry =
        new DirectoryEntry(config.Path))
    {
```

```
        entry.AuthenticationType =
            AuthenticationTypes.Anonymous;
        using (DirectorySearcher searcher =
            new DirectorySearcher(entry))
        {
            searcher.Filter = "(&(" +
                UserNameAttribute + "="
                    + userName + "))";
            searcher.PropertiesToLoad.Add
                (EmailAttribute);
            searcher.PropertiesToLoad.Add
                (UserNameAttribute);
            var result = searcher.FindOne();

// code removed for brevity
```

5. To fix the LDAP injection vulnerability, refactor the code to include a *whitelist validation* of the userName parameter:

```
public User Search(string userName)
{
    if (Regex.IsMatch(userName, "^[a-zA-Z][a-zA-Z0-
        9]*$")){
        using (DirectoryEntry entry =
            new DirectoryEntry(config.Path))
        {
            entry.AuthenticationType =
                AuthenticationTypes.Anonymous;
            using (DirectorySearcher searcher =
                new DirectorySearcher(entry))
            {
                searcher.Filter = "(&(" +
                    UserNameAttribute + "=" + userName
                        + "))";
                searcher.PropertiesToLoad.Add
                    (EmailAttribute);
                searcher.PropertiesToLoad.Add
                    (UserNameAttribute);
```

```
                    var result = searcher.FindOne();

    // code removed for brevity
```

Reusing the whitelisting technique through the use of regular expressions, we again utilize the `IsMatch` method to ascertain whether the pattern matches the input. If the input does not match the regular expression, the input is then rejected.

How it works...

In our sample solution, we have a web page that allows an admin user to search for a specific user account using the search bar:

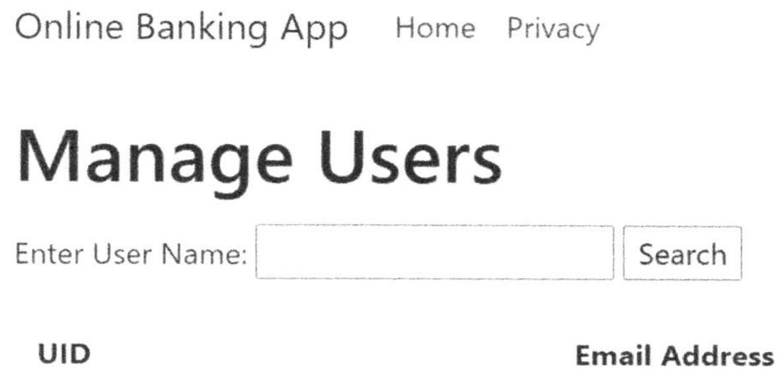

Online Banking App   Home   Privacy

Manage Users

Enter User Name: [   ] Search

UID   **Email Address**

Figure 2.7 – Manage Users page

Entering a user ID and hitting the **Search** button will send an LDAP query to the LDAP directory service to search for a user that has the exact user ID:

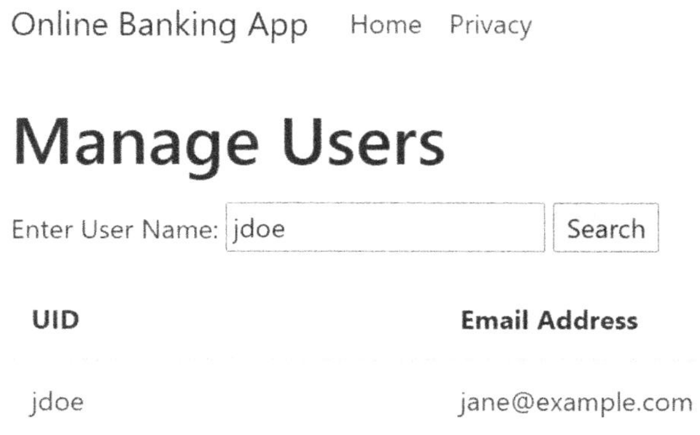

Online Banking App   Home   Privacy

Manage Users

Enter User Name: [jdoe   ] Search

UID   **Email Address**

jdoe   jane@example.com

Figure 2.8 – Search user result

> **Note**
>
> The steps on setting up your LDAP directory service are not provided in this
> book. Suppose you want a working directory server that runs in your local
> machine to work with the sample solution. In that case, I suggest you install
> **ApacheDS** and follow the steps from the **Setting up an LDAP server for
> development/testing using Apache Directory Studio** page in the official
> Crafter CMS documentation: `https://docs.craftercms.org/`
> `en/3.1/developers/cook-books/how-tos/setting-up-`
> `an-ldap-server-for-dev.html`.
>
> Change the `Ldap` entry in `appsettings.json` if necessary:
>
> ```
>   "Ldap": {
>     "Path": "LDAP://localhost:10389/
> DC=example,DC=com",
>     "UserDomainName": "example"
>   },
> ```

As the `Search` method is invoked, an LDAP query is dynamically composed, and a filter
is concatenated with the value entered in the search textbox:

```
searcher.Filter = "(&(" + UserNameAttribute + "=" + userName +
"))";
```

The `userName` parameter is not sanitized or validated, and a bad actor can exploit this
by injecting suspicious filters that could retrieve sensitive information from the LDAP
directory server.

To mitigate this risk, we used Regex's `IsMatch` method to add a whitelist validation
approach. The conditional expression will only be equivalent to true if any of the
characters in `userName` are alphanumeric:

```
public User Search(string userName)
{
    if (Regex.IsMatch(userName, "^[a-zA-Z][a-zA-Z0-9]*$")){
        using (DirectoryEntry entry = new
            DirectoryEntry(config.Path))
        {
// code removed for brevity
```

Include as part of the overall secure coding strategy the implementation of a whitelist
input validation to check user-controlled inputs, safeguarding your ASP.NET Core web
application from LDAP injection attacks.

Fixing XPath injection

Data-driven ASP.NET Core web applications can use XML databases as a means to store information and records. These data types are in XML format, and one way of navigating through the nodes of XML is by **XPath**.

Developers can, by mistake, dynamically construct XPath queries with untrusted data. This neglect can result in an arbitrary query execution or the retrieval of sensitive data from the XML database.

In this recipe, we will fix the **XPath injection** vulnerability in code.

Getting ready

Using Visual Studio Code, open the sample Online Banking app folder at `\Chapter02\ xpath-injection\before\OnlineBankingApp\`.

This example uses the following XML data:

```
<?xml version="1.0" encoding="utf-8"?>
<knowledgebase>
    <knowledge>
        <topic lang="en">Types of Transfers</topic>
        <description lang="en">
            Make transfers from checking and savings to:
            Checking and savings
            Make transfers from line of credit to:
            Checking and savings
        </description>
        <tags>transfers, transferring funds</tags>
        <sensitivity>Public</sensitivity>
    </knowledge>
    <knowledge>
        <topic lang="en">Expedited Withdrawals</topic>
        <description lang="en">
        Expedited withdrawals are available to our
        executive account holders.
        You may reach out to Stanley Jobson at
        stanley.jobson@bank.com
        </description>
        <tags>withdrawals, expedited withdrawals</tags>
```

```
      <sensitivity>Confidential</sensitivity>
   </knowledge>
</knowledgebase>
```

How to do it...

Let's take a look at the steps for this recipe:

1. Launch Visual Studio Code and open the starting exercise folder by typing the following command:

    ```
    code .
    ```

2. Navigate to **Terminal | New Terminal** in the menu or simply press *Ctrl + Shift + '* in Visual Studio Code.

3. Type the following command in the terminal to build the sample app to confirm that there are no compilation errors:

    ```
    dotnet build
    ```

4. Open the `Services/KnowledgebaseService.cs` file and locate the vulnerable part of the code in the `Search` method:

    ```
    public List<Knowledge> Search(string input)
    {
        List<Knowledge> searchResult = new
            List<Knowledge>();
        var webRoot = _env.WebRootPath;
        var file = System.IO.Path.Combine(webRoot,
            "Knowledgebase.xml");

        XmlDocument XmlDoc = new XmlDocument();
        XmlDoc.Load(file);

        XPathNavigator nav = XmlDoc.CreateNavigator();
        XPathExpression expr =
            nav.Compile(@"//knowledge[tags[contains(text()
                ,'" + input + "')] and sensitivity/text()
                ='Public']");
    ```

```
var matchedNodes = nav.Select(expr);
// code removed for brevity
```

An XPath expression is dynamically created by concatenating the user-controlled input. Without any validation or sanitization done on the `input` parameter, a malicious actor can manipulate the XPath query by injecting malicious string, changing the intent of the whole expression.

5. To fix this security bug, let's refactor the code and implement input sanitization based on the whitelisting technique. To start, add a reference to both the `System` and `System.Linq` namespaces:

```
using System;
using System.Linq;
```

6. Add a new method to the `KnowledgebaseService` class and name it `Sanitize`:

```
private string Sanitize(string input)
{
    if (string.IsNullOrEmpty(input)) {
        throw new ArgumentNullException("input",
            "input cannot be null");
    }
    HashSet<char> whitelist = new HashSet<char>
        (@"1234567890ABCDEFGHIJKLMNOPQRSTUVWXYZ
            abcdefghijklmnopqrstuvwxyz ");
    return string.Concat(input.Where(i =>
        whitelist.Contains(i))); ;
}
```

7. Call the new `Sanitize` method, passing the `input` parameter to it as an argument. Assign the result to the `sanitizedInput` variable:

```
public List<Knowledge> Search(string input)
{
    string sanitizedInput = Sanitize(input);

    List<Knowledge> searchResult = new
        List<Knowledge>();
    var webRoot = _env.WebRootPath;
```

```
var file = System.IO.Path.Combine(webRoot,
    "Knowledgebase.xml");

XmlDocument XmlDoc = new XmlDocument();
XmlDoc.Load(file);

XPathNavigator nav = XmlDoc.CreateNavigator();
XPathExpression expr =
    nav.Compile(@"//knowledge[tags[contains(text()
        ,'" + sanitizedInput + "')] and
            sensitivity/text()='Public']");

// code removed for brevity
```

The custom `Sanitize` method will now remove unnecessary and possibly dangerous characters in the input string. The output is now passed into a `sanitizedInput` variable, making the XPath expression safe from exploitation.

How it works...

As we have learned in *Chapter 1*, *Secure Coding Fundamentals*, in the *Input sanitization* section, input sanitization is a defensive technique that can be practiced to remove suspicious characters in a user-supplied input. This approach will prevent the application from processing unwanted **XPath** injected into the query.

We have created the new `Sanitize` method that will serve as our sanitizer. Inside this method is a whitelist of defined characters and a Lambda invoked to remove the characters rejected from `userName`:

```
HashSet<char> whitelist = new
HashSet<char>(@"1234567890ABCDEFGHI
JKLMNOPQRSTUVWXYZabcdefghijklmnopqrstuvwxyz ");
return string.Concat(input.Where(i =>
    whitelist.Contains(i))); ;
```

Searching for a help article with an unacceptable character will not throw an exception, and our sample Online Banking web application will also not process the string:

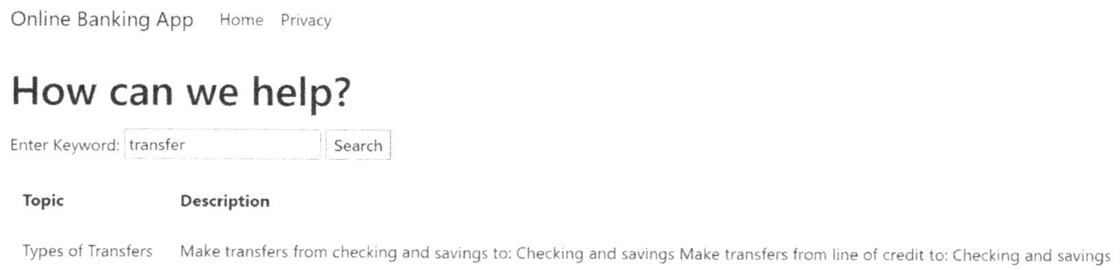

Online Banking App   Home   Privacy

How can we help?

Enter Keyword: transfer | Search |

Topic   **Description**

Types of Transfers   Make transfers from checking and savings to: Checking and savings Make transfers from line of credit to: Checking and savings

Figure 2.9 – Searching the knowledge base

There's more...

An alternative fix is to *parameterize the XPath query*. We will define a variable that will serve as a placeholder for an argument. This technique allows the data to be separated from code:

```
XmlDocument XmlDoc = new XmlDocument();
XmlDoc.Load(file);

XPathNavigator nav = XmlDoc.CreateNavigator();
XPathExpression expr =
    nav.Compile(@"//knowledge[tags[contains(text(),$input)]
        and sensitivity/text()='Public']");

XsltArgumentList varList = new XsltArgumentList();
varList.AddParam("input", string.Empty, input);

CustomContext context = new CustomContext(new NameTable(),
    varList);
expr.SetContext(context);

var matchedNodes = nav.Select(expr);

foreach (XPathNavigator node in matchedNodes)
{
    searchResult.Add(new Knowledge() {Topic =
      node.SelectSingleNode(nav.Compile("topic"))
        .Value,Description = node.SelectSingleNode
          (nav.Compile("description")).Value});
}
```

In the preceding code, the XPath expression is modified, and the $input variable is now a placeholder for the previously concatenated input value. We also used the XsltArgumentList object to create a list of arguments to include input before passing into the XpathExpression expression's custom context. In this way, the XPath query is parameterized and protected from malicious injection upon execution.

> **Note**
>
> This mitigation requires the creation of a user-defined custom context class that derives from XsltContext. There are other classes required to make this XPath parameterization possible. The class files are included in the sample solution, namely; Services\XPathExtensionFunctions.cs, Services\XPathExtensionVariable.cs, and Services\CustomContext.cs. The whole guide and source for these classes are also available online at the .NET official documentation: https://docs.microsoft.com/en-us/dotnet/standard/data/xml/user-defined-functions-and-variables.

3
Broken Authentication

Perhaps the most crucial security requirement of all – authentication – is necessary to verify and confirm identity in an ASP.NET web application. Failing to implement strong authentication allows hackers to expose this flaw and exploit it to gain forbidden access.

Weak password policies, missing brute-force attack prevention mechanisms, weakly hashed passwords, and long active sessions are a few root causes of these authentication defects. Proper credential management and session configuration are key in preventing these vulnerabilities in code. This chapter will teach us how to fix these issues.

In this chapter, we're going to cover the following recipes:

- Fixing incorrect restrictions of excessive authentication attempts
- Fixing insufficiently protected credentials
- Fixing user enumeration
- Fixing weak password requirements
- Fixing insufficient session expiration

By the end of this chapter, you will have learned how to implement **CAPTCHA** to prevent brute-force attacks, use a robust hashing algorithm to better protect your passwords, send generic messages to avoid unnecessary information being exposed, and configure sessions so that they expire in an acceptable time period.

Technical requirements

This book was written and designed to use with Visual Studio Code, Git, and .NET 5.0. Code examples in recipes are presented in ASP.NET Core Razor Pages. The sample solution also uses SQLite as the database engine for a more simplified setup. You can find the code for this chapter at `https://github.com/PacktPublishing/ASP.NET-Core-Secure-Coding-Cookbook/tree/main/Chapter03`.

Fixing the incorrect restrictions of excessive authentication attempts

An adversary will always try to gain access to the system and beat its authentication mechanism. The most prevalent way of doing this is by using compromised credentials, collected from illicit sources, or as simple as having a list of common passwords, which can be found on the web. These attacks can be executed with automation using a crafted script or a tool.

An ASP.NET Core web application must withstand this exploitation by implementing defensive measures. This helps with rejecting excessive authentication attempts and writing secure code.

In this recipe, we will identify the root cause of vulnerabilities in code and mitigate the issue by enabling the lockout feature.

Getting ready

Using Visual Studio Code, open the sample Online Banking app folder at `\Chapter03\improper-auth\before\OnlineBankingApp`.

Testing the restriction of excessive authentication attempts

Follow these steps:

1. Navigate to **Terminal | New Terminal** in the menu or simply press *Ctrl + Shift + '* in Visual Studio Code.

2. Type the following command in the Terminal to build and run the sample app:

```
dotnet run
```

3. Open a browser and go to `http://localhost:5000`.

4. The browser will display the **Log in** page:

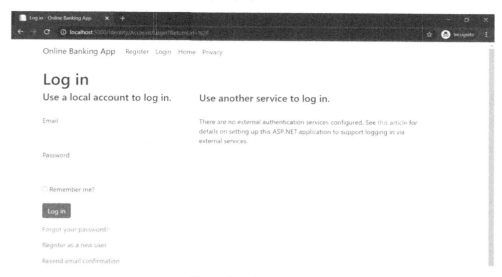

Figure 3.1 – Log in page

5. Try to log in by entering `stanley.s.jobson@lobortis.ca` as the email address and `password123` as the password.

6. You will see an error stating **Invalid login attempt**:

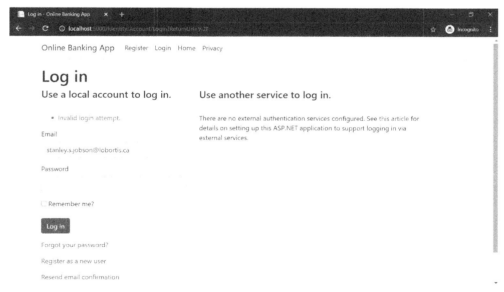

Figure 3.2 – Invalid login attempt

7. Repeat *Step 5* more than five times to try and invoke an account lockout.

After multiple failed attempts of logging in, notice that the account is not being locked. This missing lockout feature makes the ASP.NET Core web application open to brute-force attacks.

How to do it...

Let's take a look at the steps for this recipe:

1. Using the same sample solution we opened in the preceding steps, type the following command in the Terminal to build the sample app to confirm there are no compilation errors:

```
dotnet build
```

2. Open the \Chapter03\improper-auth\before\OnlineBankingApp\ Areas\Identity\Pages\Account\Login.cshtml.cs file and locate the line of code that makes a call to the PasswordSignInAsync method:

```
public async Task<IActionResult> OnPostAsync(string
    returnUrl = null)
{
    returnUrl ??= Url.Content("~/");

    ExternalLogins = (await
        _signInManager.GetExternalAuthenticationScheme
            sAsync()).ToList();

    if (ModelState.IsValid)
    {
        var result = await
            _signInManager.PasswordSignInAsync(Input.
                Email, Input.Password,
                    Input.RememberMe,lockoutOnFailure:
                        false);
        if (result.Succeeded)
        {
            _logger.LogInformation("User logged in.");
```

```
            return LocalRedirect(returnUrl);
        }
```

3. Change the last parameter in the `PasswordSignInAsync` method from `false` to `true`:

```
var result = await
_signInManager.PasswordSignInAsync(Input.Email, Input.
    Password, Input.RememberMe, lockoutOnFailure: true);
```

Changing the `lockoutOnFailure` argument from `false` to `true` will trigger a lockout on the user account when several failed password logins have been reached.

4. Next, configure the `Identity` service by setting the `DefaultLockoutTimeSpan` and `MaxFailedAttempts` properties:

```
services.AddIdentity<Customer,IdentityRole>(options => {
    options.Lockout.DefaultLockoutTimeSpan =
        TimeSpan.FromMinutes(5);
    options.Lockout.MaxFailedAccessAttempts = 3;
})
```

Setting the lockout policies will configure the lockout behavior of our sample Online Banking web application. `DefaultLockoutTimeSpan` sets the time for how long a user is locked out in minutes. The default value of this setting is 5 minutes.

The default number of failed password attempts before a user is locked out is 5. The default value can be overwritten by assigning the `MaxFailedAccessAttempts` property of `IdentityOptions`, which can be configured in the `AddIdentity` method and is invoked from the `ConfigureServices` method. `MaxFailedAccessAttempts` is set to lock the user out after *three failed login attempts*. The values of these properties should be assigned with values as per your organization's lockout policy.

How it works...

`PasswordSignInAsync` is a method call we use to log in a `Customer` using their `Input.Email` and `Input.Password` values. It expects a `lockoutOnFailure` argument that indicates whether a `Customer` should be locked out from the account if the login fails for a specified number of attempts.

The `lockoutOnFailure` parameter is set to `true` to enable a lockout on a failed sign in. This will prevent automated and excessive authentication retries by a malicious actor. The number of failed attempts can be defined using the `MaxFailedAccessAttempts` property of the `LockoutOptions` class.

> **Tips**
>
> Make sure to log failed sign-in attempts and account lockouts. These types of events should be logged and monitored for a potential brute-force attack. You will learn more about proper logging and monitoring techniques in *Chapter 11, Insufficient Logging and Monitoring*.

There's more...

Another security feature that can help prevent brute-force attacks is to implement a CAPTCHA. A **CAPTCHA** is a challenge-response test that helps determine if a human or a computer executed the action. This type of test can help detect abuse and automated login attempts.

There are various CAPTCHA systems available for web developers to use, and Google's **reCAPTCHA** is the most popular among them. To use Google's **reCAPTCHA** in your ASP.NET Core web application, follow these steps:

1. Sign up for the *reCAPTCHA* service on the Google Developer website (`https://developers.google.com/recaptcha/intro`) to get an API key pair. This API key pair will be used to integrate reCAPTCHA into our sample solution.

2. When registering localhost as the website, select the reCAPTCHA v2 **I'm not a robot** checkbox. This recipe is based on version 2 of the reCAPTCHA system.

3. Type the following command in the Terminal to install the *Google reCAPTCHA ASP.NET Core 3* library:

```
dotnet add package reCAPTCHA.AspNetCore
```

4. The *Google reCAPTCHA ASP.NET Core 3* library is a third-party and open source NuGet package that helps ASP.NET Core web developers integrate the Google reCAPTCHA system easily.

> **Warning**
>
> Using any third-party libraries comes with a risk. You may want to review the package's code before integrating it into your ASP.NET Core web application. Make sure that you are using the latest and stable version.

5. Create a new entry for the reCAPTCHA settings in the `appsettings.json` file:

```
{
  "RecaptchaSettings": {
    "SecretKey": "secret key",
    "SiteKey": "site key"
  },
  "https_port": 443,
```

6. Open the `\Chapter03\improper-auth\before\captcha\OnlineBankingApp\Startup.cs` file and add a reference to the Google ASP.NET reCAPTCHA library:

```
using reCAPTCHA.AspNetCore;
```

7. Register the reCAPTCHA service in the `ConfigureServices` method:

```
services.AddRecaptcha(Configuration.
GetSection("RecaptchaSettings"));
```

8. Select the Razor pages where you want to enable the Google reCAPTCHA. Typically, this is placed on pages where authentication or registration abuse is expected. Open the `\Chapter03\improper-auth\before\captcha\OnlineBankingApp\Areas\Identity\Pages\Account\Login.cshtml` file and add a reference to the reCAPTCHA namespaces:

```
@page
@using reCAPTCHA.AspNetCore
@using reCAPTCHA.AspNetCore.Versions;
```

9. Include a reference to `Microsoft.Extensions.Options`. A reference to this `Microsoft.Extensions.Options` namespace provides access to classes that implement the `Options` pattern, including the reCAPTCHA-related configuration settings:

```
@using Microsoft.Extensions.Options;
```

10. Add the Recaptcha HTML Helper just below the `submit` button so that the Razor page renders the reCAPTCHA and displays the challenge:

```
<div class="form-group">
<button type="submit" class="btn btn-primary">
    Log in</button>
</div>
<div class="form-group">
 @(Html.Recaptcha<RecaptchaV2Checkbox>(Recaptcha
    Settings?.Value))
</div>
```

11. Open the corresponding page model class' `\Chapter03\improper-auth\ before\captcha\OnlineBankingApp\Areas\Identity\Pages\ Account\Login.cshtml.cs` file and add a reference to the reCAPTCHA namespaces:

```
using reCAPTCHA.AspNetCore;
```

12. Using dependency injection, declare a private `readonly` object that will hold an instance of `IRecaptchaService`. Add a new parameter to the `LoginModel` constructor that will expose the injected service in the class:

```
private readonly IRecaptchaService _recaptcha;

public LoginModel(SignInManager<Customer>
        signInManager,
    ILogger<LoginModel> logger,
    UserManager<Customer> userManager,
    IRecaptchaService recaptcha)
{
    _userManager = userManager;
    _signInManager = signInManager;
    _logger = logger;
    _recaptcha = recaptcha;
}
```

13. In the `OnPostAsync` method, call where the account login verification happens and add the following highlighted lines of code to validate the reCAPTCHA response:

```
public async Task<IActionResult> OnPostAsync(string
    returnUrl = null)
{

    var recaptcha = await
        _recaptcha.Validate(this.HttpContext.Request);
    if (!recaptcha.success)
        ModelState.AddModelError("Recaptcha",
            "Error Validating Captcha");
```

14. The `Validate` method call from the reCAPTCHA service will take the current HTTP context and check whether the user's CAPTCHA response is valid.

15. Repeat *steps 1 to 7* of the *Testing the restriction of excessive authentication attempts* section and check out the results of implementing a CAPTCHA test when trying to log in:

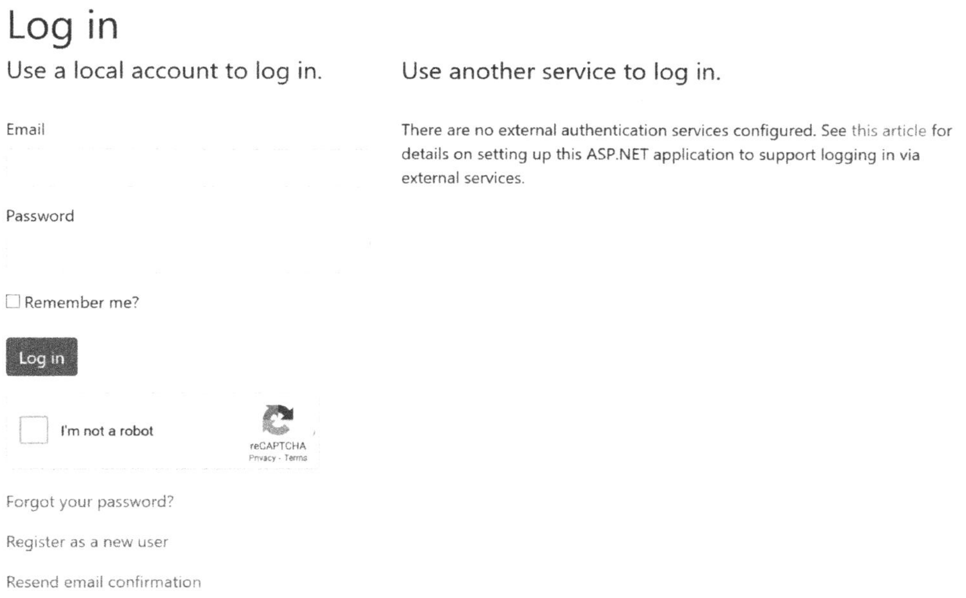

Log in

Use a local account to log in.   Use another service to log in.

Email   There are no external authentication services configured. See this article for
                                         details on setting up this ASP.NET application to support logging in via
                                         external services.
Password

☐ Remember me?

Log in

☐ I'm not a robot   reCAPTCHA
                           Privacy - Terms

Forgot your password?

Register as a new user

Resend email confirmation

Figure 3.3 – Login page with reCAPTCHA

Supplementing the ASP.NET Core web application with a reCAPTCHA service will now prevent automated attacks and brute-forcing.

Fixing insufficiently protected credentials

Password breakers and crackers are now more powerful than ever with advanced hardware and endless computing resources. Simply hashing the passwords is no longer enough, and it is now crucial to pick the right hashing function to protect the credentials from being exposed when a data breach happens.

In this recipe, we will modify the code that implements a weak hashing function and replace it with BCrypt.

Getting ready

Using Visual Studio Code, open the sample Online Banking app folder at `\Chapter03\insufficient-protected-creds\before\OnlineBankingApp`.

How to do it...

Let's take a look at the steps for this recipe:

1. Type the following command in a Terminal to build the sample app to confirm there are no compilation errors:

   ```
   dotnet build
   ```

2. Open the `\Chapter03\insufficient-protected-creds\before\OnlineBankingApp\Areas\Identity\PasswordHasher.cs` file. The `PasswordHasher` class is derived from `IPasswordHasher`, which lets you define your own custom hashing mechanism for your ASP.NET Core web application. Notice, however, that the hashing algorithm being used in the `HashPassword` method is **MD5**, which is *a known weak hashing algorithm*:

   ```
   public string HashPassword(Customer customer, string
       password)
   {
       using (var md5 = new MD5CryptoServiceProvider()) {
   ```

```
            var hashedBytes = md5.ComputeHash(System.Text
                .Encoding.UTF8.GetBytes(password));
            var hashedPassword =
                BitConverter.ToString(hashedBytes)
                    .Replace("-", "").ToLower();
            return hashedPassword;
        }

    }
```

> **Note**
>
> There are many reasons why a developer would customize their hashing process and select a weaker algorithm – migration from legacy applications and backward compatibility is one. It is still advisable and worth the effort to migrate your passwords into a more robust algorithm.

3. In the Visual Studio Code Terminal, type in the following command to install the `Bcrypt.Net` NuGet package:

```
dotnet add package BCrypt.Net-Next
```

4. `Bcrypt.Net` is a .NET library implementation of the **Bcrypt** hashing function based on the **Blowfish** cipher. The BCrypt hashing function implements a strong security measure as it adds **salt** to the hashing process. Bcrypt.Net lets developers define their own salt in the hash, but it is advisable to just let the library generate its own salt.

> **Note:**
>
> For more information and details about the **BCrypt** hashing algorithm, see the official publication titled *A Future-Adaptable Password Scheme* by the **bcrypt** algorithm designers *Niels Provos and David Mazieres* on the USENIX website:
>
> `https://www.usenix.org/legacy/events/usenix99/provos/provos_html/node1.html`.

5. Add a reference to the Bcrypt.NET namespace:

```
using BC = BCrypt.Net.BCrypt;
```

6. Register our custom IPasswordHasher service using the AddSingleton method:

```
services.AddSingleton<IEmailSender, EmailSender>();
services.Configure<AuthMessageSenderOptions>
(Configuration);
services.AddSingleton<IPasswordHasher<Customer>,
  PasswordHasher>();
```

7. Replace both the HashPassword and VerifyHashedPassword methods with the following code:

```
public class PasswordHasher : IPasswordHasher<Customer>
{
    public string HashPassword(Customer customer,
        string password)
    {
        return BC.HashPassword(password);
    }

    public PasswordVerificationResult
        VerifyHashedPassword(Customer customer,
            string hashedPassword, string password)
    {
        if (BC.Verify(password, hashedPassword))
            return PasswordVerificationResult.Success;
        else
            return PasswordVerificationResult.Failed;
    }
}
```

Here, we are using the HashPassword and Verify methods of the **BCrypt** library to hash passwords and verify the hash, respectively.

How it works...

Our sample application has customized the hashing algorithm implementation by creating a `PasswordHasher` class and inheriting from the `IPasswordHasher` interface, to modify how a password is hashed. The **MD5** hashing algorithm is known to be a weak cipher. We can replace this vulnerable hash function by implementing the **bcrypt** algorithm.

We installed the BCrypt.NET library implementation via the `BCrypt.Net-Next` NuGet package, adding a reference to the `BCrypt.Net.BCrypt` namespace and rewriting the entire `HashPassword` function to make a call to BCrypt.Net's `HashPassword` method.

> **Note:**
>
> Most security experts prefer **Argon2**, a newer hashing function introduced back in July 2015 that has a compute-intensive hard memory function, making it *resistant to hardware-based attacks*. `Isopoh.Cryptography.Argon2` is an open source project that ports the Argon2 hashing function implementation, a library that ASP.NET Core developers can use if they prefer to use this hashing method. You can follow the instructions for installing the .NET Core Argon2 library at: `https://github.com/mheyman/Isopoh.Cryptography.Argon2`.
>
> On the other hand, **Bcrypt** is still a good option since its process is time-consuming, making it hard to break; however, it can be prone to GPU-based cracking.

Fixing user enumeration

Every single piece of information is vital to a malicious actor. Knowing if a user exists in a web application gives the attacker leverage to execute a more damaging and successful attack. Protect your ASP.NET Core web application by not providing this information by displaying general messages during authentication failures.

In this recipe, we will change the code that displays the not-so generic error message to prevent user enumeration attacks.

Getting ready

Using Visual Studio Code, open the sample Online Banking app folder at `\Chapter03\user-emumeration\before\OnlineBankingApp`.

Testing user enumeration

Follow these steps:

1. Navigate to **Terminal | New Terminal** in the menu or simply press *Ctrl* + *Shift* + ' in Visual Studio Code.

2. Type the following command in the Terminal to build and run the sample app:

    ```
    dotnet run
    ```

3. Open a browser and go to `http://localhost:5000`.

4. The browser will display the login page (see *Figure 3.1*).

5. Log in using `ginger.knowles@bank.com` as the username and `password123` as the password.

6. Notice the error message **Customer does not exist**:

Figure 3.4 – User enumeration

This error message provides information to the attacker that a particular email address does not exist in the system. The attacker can then use this information to collect email addresses that have an account or record.

How to do it...

Let's take a look at the steps for this recipe:

1. Type the following command in the Terminal to build the sample app to confirm there are no compilation errors:

```
dotnet build
```

2. Open the \Chapter03\user-enumeration\before\
OnlineBankingApp\Areas\Identity\Pages\Account\Login.
cshtml.cs file and locate the line of code within the OnPostAsync method call that throws the Customer does not exist. error message:

```
if (result.IsLockedOut)
{
    _logger.LogWarning("Customer account locked out.");
    return RedirectToPage("./Lockout");
}
else
{
    var user = await
        _userManager.FindByEmailAsync(Input.Email);
    if (user == null)
    {
        ModelState.AddModelError(string.Empty,
            "Customer does not exist.");
        return Page();
    }
}
```

3. Modify the code so that it returns a generic message; that is, Invalid login attempt.:

```
if (result.IsLockedOut)
{
    _logger.LogWarning("Customer account locked out.");
    return RedirectToPage("./Lockout");
```

```
    }
    else
    {
        ModelState.AddModelError(string.Empty,
            "Invalid login attempt.");
        return Page();
    }
```

Changing the error message that's displayed on failed login attempts will prevent user enumeration attacks.

How it works...

An adversary can gather information by analyzing an application's behavior, especially on the messages that your ASP.NET Core web application displays to its users. The message *"Customer does not exist"* indicates that an email address (used as a username, in this case) does not exist in the database. This malicious actor can then come up with a list of valid usernames and email addresses that they can use for other nefarious activities.

Here, we replaced the error message in the call to the AddModel method with a generic one to avoid this enumeration. We also prevented the determination between an existing and non-existent customer account.

Fixing weak password requirements

The complexity of a user's credentials or password determines the likelihood of a successful dictionary attack. If the password is not complicated enough, it will be a matter of minutes before an adversary guesses the credentials to use to authenticate in an ASP. NET Core web application using *automation*.

In this recipe, we will change the password properties of ASP.NET Identity to implement a much stronger password policy.

Getting ready

Using Visual Studio Code, open the sample Online Banking app folder at \Chapter03\ weak-password-policy\before\OnlineBankingApp.

Testing for a weak password policy

Follow these steps:

1. Navigate to **Terminal | New Terminal** in the menu or simply press *Ctrl + Shift + '* in Visual Studio Code.

2. Type the following command in the Terminal to build and run the sample app:

    ```
    dotnet run
    ```

3. Open a browser and go to `http://localhost:5000/Identity/Account/Register`.

4. The browser will display the registration page:

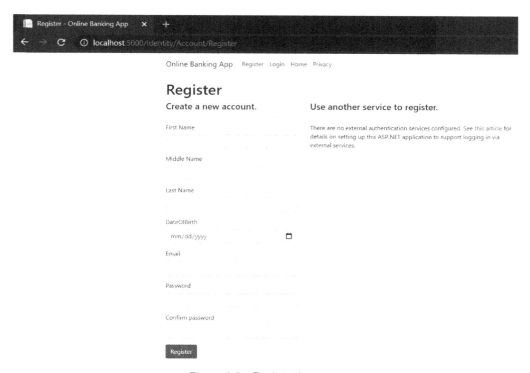

Figure 3.5 – Registration page

5. Fill in the form and enter `password123` as the password.

Notice that the web application created the account, despite the password being weak.

How to do it...

Let's take a look at the steps for this recipe:

1. Type the following command in the Terminal to build the sample app to confirm there are no compilation errors:

```
dotnet build
```

2. Open the `\Chapter03\weak-password-policy\before\` `OnlineBankingApp\Startup.cs` file, go to the `ConfigureServices` method, and examine the `Password` properties of `IdentityOptions`:

```
public void ConfigureServices(IServiceCollection
services)
{
    services.Configure<IdentityOptions>(options =>
    {
        options.Password.RequireDigit = true;
        options.Password.RequireLowercase = false;
        options.Password.RequireNonAlphanumeric =
            false;
        options.Password.RequireUppercase = false;
        options.Password.RequiredLength = 6;
        options.Password.RequiredUniqueChars = 1;
    });
```

3. ASP.NET Core's `IdentityOptions` is configured to have a weak password policy, thus overriding the default safe values for the `RequireLowercase`, `RequireNonAlphanumeric`, and `RequireUppercase` properties.

4. Change the values of the `RequireLowercase`, `RequireNonAlphanumeric`, and `RequireUppercase` properties to `true` to impose a stronger password policy:

```
public void ConfigureServices(IServiceCollection
    services)
{
    services.Configure<IdentityOptions>(options =>
    {
        options.Password.RequireDigit = true;
```

```
        options.Password.RequireLowercase = true;
        options.Password.RequireNonAlphanumeric =true;
        options.Password.RequireUppercase = true;
        options.Password.RequiredLength = 6;
        options.Password.RequiredUniqueChars = 1;
    });
```

5. Repeat steps *1 to 5* of the *Testing for a weak password policy* section and see if you can create a user account while using `pasword123` as your password.

How it works...

Not requiring lowercase, alphanumeric, and uppercase characters is no longer an acceptable password policy. A firm password policy is needed to stop successful credential-based brute-force attacks, as this helps stop our customer account being compromised. In the preceding steps, we enabled a strong password policy by setting the `RequireLowercase`, `RequireNonAlphanumeric`, and `RequireUppercase` properties of the ASP.NET Core Identity service to `true`.

Another layer of defense that you can implement in your ASP.NET Core web application is **multi-factor authentication (MFA)**. MFA in ASP.NET Core is beyond the scope of this book, but to learn more about MFA, view the *Multi-factor authentication in ASP. NET Core* topic in the official ASP.NET online documentation at `https://docs.microsoft.com/en-us/aspnet/core/security/authentication/mfa?view=aspnetcore-5.0`.

Fixing insufficient session expiration

In general, web applications create sessions to maintain users' intercommunication with the web server between multiple requests. These sessions bind a user's identity and support authenticated users being tracked. An ASP.NET Core web application must keep the length of an authenticated user's session to a minimum. This helps avoid the risk of causing a wide window of opportunity for a bad actor to take advantage in the event of a session-based attack.

In this recipe, we will shorten the validity of a session to mitigate the risk of session-based attacks.

Getting ready

Using Visual Studio Code, open the sample Online Banking app folder at `\Chapter03\improper-session\before\OnlineBankingApp`.

How to do it...

Let's take a look at the steps for this recipe:

1. Type the following command in the Terminal to build the sample app to confirm there are no compilation errors:

```
dotnet build
```

2. Open the \Chapter03\weak-password-policy\before\ OnlineBankingApp\Startup.cs file and locate the code where the application cookies have been set. Notice ExpireTimeSpan, which configures the length of time the cookie stays valid for. This is set to 24 hours:

```
services.ConfigureApplicationCookie(options =>
{
    options.LoginPath = $"/Identity/Account/Login";
    options.LogoutPath = $"/Identity/Account/Logout";
    options.AccessDeniedPath =
        $"/Identity/Account/AccessDenied";
    options.ExpireTimeSpan = TimeSpan.FromHours(24);
});
```

3. Assign the ExpireTimeSpan property with a shorter timeout:

```
services.ConfigureApplicationCookie(options =>
{
    options.LoginPath = $"/Identity/Account/Login";
    options.LogoutPath = $"/Identity/Account/Logout";
    options.AccessDeniedPath =
        $"/Identity/Account/AccessDenied";
    options.ExpireTimeSpan = TimeSpan.FromMinutes(15);
});
```

The value of ExpireTimeSpan is now shorter, which will make exploiting an open and valid session difficult for an adversary.

How it works...

An ASP.NET Core web application's cookie settings are set by invoking the `ConfigureApplicationCookie` method. This method accepts `CookieAuthenticationOptions`, including a property that determines the behavior of a cookie. The `ExpireTimeSpan` property, which specifies the session cookie's validity, has been set to 15 minutes compared to a lengthy 24 hours.

> **Note:**
>
> Your ASP.NET Core web application may be subject to an Information Security standard set by your organization or regulation due to the nature of your company's business. For instance, with the payment card industry, you must conform to the *Payment Card Industry Data Security Standard (PCI-DSS)* section 6.5.10 on broken authentication and session management requirements.
>
> To learn more about the PCI-DSS, please read the official PCI-DSS documentation: `https://www.pcisecuritystandards.org/documents/PCI_DSS_v3-2-1.pdf?agreement=true&time=1612424525744`.

4
Sensitive Data Exposure

Data protection in transit and at rest is paramount. Ensuring the use of strong transport protocols and web security directives can stop data from being compromised in transit and prevent unintended sensitive data exposure. Utilizing the latest **Transport Layer Security (TLS)** protocol version in code can help mitigate these vulnerabilities, which are brought about by the implementation flaws in lower versions of TLS, making *man-in-the-middle attacks* such as **POODLE**, **LogJam**, and **FREAK** difficult to succeed.

This chapter will help you determine if security requirements that adequately protect data in transit and at rest exist in your code. You will also learn about what additional web security mechanisms you can implement in your ASP.NET Core web application to protect you from unwanted data leakage.

In this chapter, we're going to cover the following recipes:

- Fixing insufficient protection of data in transit
- Fixing missing **HTTP Strict Transport Security (HSTS)** headers
- Fixing weak protocols
- Fixing hardcoded cryptographic keys
- Disabling caching for critical web pages

These recipes will teach you how to implement HTTPS in your ASP.NET Core web applications, enable HSTS, ensure that the latest version of TLS has been applied, and how to secure cryptographic keys. This chapter will also discuss sending the **Cache-Control** directive to disable caching on pages that contain sensitive data.

Technical requirements

This book was written and designed to use with Visual Studio Code, Git, and .NET 5.0. Code examples in recipes are presented in ASP.NET Core Razor pages. The code examples in this book's recipes are mainly presented in ASP.NET Core Razor pages. The sample solutions also use SQLite as the database engine for a more simplified setup. The complete code examples for this chapter are available at `https://github.com/ PacktPublishing/ASP.NET-Core-Secure-Coding-Cookbook/tree/main/ Chapter04`.

Fixing insufficient protection of data in transit

TLS is a network communication protocol that's used on the web to secure data and achieve privacy through cryptography. Missing or flawed implementations of this secure protocol brings an ASP.NET web application to a massive amount of risk when sensitive data being transmitted between the browser and the web server is unencrypted or potentially intercepted. Enabling TLS is the first step to adequately encrypting data in transit. The succeeding recipes in this chapter will add even more protection.

Not enabling TLS in your ASP.NET Core web application puts your confidential data in transit between the clients and servers at risk. You must ensure that **HTTPS** has been configured for the best protection.

In this recipe, we will learn how to correctly mitigate the risk of a missing security protocol implementation and support for HTTPS.

Getting ready

To complete the recipes in this chapter, we will need a sample Online Banking app.

Open the command shell and download the sample Online Banking app by cloning the ASP.NET Secure Coding Cookbook repository, as follows:

```
git clone https://github.com/PacktPublishing/ASP.NET-Core-
Secure-Coding-Cookbook.git
```

Run the sample app to verify that there are no build or compile errors. In your command shell, navigate to the sample app folder at `\Chapter04\insufficient-transport-protection\before\OnlineBankingApp` and run the following command:

```
dotnet build
```

The `dotnet build` command will build our sample `OnlineBankingApp` project and its dependencies.

How to do it…

Let's take a look at the steps for this recipe:

1. From the starting exercise folder, launch Visual Studio Code by typing in the following command:

    ```
    code .
    ```

2. Open the `Startup.cs` class file and add the following code before the closing braces of the `ConfigureServices` method:

    ```
    if (Environment.IsDevelopment())
    {
        services.AddHttpsRedirection(options =>
        {
            options.RedirectStatusCode =
                StatusCodes.Status307TemporaryRedirect;
            options.HttpsPort = 5001;
        });
    }
    else
    {
        services.AddHttpsRedirection(options =>
        {
            options.RedirectStatusCode =
                StatusCodes.Status308PermanentRedirect;
            options.HttpsPort = 443;
        });
    }
    ```

We added a conditional statement checking if the current environment is running in development or production. This check will help us determine if we must perform temporary redirection or permanent redirection using the standard HTTPS port 443.

3. Add a call to the `UseHttpsRedirection` method just before the call to `UseStaticFiles` in the `Configure` method:

```
app.UseHttpsRedirection();
```

4. Open the `launchsettings.json` file and change the values in `applicationUrl` and `environmentVariables`, as shown in the following highlighted code:

```
"OnlineBankingApp": {
    "commandName": "Project",
    "dotnetRunMessages": "true",
    "launchBrowser": true,
    "applicationUrl": "https://localhost:5001",
    "environmentVariables": {
        "ASPNETCORE_ENVIRONMENT": "Development",
        "ASPNETCORE_URLS":
            "http://localhost:5000;https://localhost:5001
    }
```

The `launchsettings.json` file is a configuration file that allows you to work on multiple environments during development. This file is not included when deploying to production. If you have a setting for `IISExpress`, you may also want to change the `ASPNETCORE_URLS` environment variable and `applicationURL`.

5. Navigate to **Terminal | New Terminal** in the menu or simply press *Ctrl + Shift + '* in Visual Studio Code.

6. Type the following command in the Terminal to build and run the sample app:

```
dotnet run
```

7. Open a browser and go to `http://localhost:5000`:

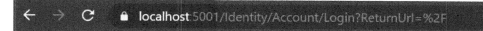

localhost:5001/Identity/Account/Login?ReturnUrl=%2F
Online Banking App
Register
Login
Home
Privacy

Figure 4.1 – HTTPS enabled

Notice that the sample solution is redirected to `https://localhost:5001`.

> **Note**
>
> Web APIs are beyond the scope of this book, but it is important to note that HTTP redirection *must be disabled in APIs*. Web APIs should also *reject requests in HTTP* and *return a* `HTTP 400` *status code.*

How it works...

In the `Startup` class, we call the `AddHttpsRedirection` method to register `UseHttpsRedirection` to the service collection. We configure the middleware options by setting two properties: `RedirectStatusCode` and `HttpsPort`. By default, `RedirectStatusCode` is `Status307TemporaryRedirect`, but it should be changed to `Status308PermanentRedirect` in production environments to prevent user-agents (also known as browsers) from changing the HTTP methods from `POST` to `GET`. We must also specify the HTTPS standard port of `443`:

```
services.AddHttpsRedirection(options =>
{
    options.RedirectStatusCode =
        StatusCodes.Status308PermanentRedirect;
    options.HttpsPort = 443;
});
```

> **Tip**
>
> The call to `AddHttpsRedirection` is optional unless you need a different redirect status code or a different port other than 443.

To redirect HTTP requests to HTTPS, we must add the HTTPS middleware in `Configure` with a call to the `UseHttpsRedirection` method.

> **Note**
>
> **Secure Socket Layer**, also known as **SSL**, is a predecessor of TLS. Other references describe SSL and TLS as one and the same, but TLS has been used in this book to suggest the latest version of the cryptographic protocol.
>
> However, TLS supports a *wide variety of cipher suites* and not all are created equal. Some offer better security, such as the *GCM ciphers*, which is the ideal choice. For more information about ciphers, please see the *TLS Cipher String Cheat Sheet* from OWASP: `https://cheatsheetseries.owasp.org/cheatsheets/TLS_Cipher_String_Cheat_Sheet.html`.

Fix missing HSTS headers

HTTP Strict Transport Security or **HSTS** is another web application security mechanism that helps prevent *man-in-the-middle attacks*. It allows web servers to send a special HTTP Response header that informs supporting browsers that the subsequent communication and transmission of data should only be done over HTTPS; otherwise, succeeding connections will not be allowed.

Failing to opt-in HSTS as an additional security policy does not eliminate the threat of sensitive data interception. Supplementing HTTPS with HSTS will thwart the risk of a user being exposed to an unencrypted channel.

This recipe will teach us how to enable the missing HSTS in our sample ASP.NET Core web application to force the client to communicate over HTTPS entirely.

Getting ready

We will be using the Online Banking app we used in the previous recipe. Using Visual Studio Code, open the sample Online Banking app folder at `\Chapter04\missing-hsts\before\OnlineBankingApp\`.

You can perform the steps in this folder to fix the missing HSTS headers.

How to do it...

Let's take a look at the steps for this recipe:

1. From the starting exercise folder, launch Visual Studio Code by typing the following command:

    ```
    code .
    ```

2. Open the `Startup.cs` class file and add the following code before the `AddHttpsRedirection` call of the `ConfigureServices` method:

    ```
        services.AddHsts(options =>
        {
            options.ExcludedHosts.Clear();
            options.Preload = true;
            options.IncludeSubDomains = true;
            options.MaxAge = TimeSpan.FromDays(60);
        });
    if (Environment.IsDevelopment())
    {
        services.AddHttpsRedirection(options =>
        {
            options.RedirectStatusCode =
                StatusCodes.Status307TemporaryRedirect;
            options.HttpsPort = 5001;
        });
    }
    else
    {
        services.AddHttpsRedirection(options =>
        {
            options.RedirectStatusCode =
                StatusCodes.Status308PermanentRedirect;
            options.HttpsPort = 443;
        });

    }
    ```

> **Tip**
>
> The call to the `Clear` method of `ExcludedHostsProperty` is used for the purposes of testing HSTS locally and in development. This method stops `localhost` from being excluded since it's a loopback host. This code *must be removed* in the *production environment*.
>
> You can also add exclude options for localhost and/or development environment hosts as an alternative:
>
> `options.ExcludedHosts.Add("localhost");`
>
> Testing HSTS locally can lead to some unexpected errors when it is set up incorrectly. When you encounter errors, you will have to clear the HSTS cache.

3. Add a call to the `UseHsts` method:

```
if (webHostEnv.IsDevelopment())
{
    appBuilder.UseDeveloperExceptionPage();
}
else
{
    appBuilder.UseExceptionHandler("/Error");
    appBuilder.UseHsts();
}
```

4. For the `IsDevelopment` method to return `false` and for us to be able to test HSTS locally, we need to *temporarily* change the environment variable. Open \Chapter04\missing-hsts\before\OnlineBankingApp\Properties\launchSettings.json and locate the `ASPNETCORE_ENVIRONMENT` node. Change the value from `Development` to `Staging`:

```
"environmentVariables": {
"ASPNETCORE_ENVIRONMENT": "Staging",
"ASPNETCORE_URLS":
    "http://localhost:5000;https://localhost:5001"
}
```

5. Navigate to **Terminal | New Terminal** in the menu or simply press *Ctrl + Shift + '* in Visual Studio Code.

6. Type the following command in the Terminal to build and run the sample app:

```
dotnet run
```

7. Press *F12* to open the browser's developer tools.

8. Go to the **Network** tab and monitor the upcoming traffic.

9. Open a browser and go to `http://localhost:5000`.

   Your browser will automatically redirect you to `https://localhost:5001`.

10. In the **Network** tab of the developer tools pane, select the second set of HTTP traffic that's been sent to the localhost and examine the HTTP Response header:

Figure 4.2 – Strict-Transport-Security HTTP header

A new HTTP header is included in the response. The Strict-Transport-Security HTTP header enables HSTS in your ASP.NET Core web application.

How it works...

To enable HSTS in our ASP.NET Core web application, we need to add the HSTS service by making a call to `AddHsts`. The following properties of the HSTS service are configured here:

- `Preload`: Sends the preload flag as part of the Strict-Transport-Header. It directs the supporting browser to include your ASP.NET Core web application's domain in the preloaded list, thus preventing users access over HTTP.

- `IncludeSubdomains`: Another directive that lets the subdomains have HSTS enabled, not just the top-level domain name.

- `MaxAge`: A property that determines the max-age directive of the Strict-Transport-Security header. This dictates how long the browser will remember to send requests for over HTTPS in seconds.

> **Note**
>
> Setting the `MaxAge` property value to 31,536,000 seconds guarantees that the **max-age** attribute in the **HSTS** header is enforced for *at least a year*, and it also prevents users from manually accepting an untrusted SSL certificate.

Finally, a call to the `UseHsts` method adds the middleware for HSTS.

There's more...

Using the `preload` flag in the **Strict-Transport-Security** header can have undesirable outcomes for your users. Tread lightly when you're enabling this property while setting up the HSTS middleware. For instance, try browsing the site for a second time over HTTP:

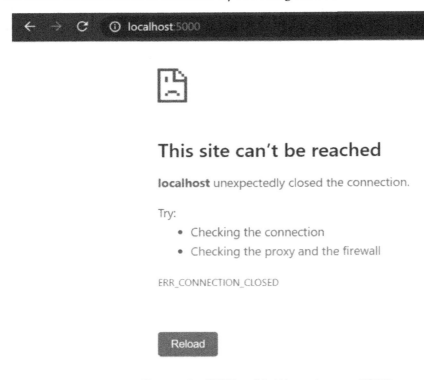

Figure 4.3 – HSTS enabled/ browsing over HTTP

Notice that the browser is preventing you from using the sample ASP.NET web application.

> **Note**
>
> Not all browsers support the HSTS header. To see the list of browsers that support HSTS, see the *Strict-Transport-Security Browser Compatibility* table on the official Mozilla Developer website: `https://developer.mozilla.org/en-US/docs/Web/HTTP/Headers/Strict-Transport-Security#browser_compatibility`.

Fixing weak protocols

The cryptographic protocol known as TLS has evolved over the years and initially started as **Secure Sockets Layer**, most commonly known as **SSL**. This is now deprecated, and so its successors have been discovered to have vulnerabilities in their design. The latest version of the Transport Layer Security protocol, TLS 1.3, was created to solve these problems.

Enabling HTTPS and using TLS is not enough to protect your ASP.NET Core web applications from accidental data exposure. An adversary can potentially exploit a weak version of TLS. To overcome this, you must employ the latest and greatest versions of cryptographic ciphers and protocols.

This recipe will teach you how to change an outdated version of TLS and write code to utilize the TLS 1.3 version of the protocol.

Getting ready

Using Visual Studio Code, open the sample Online Banking app folder at `\Chapter02\weak-protocol\before\OnlineBankingApp\`.

You can perform the steps in this folder to fix weak protocols.

How to do it...

Let's take a look at the steps for this recipe:

1. From the starting exercise folder, launch Visual Studio Code by typing the following command:

    ```
    code .
    ```

2. Open the `Program.cs` class file. This class sets up the host and, by default, uses *Kestrel* as the web server. The `CreateHostBuilder` method call is where you can locate the line where the `SslProtocols` property is being assigned with a lower version of TLS. The current value indicates that the TLS version being used is version *TLS 1.0*:

    ```
    public static IHostBuilder CreateHostBuilder(string[]
      args) =>
        Host.CreateDefaultBuilder(args)
          .ConfigureWebHostDefaults(host =>
          {
              host.UseKestrel(options =>
                {
                      options.ConfigureHttpsDefaults
                      (https =>
                      {
                          https.SslProtocols =
                              SslProtocols.Tls;
                      });
                });
          });
          host.UseStartup<Startup>();
        });
    ```

3. Assign the `SslProtocols` property, along with a much stronger version of TLS:

    ```
    options.ConfigureHttpsDefaults(https =>
    {
        https.SslProtocols = SslProtocols.Tls12 |
            SslProtocols.Tls13;
    });
    ```

4. Navigate to **Terminal | New Terminal** in the menu or simply press *Ctrl + Shift + '* in Visual Studio Code.

5. Type the following command in the Terminal to build and run the sample app:

```
dotnet run
```

6. Press *F12* to open the browser's developer tools.

7. Go to the **Network** tab and monitor the upcoming traffic.

8. Open a browser and go to `http://localhost:5000`. Your browser will automatically redirect you to `https://localhost:5001`.

9. Go to the **Security** tab of the developer tools pane and look at the secure connection details:

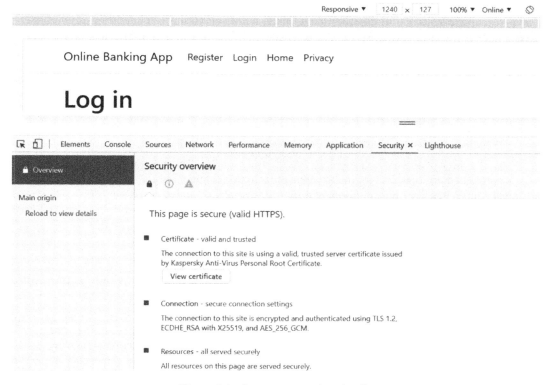

Figure 4.4 – Secure connection details

The **Security** tab shows details of the version of the TLS protocol being used, as well as the cipher.

How it works...

The current version of the code is using a lower and vulnerable version of TLS. `SslProtocols` is assigned an enum value of `SslProtocols.Tls`, which is equivalent to **TLS 1.0**. TLS 1.0 is deprecated *as of March 2020*.

The default web server being used in this sample ASP.NET Core web application is **Kestrel**. Within the code, we configured the settings of Kestrel with `UseKestrel`, passing the property values as options.

One of these properties is `SslProtocols`, which we should assign with the`SslProtocols.Tls12` and `SslProtocols.Tls13` piped enum values to specify that only **TLS 1.2** and **TLS 1.3** are allowed. These will be set to our defaults.

Fixing hardcoded cryptographic keys

Cryptographic keys are an essential part of the whole ecosystem of cryptography. This string is vital for encrypting and decrypting sensitive data. In particular, asymmetric cryptographic algorithms have private keys (as part of the public-private key pair exchange) that are meant to be kept secure from prying eyes. If these secret keys fall into the wrong hands or get leaked, an attacker will be able to successfully perform sensitive data decryption.

> **Note**
>
> The topic of applied cryptography is wide and complex. This book briefly touched on weak cryptographic algorithms in this chapter, but for a more comprehensive understanding of how cryptography is implemented in .NET, please read *.NET Cryptography Model* from the official Microsoft online documentation: `https://docs.microsoft.com/en-us/dotnet/standard/security/cryptography-model`.

The following recipe will help us find the security flaw in our code that would compromise these cryptographic private keys and remediate the risk with a code fix.

Getting ready

Using Visual Studio Code, open the sample Online Banking app folder at `\Chapter04\hard-coded-key\before\OnlineBankingApp\`.

You can perform the steps in this folder to fix hardcoded cryptographic keys.

How to do it...

Let's take a look at the steps for this recipe:

1. From the starting exercise folder, launch Visual Studio Code by typing the following command:

```
code .
```

2. Open the `\Areas\Identity\Pages\Account\Register.cshtml.cs` file and go to the `OnPostAsync` method definition:

```
public async Task<IActionResult> OnPostAsync(string
returnUrl = null)
{
    returnUrl ??= Url.Content("~/");
    ExternalLogins = (await
        _signInManager.GetExternalAuthenticationScheme
            sAsync()).ToList();
    if (ModelState.IsValid)
    {
        var user = new Customer {
            FirstName = _cryptoService.Encrypt
                (Input.FirstName, key),
            MiddleName = _cryptoService.Encrypt
                (Input.MiddleName, key),
            LastName = _cryptoService.Encrypt
                (Input.LastName, key),
            DateOfBirth = Input.DateOfBirth,
            UserName = Input.Email,
            Email = Input.Email
        };
```

> **Note**
> The complete code can be found in this book's GitHub repository at
> `https://github.com/PacktPublishing/ASP.NET-Core-Secure-Coding-Cookbook\Chapter04`.

3. Notice that the call to the _cryptoService.Encrypt method has a second argument that accepts a string. This parameter expects to receive a key, but the key that is being passed is hardcoded in code. The key class field is declared and assigned with a hardcoded value of BGw3UHkI4z:

```
[AllowAnonymous]
public class RegisterModel : PageModel
{
    private readonly SignInManager<Customer>
        _signInManager;
    private readonly UserManager<Customer>
        _userManager;
    private readonly ILogger<RegisterModel> _logger;
    private readonly IEmailSender _emailSender;
    private readonly ICryptoService _cryptoService;
    private const string key = "BGw3UHkI4z";
```

4. We can remediate this issue by retrieving the key from a secure environment such as an environment variable. *Environment variables* are variables in your operating system that are used in a variety of applications and services:

```
FirstName = _cryptoService.Encrypt(Input.FirstName,
    Environment.GetEnvironmentVariable("securekey",
        EnvironmentVariableTarget.Machine)),
MiddleName = _cryptoService.Encrypt(Input.MiddleName,
    Environment.GetEnvironmentVariable("securekey",
        EnvironmentVariableTarget.Machine)),
LastName = _cryptoService.Encrypt(Input.LastName,
    Environment.GetEnvironmentVariable("securekey",
        EnvironmentVariableTarget.Machine)),
```

5. We can use the Environment.GetEnvironmentVariable method to retrieve the value of the key stored in the securekey environment variable.

6. Create the new `securekey` environment variable.

If you are a Windows user, follow these steps:

a) Open the Windows **Run** prompt, type `sysdm.cpl`, and press **OK** or *Enter*:

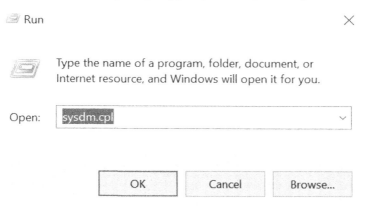

Figure 4.5 – Windows Run prompt

b) Click the **Advanced** tab and then click the **Environment Variables** button:

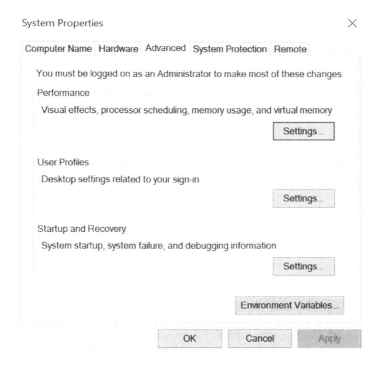

Figure 4.6 – Advanced System Properties

c) Under **System variables**, click **New** to create a new system-wide variable:

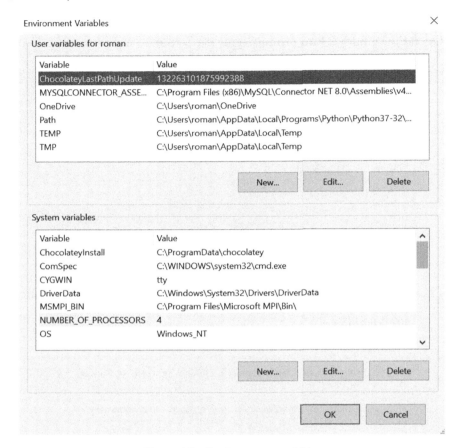

Figure 4.7 – Environment variables

d) Specify the name of the system variable as `securekey` and its value as `BGw3UHkI4z`:

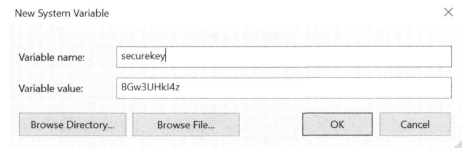

Figure 4.8 – securekey system variable

e) Test whether the new system variable has been created by typing the following command in the command line:

```
echo %securekey%
```

The preceding command will show the value of the `securekey` system variable in the command prompt.

If you are a Linux/MacOS user, follow these steps:

a) Open the `.bashrc` file in your home directory. Type the following command to open the `.bashrc` file with either the gedit text editor:

```
gedit ~/.bashrc
```

Type the following command to open the `.bashrc` file with the vim text editor:

```
vi  ~/.bashrc
```

`.bashrc` is a shell script that Bash executes to initialize an interactive shell session.

The following screenshot shows the `.bashrc` file open in **gedit**, the default text editor in GNOME-based desktop environments. It is commonly seen on Linux:

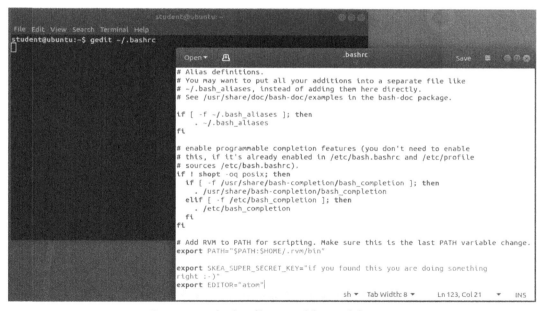

Figure 4.9 – .bashrc file opened for modification

b) Using a code editor of your choice (vim or gedit), add the following line to your `.bashrc` file:

```
export securekey=" BGw3UHkI4z"
```

The following screenshot shows the gedit text editor with the new environment variable added:

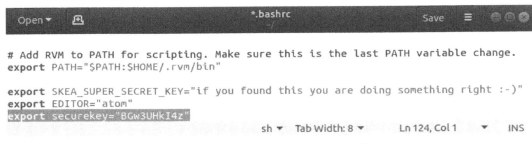

Figure 4.10 – New environment variable

c) Save the `.bashrc` file to apply the changes.

d) Open a new Terminal and type following the command to verify that the environment variable now exists:

```
echo $securekey
```

The following screenshot shows that the new `securekey` environment variable has been successfully added:

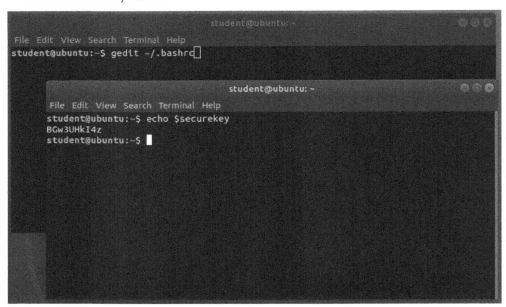

Figure 4.11 – New Terminal

7. Lastly, remove the following line, which declares the `key` variable:

```
private const string key = "BGw3UHkI4z";
```

> **Tip**
>
> For large-scale deployments, storing the secrets and keys in the environment variable may not be ideal. As an option, use cloud-based key stores such as *Azure Key Vault*. Follow the quick start instructions to store your secrets in Azure Key Vault: `https://docs.microsoft.com/en-us/azure/key-vault/secrets/quick-create-net`.

Now, let's understand how this recipe works.

How it works...

In the event that an attacker can get hold of the code repository, there is a risk that the bad actor will be able to see the private key in the code. We must protect these secret keys and they must be stored externally from the code repository, thus limiting who can see them to anyone who has access to the system. In our sample Online Banking app, the key was plainly declared as a variable in code:

```
private const string key = "BGw3UHkI4z";
```

This is a risk for accidental exposure through unauthorized access, but this can be remediated by storing the key in an environment variable.

Here, we created a system variable, making it accessible machine-wide, and retrieved the key by invoking the `Environment.GetEnvironmentVariable` method:

```
FirstName = _cryptoService.Encrypt(Input.FirstName,
    Environment.GetEnvironmentVariable("securekey",
        EnvironmentVariableTarget.Machine)),
```

The first parameter is the name of the environment variable, while the second parameter specifies the location where the key is stored. The possible enum values are `EnvironmentVariableTarget.Machine`, `EnvironmentVariableTarget.Process`, and `EnvironmentVariableTarget.User`.

We used `EnvironmentVariableTarget.Machine` to indicate that our variable is stored in the Windows registry. Its exact location is the Windows registry is `HKEY_LOCAL_MACHINE\System\CurrentControlSet\Control\Session Manager\Environment`.

> **Note**
> You can automate the process of adding an environment variable to the web server using your build pipeline. If you're using *Azure Pipelines*, you can learn more by reading the *Define Variables* section of the Microsoft documentation: `https://docs.microsoft.com/en-us/azure/devops/pipelines/process/variables?view=azure-devops&tabs=yaml%2Cbatch`.

There's more...

Another option for ASP.NET Core web application developers is to use a cloud-based service that can store keys and secrets. Major cloud providers offer this type of service and allow you to manage cryptographic keys that use hardware security modules.

To integrate any of these services in your ASP.NET web application, you must have a subscription and use their specific Software Development Kits. Here are two of them:

- **Azure Key Vault**: Integrating with this service requires that you install the *Azure SDK* and use the *Azure Key Vault Configuration Provider* for ASP.NET Core to retrieve the keys.
- **AWS Key Management Services (KMS)**: *AWS SDK for .NET* will help you quickly add the KMS service to your ASP.NET Core web application.

Now, let's move on to the next recipe.

Disabling caching for critical web pages

Performance is one of the critical metrics for ASP.NET Core web applications. As developers, we find ways to make pages load faster, and the concept of caching resources and pages is nothing new. Browsers implement caching based on the **Cache-Control** directive they receive from the server. However, there is a risk associated with caching pages that contain sensitive data. We must selectively determine which pages are in danger of leaking information and disable caching from these pages.

Getting ready

We will be using the Online Banking app we used in the previous recipe. Using Visual Studio Code, open the sample Online Banking app folder at `\Chapter04\cache-data\before\OnlineBankingApp\`.

You can perform the steps in this folder to disable caching on the **Manage profile** page.

How to do it...

Let's take a look at the steps for this recipe:

1. From the starting exercise folder, launch Visual Studio Code by typing the following command:

    ```
    code .
    ```

2. Open the `Areas\Identity\Pages\Account\Manage\Index.cshtml.cs` file. Notice that there is no annotation for the page model, which typically controls response caching:

    ```
    namespace OnlineBankingApp.Areas.Identity.Pages.Account.
    Manage
    {
        public partial class IndexModel : PageModel
        {
    ```

    This page allows you to manage your profile and change your personal details, such as your First Name, Last Name, and Date of Birth. Viewing these pages while caching is turned on can lead to information leakage as the browser caches the data unless it's instructed not to do so.

3. To disable caching on this particular Razor page, let's annotate the page mode with the `ResponseCache` attribute:

    ```
    namespace OnlineBankingApp.Areas.Identity.Pages.Account.
      Manage
    {
        [ResponseCache(Duration = 0, Location =
            ResponseCacheLocation.None, NoStore = true)]
        public partial class IndexModel : PageModel
        {
            private readonly UserManager<Customer>
                _userManager;
            private readonly SignInManager<Customer>
                _signInManager;
    ```

    Adding the `ResponseCache` attribute will set the directive of the **Cache-Control** response header.

Now, let's verify that **Cache-Control** has been set to **no-cache, no-store** as part of the HTTP response.

Validating the Cache-Control HTTP response header

Let's get started:

1. Navigate to **Terminal** | **New Terminal** in the menu or simply press *Ctrl* + *Shift* + *'* in Visual Studio Code.

2. Type the following command in the Terminal to build and run the sample app:

```
dotnet run
```

3. Open a browser and go to `https://localhost:5001/`.

4. Log in using the following credentials:

    a). Email: `stanley.s.jobson@lobortis.ca`

    b). Password: `rUj5jtV8jrTyHnx!`

5. Once authenticated, you will be redirected to the home page:

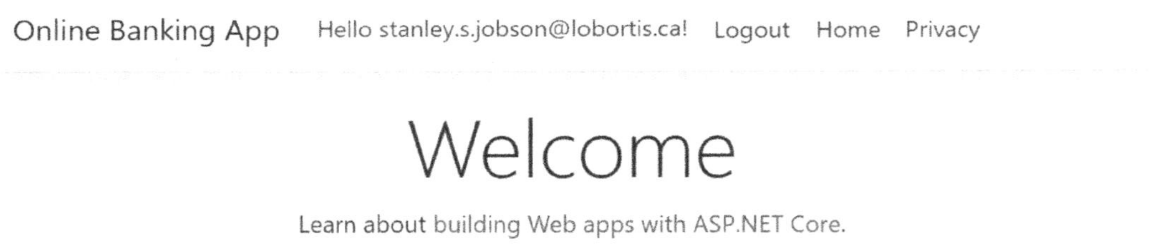

Online Banking App   Hello stanley.s.jobson@lobortis.ca!   Logout   Home   Privacy

Welcome

Learn about building Web apps with ASP.NET Core.

Figure 4.12 – Home page authenticated

6. Click **stanley.s.jobson@lobortis.ca** from the banner to go to the customer's profile page:

Online Banking App   Hello stanley.s.jobson@lobortis.ca!   Logout   Home   Privacy

Profile

First Name

| Stanley |

Middle Name

| Sybil |

Last Name

| Jobson |

DateOfBirth

| 10/11/1933 |

Figure 4.13 – Profile page

7.   Press *F12* to open the browser's developer tools.

8.   Go to the **Network** tab and select the first piece of HTTP traffic in the traffic list.

9.   Once **single HTTP traffic** has been selected, scroll through the right pane to view the corresponding HTTP response security headers:

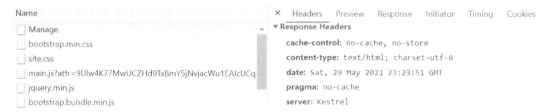

Figure 4.14 – Cache-Control

The **Cache-Control** header has now been added as part of the HTTP response that was sent from our sample Online Banking web application.

How it works...

Setting **Cache-Control** to **no-store, no-cache** tells the browser to not cache the response. You can achieve this by using the ResponseCache attribute with the following properties and their corresponding values and annotating IndexModel:

```
[ResponseCache(Duration = 0, Location = ResponseCacheLocation.
None, NoStore = true)]
```

Duration is set to 0 seconds, thus setting its matching max-age directive with the same value. Assigning max-age with a value of 0 seconds indicates that resources should be retrieved fresh from the web server.

Location is assigned with an enum value of ResponseCacheLocation.None, which specifies that the browser won't cache the resources.

NoStore, when set to true, configures the no-store directive HTTP response header and tells the client that the resource is not to be cached.

> **Tip:**
>
> You can configure the caching behavior of an ASP.NET Core web application centrally by creating CacheProfiles:
>
> ```
> using Microsoft.AspNetCore.Mvc;
>
> . . .
>
> public void ConfigureServices(IServiceCollection services)
> {
>
> . . .
>
>     services.AddMvc(options =>
>     {
>         options.CacheProfiles.Add("NoCache",
>             new CacheProfile()
>             {
>                 Duration = 30,
>                 Location = ResponseCacheLocation.None,
>                 NoStore = true
>             });
>     });
> ```

The same values from the preceding recipe have been passed into the CacheProfile instance to disable caching.

5
XML External Entities

eXtensible Markup Language (XML) is a standard markup language that's used to define data. XML is also a format that an ASP.NET Core web application can use to parse information. To achieve this, a developer can use any number of .NET XML parsers readily available in the framework.

XML being a source of input is likely to be prone to malicious data injection. A feature called **XML External Entity** (**XXE**) allows XML to define a custom entity using a URL or file path. This ability to represent external entities in XML can be abused or exploited. Unrestricted external entity references can allow attackers to send sensitive information and files outside the applications' trusted domains and into the perpetrator-controlled server. The existence of this vulnerability can lead to **Denial-of-Service** (**DoS**) attacks, making the whole application inaccessible because of flooded requests, or file inclusion attacks, where an adversary can gain unauthorized access to files.

To ensure security in code and to prevent these types of XML-based injection attacks, you must validate XML using **XML Schemas** (**XSD**). The use of XSDs ensures the conformance of the XML with the desired format. Also, choosing which .NET parser to use must be carefully configured and set to avoid any unexpected behavior from the XML parser.

In this chapter, we're going to cover the following recipes:

- Enabling XML validation
- Fixing XXE injection with `XmlDocument`
- Fixing XXE injection with `XmlTextReader`
- Fixing XXE injection with **LINQ** to **XML**

These recipes will teach us how to add XML schema validation to our ASP.NET Core web applications, as well as how to fix a variety of vulnerabilities in code that allow external XML entities to be injected and processed.

Technical requirements

This book was written and designed to use with Visual Studio Code, Git, and .NET 5.0. Code examples in recipes are presented in ASP.NET Core Razor pages. The sample solutions also use SQLite as the database engine for a more simplified setup. The complete code examples for this chapter are available at `https://github.com/PacktPublishing/ASP.NET-Core-Secure-Coding-Cookbook/tree/main/Chapter05`.

Enabling XML validation

An **XSD** specifies how XML should be composed. The schema helps define an XML structure and, with it, prevents unwanted elements, attributes, and text. Without an XSD, a .NET parser will blindly process the XML data and increase the risk of an XXE injection vulnerability in code.

This recipe will teach you how to create the use XSD and validate XML data.

Getting ready

To complete the recipes in this chapter, we will need the sample Online Banking app.

Open the command shell and download the sample Online Banking app by cloning the ASP.NET Secure Coding Cookbook repository, as follows:

```
git clone https://github.com/PacktPublishing/ASP.NET-Core-
Secure-Coding-Cookbook.git
```

Run the sample app to verify that there are no build or compile errors. In your command shell, navigate to the sample app folder at `\Chapter05\missing-validation\before\OnlineBankingApp` and run the following command:

```
dotnet build
```

The `dotnet build` command will build our sample `OnlineBankingApp` project and its dependencies.

How to do it...

Let's take a look at the steps for this recipe:

1. From the starting exercise folder, launch Visual Studio Code by typing in the following command:

    ```
    code .
    ```

2. Under the `wwwroot` directory, *right-click* and select **New File**. Name the file `Knowledgebase.xsd`:

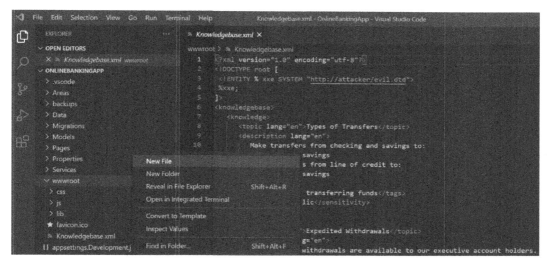

Figure 5.1 – Adding a new file

3. Add the following markup to the `Knowledgebase.xsd` file (the entirety of this xsd file can be found in the completed exercise folder, under `\Chapter05\ missing-validation\after\OnlineBankingApp`):

```xml
<?xml version="1.0" encoding="utf-8"?>
<xs:schema attributeFormDefault="unqualified"
elementFormDefault="qualified" xmlns:xs="http://www.
w3.org/2001/XMLSchema">
  <xs:element name="knowledgebase">
    <xs:complexType>
      <xs:sequence>
        <xs:element maxOccurs="unbounded"
        name="knowledge">
          <xs:complexType>
            <xs:sequence>
              <xs:element name="topic">
                <xs:complexType>
                  <xs:simpleContent>
                    <xs:extension base="xs:string">
                      <xs:attribute name="lang"
                      type="xs:string" use="required"
                      />
                    </xs:extension>
                  </xs:simpleContent>
                </xs:complexType>
              </xs:element>

// markup removed for brevity
```

4. Now that we have created the schema, we will use this `xsd` file to validate the format of `Knowledgebase.xml`, which contains the data for our knowledge base.

5. Open `\Services\KnowledgebaseServices.cs` and add a reference to the following namespaces:

```csharp
using System.Xml.Schema;
using System.IO;
```

6. These namespaces allow you to use the classes you need to validate the XML schema and provide some methods for file input-output operations on XML files.

7. We will need to refactor code in the `Search` method so that it can use the schema we created in *step 3*. Insert the following code just after where the `webroot` variable is declared and just before where `file` is declared:

```
var webRoot = _env.WebRootPath;
var schemaSet = new XmlSchemaSet();
var xsdFile = System.IO.Path.Combine(webRoot,
    "Knowledgebase.xsd");
using (System.IO.FileStream stream =
    File.OpenRead(xsdFile))
{
    schemaSet.Add(XmlSchema.Read(stream, (s, e) =>
    {
        var x = e.Message;
    }));
}


XmlReaderSettings settings = new XmlReaderSettings();
settings.ValidationType = ValidationType.Schema;
settings.Schemas = schemaSet;


settings.DtdProcessing = DtdProcessing.Ignore;


var file = System.IO.Path.Combine(webRoot,
    "Knowledgebase.xml");
```

8. Declare an `XmlReader` object that will take `file` and `settings` as arguments from the preceding lines of code:

```
XmlReader reader = XmlReader.Create(file, settings);
```

9. Modify this line of code so that the `XmlDocument` instance will load the reader instead of the file:

```
xmlDoc.Load(reader);
```

The `XmlDocument` object now loads `XmlReader`, which includes schema validation.

How it works...

The `knowledgebase.xsd` file contains the valid elements and attributes that are allowed in `knowledgebase.xml`. This XSD also describes the expected data type of the elements. For instance, `<xs:element name="sensitivity" type="xs:string" />` expects that the `sensitivity` element is of the `string` data type. The `knowledgebase.xml` file is expected to follow this format. Otherwise, the validation process will fail.

We added a reference to the `System.Xml.Schema` namespace in `\Services\KnowledgebaseServices.cs`, which holds the classes we need for validation. From this reference, we used the `XmlSchemaSet` class to store the `knowledgebase.xsd` schema. The `XmlSchemaSet` class can contain more than one schema, but we will only use one for our recipe.

Then, we created a `FileStream` object with the `File.OpenRead(xsdFile)` method. The `xsdFile` object represents `knowledgebase.xsd` and is passed to `File.OpenRead` as an argument. The `FileStream` object is then supplied to the `XmlSchema.Read` method, adding `knowledgebase.xsd` to the `schemaSet` collection.

The `XmlReaderSettings` property's `ValidationType` is assigned with a value of `ValidationType.Schema`, which sets the new `XmlReader` to perform validation using the XSD schema.

With the `XmlReader.Create` method, we created a `reader` instance of `XmlReader` using the `XmlReaderSettings` property we defined in the preceding lines. Lastly, we passed the reader object to the `XmlDocument` instance for the application to start parsing the `knowledgebase.xml` file.

> **Note**
> Similar to XML, XSDs can also have external references and can come from untrusted resources. Additional verification is needed to ensure that the source is trusted and that you are not using malicious strings from a rogue XSD.

There's more...

Another form of XML is **eXtensible Stylesheet Language Transformation**, or **XSLT** for short. This language is used to transform XML documents into other document formats, such as plain text files or HTML.

You can load an XSLT into your ASP.NET web application by using the `XslCompiledTransform` class from the `System.Xml.Xsl` namespace. Call the `Load` and `Transform` methods to load the XSLT and transform it into a certain format:

```
XslCompiledTransform xslt = new XslCompiledTransform();
xslt.Load("Knowledgebase.xsl");
xslt.Transform("Knowledgebase.xml", "Knowledgebase.html");
```

However, just like with any form of input, XSLT can be tainted or compromised to load malicious XXEs. To safely compile XSLT, pass a `null` `XmlResolver` to stop resolving external resources and set the XmlReaderSetting's `DtdProcessing` to `Ignore`.

To prevent XSLTs from embedding script blocks and using the dangerous `document()` function, we set the xsltSetting's `EnableScript` and `EnableDocumentFunction` to `false`:

```
XslCompiledTransform xslt = new XslCompiledTransform();
XmlReaderSettings settings = new XmlReaderSettings();
settings.DtdProcessing = DtdProcessing.Ignore;
var file = System.IO.Path.Combine(webRoot,
    "Knowledgebase.xsl");
XmlReader reader = XmlReader.Create(file, settings);
XsltSettings xsltSettings = new XsltSettings();
xsltSettings.EnableDocumentFunction = false;
xsltSettings.EnableScript = false;
xslt.Load(reader, xsltSettings, null);
```

> **Note**
> By default, the `EnableDocumentFunction` and `EnableScript` properties are disabled and set to `false`.

Configuring these objects with proper settings before passing them into the overloaded `Load` method helps prevent XSLT injection and XXE attacks.

Fixing XXE injection with XmlDocument

The `XmlDocument` class has been the de facto XML parser for .NET applications. This XML parser object is often used to load, modify, and delete XML in-memory. It has an `XmlResolver` property, which enables the use of external XML resources such as DTDs.

Document Type Definition, most commonly known as **DTD**, is similar to XML files but holds information about an XML's composition or structure. It can have an `ENTITY` element, which can be internal or external. When an `XDocument` parses an XML file with a DTD, this XML parser will process it, along with its `ENTITY` declarations.

Let's look at some content of an XML file with malicious injected `ENTITY` declarations. This is a known classic example of the *Billion Laughs attack*, which is a **Denial-of-Service (DoS)** attack that targets XML parsers such as `XmlDocument`. Loading this XML will cause your ASP.NET Core web app to crash or become unresponsive:

```
<?xml version="1.0"?>
<!DOCTYPE lolz [
<!ENTITY lol "lol">
<!ENTITY lol2 "&lol;&lol;&lol;&lol;&lol;&lol;&lol;&lol;&lol;&l
ol;">
<!ENTITY lol3 "&lol2;&lol2;&lol2;&lol2;&lol2;&lol2;&lol2;&lol2;
&lol2;&lol2;">
]>
<lolz>&lol3;</lolz>
```

Also, accidentally setting your unsafe custom `XmlResolver` could allow DTDs from an untrusted source or host to be included in `knowledgebase.xml` parsed, potentially leading to **XXE injections**.

This recipe will show you how to disable DTDs, thus making your code safer when parsing XML.

Getting ready

Using Visual Studio Code, open the sample Online Banking app folder at `\Chapter05\ xxe-injection01\before\OnlineBankingApp\`.

How to do it...

Let's take a look at the steps for this recipe:

1. From the starting exercise folder, launch Visual Studio Code by typing the following command:

```
code .
```

2. Open the `Services\KnowledgebaseService.cs` file and notice the line that gets assigned to the `XmlUrlResolver` object:

```
XmlUrlResolver resolver = new XmlUrlResolver();
XmlDocument xmlDoc = new XmlDocument();
xmlDoc.XmlResolver = resolver;
xmlDoc.Load(file);
```

3. Assign the `XmlResolver` property of `xmlDoc` to `null`:

```
XmlDocument xmlDoc = new XmlDocument();
xmlDoc.XmlResolver = null;
xmlDoc.Load(file);
```

Setting `XmlResolver` to `null` will disable DTDs from loading inside the `knowledgebase.xml` file.

> **Note**
>
> When an external entity or **DTD** exists in an XML document, an `XMLException` is thrown when your application tries to parse the **XML**.

How it works...

In our `OnlineBankApp` sample application, an `XMLResolver` gets instantiated and assigned to the xmlDoc's `XmlResolver` property. Setting a value for the `XmlResolver` property indicates that loading DTDs or resolving external entity references is allowed.

However, to mitigate this vulnerability in code, we must nullify `XmlResolver` references, thus preventing nefarious DTDs from being loaded.

There's more...

If it's necessary to parse DTDs in your ASP.NET Core web application, you must use the `XmlSecureResolver` class and assign its instance to the `XmlResolver` property of `XmlDocument`. `XmlSecureResolver` is a secure implementation of the `XmlResolver` class that limits access to resources.

To achieve safe DTD parsing with this class, define the allowed resource by simply passing the URL as the second argument of the `XmlSecureResolver` constructor. The `https://localhost:5001` URL is explicitly declared to indicate that we only allow resources that come from this URL:

```
XmlSecureResolver resolver =
    new XmlSecureResolver(new XmlUrlResolver(),
        "https://localhost:5001");


XmlDocument xmlDoc = new XmlDocument();
xmlDoc.XmlResolver = resolver;
xmlDoc.Load(file);
```

The `XmlSecureResolver` object wraps the `XmlResolver` object with a `PermissionSet` that specifies the access that's allowed. Internally, it makes a call to the `PermitOnly` method, which, as its name implies, sets permissions that do not cause the invoking code to fail.

Fixing XXE injection with XmlTextReader

Similar to `XmlDocument`, another fast, non-cached, forward-only parser to XML option is `XmlTextReader`. A major drawback of this high-performance parser is its lack of data validation. `XmlTextReader` also allows you to process DTDs by default, which can be a concern if your XML sources are untrusted.

This recipe will show you how to disable DTD processing with `XmlTextReader`.

Getting ready

Using Visual Studio Code, open the sample Online Banking app folder at `\Chapter05\xxe-injection02\before\OnlineBankingApp\`.

How to do it...

Let's take a look at the steps for this recipe:

1. From the starting exercise folder, launch Visual Studio Code by typing the following command:

   ```
   code .
   ```

2. Open the `Services\KnowledgebaseService.cs` file. This version of the `OnlineBankingApp` sample solution is using `XmlTextReader` to parse the `Knowledgebase.xml` file:

   ```
   XmlTextReader xmlReader = new XmlTextReader(file);
   xmlReader.DtdProcessing = DtdProcessing.Parse;
   XPathDocument xmlDoc = new XPathDocument(xmlReader);
   ```

   Assign the `DtdProcessing` property of `xmlReader` to the enum value of `DtdProcessing.Ignore`:

   ```
   XmlTextReader xmlReader = new XmlTextReader(file);
   xmlReader.DtdProcessing = DtdProcessing.Ignore;
   XPathDocument xmlDoc = new XPathDocument(xmlReader);
   ```

   Setting the `DtdProcessing` property to `DtdProcessing.Ignore` will prevent DTDs from being processed and disregard the `DOCTYPE` tag. `DOCTYPE` is a form of markup that informs the browser of what version of HTML the document is using.

How it works...

Follow these steps:

1. When the XmlTextReader's `DtdProcessing` property is set to an enum value of `DtdProcessing.Parse`, this designates that DTDs will be processed. Allowing DTDs to be processed could be dangerous if a bad actor injects malicious entity reference nodes into the `knowledgebase.xml` file.

2. Specifying the `DtdProcessing` property of `DtdProcessing.Ignore` makes processing DTDs impossible, hence making your code secure.

Fixing XXE injection with LINQ to XML

Language-Integrated Query or **LINQ** is an API within the .NET framework that provides query-like syntax for writing declarative code. LINQ comes in different flavors, and LINQ to XML is one of them. LINQ to XML is an in-memory XML parser that allows you to perform XML transformations – from modifying elements and nodes to serialization.

In general, LINQ to XML is safe from XXE injection. The XDocument class *has DTD processing disabled by default*. However, this can be unsafe when it's instantiated with an insecure XML parser such as XmlReader. This recipe will show you how to find a security flaw in your LINQ to XML code and fix the bug by disabling DTD processing.

Getting ready

Using Visual Studio Code, open the sample Online Banking app folder at \Chapter05\ xxe-injection03\before\OnlineBankingApp\.

You can perform the steps for fixing XXE injections with LINQ to XML in this folder.

How to do it...

Let's take a look at the steps for this recipe:

1. From the starting exercise folder, launch Visual Studio Code by typing the following command:

   ```
   code .
   ```

2. Open the Services\KnowledgebaseService.cs file. This version of the OnlineBankingApp sample solution is using Linq to XML to parse the Knowledgebase.xml file.

   Notice the use of the XDocument class and the query-like method of parsing XML:

   ```
   XmlReaderSettings settings = new XmlReaderSettings();
   settings.DtdProcessing = DtdProcessing.Parse;
   settings.MaxCharactersFromEntities = 1024;
   settings.MaxCharactersInDocument = 2048;


   XmlReader reader = XmlReader.Create(file, settings);
   XDocument xmlDoc = XDocument.Load(reader);
   ```

```
var query = from i in xmlDoc.Element("knowledgebase")
    .Elements("knowledge")
    where
    (i.Element("topic").ToString()
        .Contains(input) == true ||
    i.Element("description").ToString()
        .Contains(input) == true) &&
    i.Element("sensitivity").ToString()
        .Contains("Public") == true
    select new
    {
        Topic = (string)i.Element("topic"),
        Description =
            (string)i.Element("description")
    };
```

3. The `Create` method of the `XmlReader` class is invoked with a vulnerable `XmlReaderSettings`. As we saw in the previous recipes, we must disable DTD processing. This can be done by setting `DtdProcessing` to an enum value of `DtdProcessing.Prohibit`:

```
XmlReaderSettings settings = new XmlReaderSettings();
settings.DtdProcessing = DtdProcessing.Prohibit;
settings.MaxCharactersFromEntities = 1024;
settings.MaxCharactersInDocument = 2048;
```

4. Changing the `DtdProcessing` property of the `XmlReaderSettings` object from `DtdProcessing.Parse` to `DtdProcessing.Prohibit` will prevent DTD processing, and it will also throw an `XmlException` in the presence of a DTD in the XML.

5. Now, we must assign `MaxCharactersFromEntities` of the `XmlReaderSettings` instance with a value of `1024`:

```
XmlReaderSettings settings = new XmlReaderSettings();
settings.DtdProcessing = DtdProcessing.Prohibit;
settings.MaxCharactersFromEntities = 1024;
settings.MaxCharactersInDocument = 2048;
```

6. Assigning `MaxCharactersFromEntities` will restrict the size of the expanded entities and prevent abuse.

7. We must also explicitly assign `MaxCharactersInDocument` of the `XmlReaderSettings` object with a value of `2048`:

```
XmlReaderSettings settings = new XmlReaderSettings();
settings.DtdProcessing = DtdProcessing.Prohibit;
settings.MaxCharactersFromEntities = 1024;
settings.MaxCharactersInDocument = 2048;
```

Assigning the `MaxCharactersInDocument` property with a value of `2048` indicates that the maximum allowable number of characters in an XML file is `2048`. Again, this helps prevent potential abuse from an attacker.

> **Note**
>
> Add a `try-catch` statement to handle the possibility of an `XmlException`. Always practice secure error handling in your code. The last chapter of this book will cover this best practice in detail.

How it works...

In the `KnowledgebaseService` class, we have a `Search` method that performs a search on the entire `Knowledgebase.xml` file, which contains the **Help** inquiry data. When a user hits search on the web page, it invokes this method and creates an instance of both the `XmlReader` and `XDocument` classes.

XDocument is instantiated with XmlReader. The properties of XmlReader are based on the Knowledgebase XML data and its XmlReaderSettings. While this is an efficient way of populating the parser with the XML data, XmlReaderSettings of XmlReader have the DtdProcessing property set to DtdProcessing.Parse, thus setting the XDocument object with an unsafe parser. This setting causes the code to be vulnerable to XXE injection.

To remediate this, we must choose a better property value – either DtdProcessing. Ignore or DtdProcessing.Prohibit – and assign it to DtdProcessing of XmlReaderSettings. Either value can prevent risky DTD processing. We covered the DtdProcessing.Ignore property value in a previous recipe, so we picked DtdProcessing.Prohibit here.

To manage the occurrence of a DTD occurring via your XML parser, pick the DtdProcessing.Prohibit property value over DtdProcessing.Ignore. Having DtdProcessing.Prohibit raises XmlExceptions that you can handle with a try-catch block, while DtdProcessing.Ignore completely ignores the DTDs.

Suppose an attacker was able to input an arbitrary XML file with a huge amount of data. This could cause the system to consume many computing resources that could lead to a DOS attack. We can prevent this from happening by assigning a reasonable value to both the MaxCharactersFromEntities and MaxCharactersInDocument properties of XmlReaderSettings. These properties limit the expansion size of the XML, along with its elements and attributes.

6
Broken Access Control

Authorization is just as significant and essential as authentication. It defines what an authenticated user can perform and execute, and resources and web pages need to have defined privileges to limit unauthorized access. Permission bypass and missing or improper access controls are some of the broken access control vulnerabilities discovered in an ASP.NET Core web application.

In this chapter, we're going to cover the following recipes:

- Fixing **insecure direct object references (IDOR)**
- Fixing improper authorization
- Fixing missing access control
- Fixing open redirect vulnerabilities

By the end of this chapter, you will have learned how to use the built-in authorization mechanism in ASP.NET Core. You will properly implement role-based authorization to prevent unauthorized access to resources in your web application. Also, you will see how to utilize safer redirection methods to prevent open redirection attacks.

Technical requirements

This book was written and designed to use with Visual Studio Code, Git, and .NET 5.0. Code examples in recipes are presented in ASP.NET Core Razor pages. The sample solution also uses SQLite as the **database** (**DB**) engine for a more simplified setup. The complete code examples for this chapter are available at `https://github.com/PacktPublishing/ASP.NET-Core-Secure-Coding-Cookbook/tree/main/Chapter06`.

Fixing IDOR

When accessing a record in a DB, we often use a form of **identifier** (**ID**) that uniquely identifies a dataset. The DB design and structure rely on these keys, and sometimes they can be easily guessed or enumerated. Adversaries can find these identifiers in your requests to your ASP.NET Core web pages. If not adequately safeguarded with access controls, a malicious user can view, modify, or— at worst—delete these records.

In this recipe, we will discover the IDOR vulnerability in our code and mitigate the problem by using the identity of the authenticated customer.

Getting ready

For the recipes of this chapter, we will need the sample Online Banking app.

Open the command shell and download the sample Online Banking app by cloning the `ASP.NET-Core-Secure-Coding-Cookbook` repository, as follows:

```
git clone https://github.com/PacktPublishing/ASP.NET-Core-
Secure-Coding-Cookbook.git
```

Run the sample app to verify that there are no build or compile errors. In your command shell, navigate to the sample app folder at `\Chapter06\insecure-direct-object-references\before\OnlineBankingApp` and run the following command:

```
dotnet build
```

The `dotnet build` command will build our sample `OnlineBankingApp` project and its dependencies.

Let's see in action how IDOR vulnerabilities can be exploited.

Testing IDOR

Here are the steps:

1. Navigate to **Terminal | New Terminal** in the menu or do this by simply pressing *Ctrl + Shift + '* in VS Code.

2. Type the following command in the terminal to build and run the sample app:

```
dotnet run
```

3. Open a browser and go to `https://localhost:5001/Fundtransfers/Details?id=1`.

4. Log in using the following credentials:

   a) Email: `stanley.s.jobson@lobortis.ca`

   b) Password: `rUj5jtV8jrTyHnx!`

5. Once authenticated, you will be redirected to Stanley's fund transfer details page, as shown in the following screenshot:

Online Banking App   Hello stanley.s.jobson@lobortis.ca!   Logout   Home   Privacy

Details
Fund Transfer

Account From	1
Account To	2
TransactionDate	6/12/2021
Amount	510.00
Note	Transfer between accounts

Back to List

Figure 6.1 – Fund transfer details page

6. Click on **Logout** to log out from the sample solution, as shown in the following screenshot:

Figure 6.2 – Logout link

7. Go to https://localhost:5001/FundTransfers/Details?id=1.

8. Now, log in using Axl's credentials:

    a) Email: axl.l.torvalds@ut.net

    b) Password: 6GKqqtQQTii92ke!

9. Notice in the following screenshot that Axl is able to see Stanley's fund transfer details page:

Details
Fund Transfer

Account From	1
Account To	2
TransactionDate	6/12/2021
Amount	510.00
Note	Transfer between accounts

Back to List

Figure 6.3 – Unauthorized access

The preceding test shows that this page is susceptible to an IDOR security bug.

In this recipe, we will fix the IDOR vulnerability in code by adding a validation check to ascertain whether a specific user can see the fund transfer details page.

How to do it...

Let's take a look at the steps for this recipe:

1. From the starting exercise folder, launch VS Code by typing the following command:

```
code .
```

2. Open `Models\FundTransfer.cs` and change the `ID` property from `int` to a `Guid` type. **Globally unique identifiers (GUIDs)** are unique identifiers and are harder to guess:

```
[Key]
public Guid ID { get; set; }
```

Annotating the `ID` property with the `Key` attribute makes this property the primary key for Entity Framework to identify.

3. Under the `Services` folder, create a new file and name it `FundTransferIsOwnerAuthorizationHandler.cs`.

4. In `FundTransferIsOwnerAuthorizationHandler.cs`, add references to the following namespaces:

```
using Microsoft.AspNetCore.Authorization;
using Microsoft.AspNetCore.Identity;
using System.Threading.Tasks;
using OnlineBankingApp.Models;
```

5. Next, define a `FundTransferIsOwnerAuthorizationHandler` class that inherits from `AuthorizationHandler`:

```
namespace OnlineBankingApp.Authorization {
    public class
        FundTransferIsOwnerAuthorizationHandler
            : AuthorizationHandler<
                FundTransferOwnerRequirement,
                FundTransfer>{

    }
}
```

An authorization handler—as the name implies—handles authorization, and in our preceding highlighted code, it determines whether a user will have access or not.

6. Using **dependency injection (DI)**, use the `UserManager` service to be able to retrieve the user ID information from the currently logged-in customer:

```
UserManager<Customer> _userManager;
public FundTransferIsOwnerAuthorizationHandler
    (UserManager<Customer>
    userManager) {
    _userManager = userManager;
}
```

7. Inside the `FundTransferIsOwnerAuthorizationHandler` class, define a `Task` object that will handle the authorization check using the passed `requirement` and `resource` arguments:

```
protected override Task
HandleRequirementAsync (AuthorizationHandlerContext
    context,
FundTransferOwnerRequirement requirement,
FundTransfer resource) {
    if (context.User == null || resource == null)
{
        return Task.CompletedTask;
    }
    if (resource.CustomerID ==
            _userManager.GetUserId
                (context.User)) {
        context.Succeed(requirement);
    }
    return Task.CompletedTask;
}
}
```

8. Define a `FundTransferOwnerRequirement` class that will inherit from the `IauthorizationRequirement` empty marker interface within the same `FundTransferIsOwnerAuthorizationHandler.cs` file:

```
public class FundTransferOwnerRequirement :
    IAuthorizationRequirement { }
}
```

`FundTransferOwnerRequirement` doesn't need to have any properties or data, so we will leave the class empty.

9. Open `Startup.cs` and include the following namespace references:

```
using OnlineBankingApp.Authorization;
using Microsoft.AspNetCore.Authorization
.Infrastructure;
```

10. In `ConfigureServices`, add a new authorization policy and register the authorization handler we created in *Step 3*:

```
services.AddAuthorization(options => {
    options.AddPolicy("Owner", policy =>
        policy.Requirements.Add(new
            FundTransferOwnerRequirement()));
});
services.AddScoped<IAuthorizationHandler,
    FundTransferIsOwnerAuthorizationHandler>();
```

11. Next, open the `\Pages\FundTransfers\Details.cshtml.cs` file and add the following namespace references:

```
using Microsoft.AspNetCore.Authorization;
using Microsoft.AspNetCore.Identity;
```

12. Through DI, add the following highlighted code from the authorization service we registered in *Step 5* into the `DetailsModel` constructor:

```
protected IAuthorizationService _authorizationService
    { get; }
protected UserManager<Customer> _userManager { get; }
public DetailsModel(OnlineBankingApp.Data
    .OnlineBankingAppContext context,
            IAuthorizationService authorizationService,
            UserManager<Customer> userManager)
{
    _context = context;
    _userManager = userManager;
    _authorizationService = authorizationService;
}
```

13. Refactor the whole code under the `OnGetAsync` page handler:

```
public async Task<IActionResult> OnGetAsync(Guid? id)
{
    if (!id.HasValue){
        return NotFound();
    }
    if (!User.Identity.IsAuthenticated){
        return Challenge();
    }
    fundTransfer = await _context.FundTransfer
                .Where(f => f.ID == id)
                .Include(f => f.Customer)
                .OrderBy(f => f.TransactionDate)
                .FirstOrDefaultAsync<FundTransfer>();
    var isAuthorized = await
        _authorizationService.AuthorizeAsync
                (User, fundTransfer,"Owner");
    if (!isAuthorized.Succeeded){
        return Forbid();
    }
    return Page();
}
```

With the steps we performed, we have implemented a more robust way of authorization using a policy-based authorization approach.

Repeat the steps in the *Testing IDOR* section to verify that the fix worked, but instead of using the IDOR-vulnerable **Uniform Resource Locator (URL)**, go to `https://localhost:5001/FundTransfers/Details?id=7c281d46-f2ab-4027-a4d4-3bb97a60012c`, and you should see the following message on your screen:

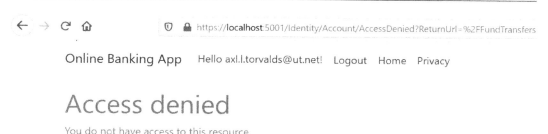

Online Banking App   Hello axl.l.torvalds@ut.net!   Logout   Home   Privacy

Access denied

You do not have access to this resource.

Figure 6.4 – Access denied message

Notice that Axl's account no longer has access to Stanley's fund transfer details page and was redirected to the **Access denied** page.

How it works...

First, we change our `FundTransfer` primary key into a type that cannot be guessed easily. We use the `Guid` type to allow us to have a **unique ID (UID)** as our `Key` for each fund transfer:

```
[Key]
public Guid ID { get; set; }
```

We then implement *policy-based authorization* by first creating an authorization handler. Inside the `FundTransferIsOwnerAuthorizationHandler` class is the code that determines if the resource's (fund transfer's) `CustomerID` matches that of the customer's user ID. If the requirement is satisfied, a call to the `Succeed` method of `AuthorizationHandlerContext` indicates a successful evaluation:

```
if (resource.CustomerID ==
    _userManager.GetUserId(context.User)){
    context.Succeed(requirement);
}
```

The authorization handler is registered as a service, and a preconfigured policy is added using the `AddScoped` and the `AddPolicy` methods respectively:

```
services.AddAuthorization(options => {
    options.AddPolicy("Owner", policy =>
        policy.Requirements.Add(new
            FundTransferOwnerRequirement()));
});
```

```
services.AddScoped<IAuthorizationHandler,
    FundTransferIsOwnerAuthorizationHandler>();
```

We utilize these services via DI in our `DetailsModel` page model.

Fixing improper authorization

Incorrectly using ASP.NET Core's authorization components could lead to insecure code. The authorization feature offers a simple and declarative way to impose authorization, but mistakes can occur in implementing this. In this recipe, we will correctly implement the role-based authorization feature of ASP.NET Core in our sample Online Banking application.

Run the sample app to verify that there are no build or compile errors. In your command shell, navigate to the sample app folder at `\Chapter06\improper-authorization\before\OnlineBankingApp`.

Let's see in action how improper authorization can lead someone to use functions a customer is not authorized to use.

Testing improper authorization

Here are the steps:

1. Navigate to **Terminal | New Terminal** in the menu or do this by simply pressing *Ctrl + Shift + '* in VS Code.

2. Type the following command in the terminal to build and run the sample app:

   ```
   dotnet run
   ```

3. Open a browser and go to `https://localhost:5001/FundTransfers/Create`.

4. Log in using the following credentials:

   a) Email: `axl.l.torvalds@ut.net`

   b) Password: `6GKqqtQQTii92ke!`

5. Once authenticated, you will be redirected to a page where you can make a fund transfer.

Our sample Online Banking solution had only created Axl's customer account; thus, his roles are `Customer` and `PendingCustomer`. Until Axl's account moves into an `ActiveCustomer` role, he shouldn't be able to make a fund transfer.

Getting ready

We will use the Online Banking app we used in the previous recipe. Using VS Code, open the sample Online Banking app folder at `\Chapter06\missing-access-control\before\OnlineBankingApp\`.

You can also perform the steps in this folder for *Fixing improper authorization* recipe.

How to do it...

Let's take a look at the steps for this recipe:

1. From the starting exercise folder, launch VS Code by typing the following command:

   ```
   code .
   ```

2. Open the `\Pages\FundTransfers\Create.cshtml.cs` file and notice the `Authorize` annotation on top of the `CreateModel` class:

   ```
   namespace OnlineBankingApp.Pages.FundTransfers
   {
       [Authorize(Roles = "Customer,ActiveCustomer")]
       public class CreateModel : AccountPageModel
       {
           private readonly OnlineBankingApp.Data
               .OnlineBankingAppContext _context;

           public CreateModel (OnlineBankingApp.Data
               .OnlineBankingAppContext context)
           {
               _context = context;
           }
   // code removed for brevity
   ```

The `Authorize` annotation appears to have been used properly, but not quite. The `CreateModel` page model would only be open to customers who have a `Customer` *OR* an `ActiveCustomer` role. Setting the `Authorize` annotation in this format means customers with either role can send money, which is not what we expect based on our business rule, allowing only active customers to make fund transfers.

3. Change the way the `Authorize` annotation is formatted using the following code:

```
namespace OnlineBankingApp.Pages.FundTransfers
{
    [Authorize(Roles = "Customer")]
    [Authorize(Roles = "ActiveCustomer")]
    public class CreateModel : AccountPageModel
    {
        private readonly OnlineBankingApp.Data
            .OnlineBankingAppContext _context;

        Public CreateModel(OnlineBankingApp.Data
            .OnlineBankingAppContext context)
        {
            _context = context;
        }
// code removed for brevity
```

4. Navigate to **Terminal | New Terminal** in the menu or do this by simply pressing *Ctrl + Shift + '* in VS Code.

5. Type the following command in the terminal to build and run the sample app:

```
dotnet run
```

6. Open a browser and go to `https://localhost:5001/Fundtransfers/Create`.

7. Log in with the following credentials:

    a). Email: `axl.l.torvalds@ut.net`

    b). Password: `6GKqqtQQTii92ke!`

8. Notice that you will be redirected to the **Access denied** page, as shown in the following screenshot:

Figure 6.5 – Access denied page

Setting the `AuthorizeAttribute` property configures the necessary authorization in the `CreateModel` page model. This requires that an authenticated user has both `Customer` *AND* `ActiveCustomer` roles.

How it works...

Declarative role checks enable web developers to add authorization in a page model easily, but there is a big difference between the annotations. For example, have a look at this one:

```
[Authorize(Roles = "Customer,ActiveCustomer")]
```

Now, contrast it with these annotations:

```
[Authorize(Roles = "Customer")]
[Authorize(Roles = "ActiveCustomer")]
```

The first one indicates that an authenticated user with either a `Customer` or an `ActiveCustomer` role can access the fund transfer page. The latter specifies that a customer needs *both roles* to have the authority to send money.

> **Tip**
> A *policy-based authorization* check is also a necessary technique to accompany declarative authorization, to ensure a user is authorized to view a fund transfer. Please refer to the *Fixing IDOR* recipe for more information and details on how to implement this type of authorization.

Fixing missing access control

An access control vulnerability can allow a malicious actor to access your ASP.NET Core web application just by simply registering an account and getting authenticated. This security flaw can lead to unauthorized access to sensitive information.

In this recipe, we add roles to the sample Online Banking app to integrate a **policy-based** authorization.

Getting ready

We will use the Online Banking app we used in the previous recipe. Using VS Code, open the sample Online Banking app folder at \Chapter06\missing-access-control\ before\OnlineBankingApp\.

You can also perform the steps in this folder for the *Fixing missing access control* recipe.

How to do it...

Let's take a look at the steps for this recipe.

1. From the starting exercise folder, launch VS Code by typing the following command:

```
code .
```

2. Open the \Pages\FundTransfers\Create.cshtml.cs file and notice the Authorize annotation on top of the CreateModel class:

```
namespace OnlineBankingApp.Pages.FundTransfers
{
    [Authorize]
    public class CreateModel : AccountPageModel
    {
        private readonly OnlineBankingApp.Data
            .OnlineBankingAppContext _context;

        public CreateModel(OnlineBankingApp.Data
            .OnlineBankingAppContext context)
        {
            _context = context;
        }
// code removed for brevity
```

The `Authorize` attribute in the `CreateModel` class provides the most basic authorization indicating that this Razor pages model requires authorization. However, a lack of defined roles as to which types of customers can make a fund transfer opens up an opportunity for an adversary to abuse this.

3. We need to implement policy-based authorization with criteria defined based on the current roles that our customer has. Under the `Models` folder, create a new file, name it `PrincipalPermission.cs`, and add the following code:

```
using System;
using System.Collections.Generic;
using Microsoft.AspNetCore.Authorization;
using OnlineBankingApp.Models;

namespace OnlineBankingApp.Authorization{
    public static class PrincipalPermission{
        public static List
            <Func<AuthorizationHandlerContext, bool>>
                Criteria = new List<Func
                <AuthorizationHandlerContext, bool>>
        {

            CanCreateFundTransfer

        };

        public static bool CanCreateFundTransfer
            (this AuthorizationHandlerContext ctx){
            return ctx.User.IsInRole
                (Role.ActiveCustomer.ToString());
        }

    }
}
```

In the preceding code snippet, we used `Func` to fulfill a policy. `Func` is a delegate that will point to our `CanCreateFundTransfer` method. We also created an instance of `List<Func<AuthorizationHandlerContext, bool>>` to configure a `Criteria` list for our policy. We defined the `CanCreateFundTransfer` method as one of our criteria, indicating that only customers with an `ActiveCustomer` role can create fund transfers.

> **Note**
>
> You can define more criteria for a customer to be able to submit fund transfers, but to simplify the example, we will use the customer's current role.

4. Open `Startup.cs`, and in `ConfigureServices`, add a reference to `OnlineBankingApp.Authorization`, which is the namespace for our `PrincipalPermission` class:

```
using OnlineBankingApp.Authorization;
```

5. Include the following highlighted code in the authorization middleware:

```
services.AddAuthorization(options =>
{
    options.FallbackPolicy = new
        AuthorizationPolicyBuilder()
            .RequireAuthenticatedUser()
            .Build();

    foreach (var criterion in PrincipalPermission
        .Criteria)
    {
        options.AddPolicy(criterion.Method.Name,
            policy =>
                policy.RequireAssertion(criterion));
    }
});
```

We loop into each of the criteria lists we defined and create an authorization policy for each.

6. Open `Pages\FundTransfers\Create.cshtml.cs` and annotate the `CreateModel` page model with the highlighted code:

```
namespace OnlineBankingApp.Pages.FundTransfers
{
    [Authorize(Policy =
        nameof(PrincipalPermission
            .CanCreateFundTransfer))]
    public class CreateModel : AccountPageModel
```

```
    {
        // code removed for brevity
```

Placing the preceding highlighted attribute will apply the authorization policy that we added to the authorization service.

7. Navigate to **Terminal | New Terminal** in the menu or do this by simply pressing *Ctrl + Shift + '* in VS Code.

8. Type the following command in the terminal to build and run the sample app:

```
    dotnet run
```

9. Open a browser and go to `https://localhost:5001/Fundtransfers/Create`.

10. Log in with the following credentials:

    a) Email: `axl.l.torvalds@ut.net`

    b) Password: `6GKqqtQQTii92ke!`

    Notice that the user is redirected to the `https://localhost:5001/Identity/Account/AccessDenied?ReturnUrl=%2FFundTransfers%2FCreate` **Access denied** URL:

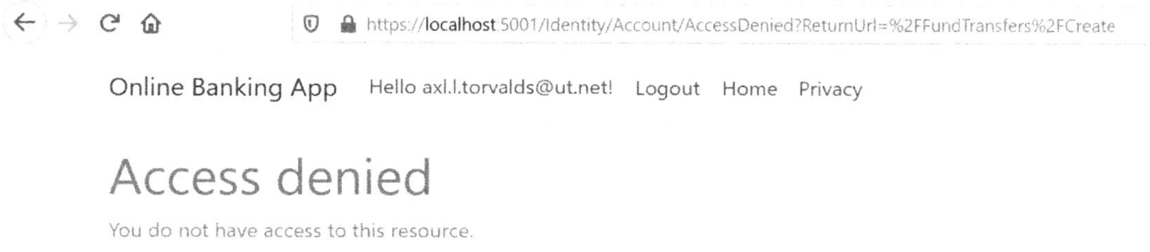

← → C ⌂   🛈 🔒 https://localhost:5001/Identity/Account/AccessDenied?ReturnUrl=%2FFundTransfers%2FCreate

Online Banking App   Hello axl.l.torvalds@ut.net!   Logout   Home   Privacy

Access denied
You do not have access to this resource.

Figure 6.6 – Access denied page for users with PendingCustomer roles

Axl is pre-assigned a `PendingCustomer` role (see `Models\SeedData.cs`), which prevents him from submitting a fund transfer based on the policy we created.

How it works...

The policy-based approach gives ASP.NET Core web developers the granularity needed to define authorization matrices. In our preceding recipe, we used a simple example of using roles as criteria for our authorization policy. In fulfilling a policy, we supplied a `List` of `Func<AuthorizationHandlerContext, bool>` that holds each of the `Criteria` we defined:

```
public static List<Func<AuthorizationHandlerContext, bool>>
        Criteria = new List<Func
            <AuthorizationHandlerContext, bool>>
{
    CanCreateFundTransfer,
    CanViewFundTransfer
};
```

The `Criteria` represent a delegate that will be used to set the conditional access. In our case, we will use the customer's role as a criterion, but you can expand it if necessary:

```
public static bool CanCreateFundTransfer(this
        AuthorizationHandlerContext ctx)
{
    return ctx.User.IsInRole(Role.ActiveCustomer
        .ToString());
}
```

Finally, we use the `RequireAssertion` policy to build our policies with our `List` of `Criteria`:

```
foreach (var criterion in PrincipalPermission.Criteria)
{
    options.AddPolicy(criterion.Method.Name,
        policy => policy.RequireAssertion(criterion));
}
```

Fixing open redirect vulnerabilities

A user can be tricked into clicking a link generated from your ASP.NET Core web application, but this can eventually redirect them to a malicious website. Open redirection can happen when a user-controlled parameter determines that the URL to redirect to has no validation or whitelisting. In this recipe, we will remediate the risk of open redirect attacks in code by utilizing safer redirect methods.

First, let's take a look at how an open redirect vulnerability is exploited.

Getting ready

We will use the Online Banking app we used in the previous recipe. Using VS Code, open the sample Online Banking app folder at `\Chapter06\unvalidated-redirect\ before\OnlineBankingApp\`.

You can also perform the steps in this folder for the *Fixing open redirect vulnerability* recipe.

Testing open redirection

Here are the steps:

1. Navigate to **Terminal | New Terminal** in the menu or do this by simply pressing *Ctrl + Shift + '* in VS Code.

2. Type the following command in the terminal to build and run the sample app:

    ```
    dotnet run
    ```

3. Open a browser and go to `https://localhost:5001/Identity/Account/ Login?ReturnUrl=https://www.packtpub.com`.

4. Log in using the following credentials:

    a) Email: `stanley.s.jobson@lobortis.ca`

    b) Password: `rUj5jtV8jrTyHnx!`

5. Once authenticated, you will be redirected to the *Packt Publishing* website.

    The preceding test shows that this page is vulnerable to an open redirect attack.

How to do it...

Let's take a look at the steps for this recipe.

1. From the starting exercise folder, launch VS Code by typing the following command:

```
code .
```

2. Open `Areas\Identity\Pages\Account\Login.cshtml.cs` and notice the `Redirect` method call:

```
public async Task<IActionResult> OnPostAsync(string
    url = null)
{

    . . . .


// code removed for brevity
    var signInResult = await _signInManager
        .PasswordSignInAsync(Input.Email,
            Input.Password, Input.RememberMe,
                lockoutOnFailure: false);
    if (signInResult .Succeeded)
    {
        _log.LogInformation("User logged in.");

        if (string.IsNullOrEmpty(HttpContext
            .Session.GetString(SessionKey)))
        {
            HttpContext.Session.SetString(SessionKey,
                Input.Email);
        }

        return Redirect(url);
    }
// code removed for brevity
```

The `Redirect` method, when invoked, sends a temporary redirect response to the browser. With no URL validation in place, the URL redirection can be abused and sent to a website controlled by an attacker whenever a tricked customer clicks a malicious URL.

3. Another security flaw found in this sample Online Banking app is in its logout page redirection. Open `Areas\Identity\Pages\Account\Logout.cshtml.cs` and go to the `OnGet` method of the page method:

```
public async Task<IActionResult> OnGet(string url =
   null)
{
    await _signInManager.SignOutAsync();
    _log.LogInformation("User logged out.");
    if (url != null)
    {
        return Redirect(url);
    }
    else
    {
        return RedirectToPage();
    }
}
// code removed for brevity
```

Again, the redirection is invalidated, and an adversary can craft a URL that could redirect to a hacker-controlled website delivered through phishing or some other deceptive means.

4. To remediate these security flaws, open `Areas\Identity\Pages\Account\Login.cshtml.cs` and change the `Redirect` method to `LocalRedirect`:

```
if (ModelState.IsValid)
{
    // This doesn't count login failures towards
    account lockout
    // To enable password failures to trigger account
    lockout, set lockoutOnFailure: true
    var signInResult = await _signInManager
        .PasswordSignInAsync(Input.Email,
            Input.Password, Input.RememberMe,
                lockoutOnFailure: false);
    if (signInResult.Succeeded)
    {
```

```
        _log.LogInformation("User logged in.");

        if (string.IsNullOrEmpty
          (HttpContext.Session.GetString(SessionKey)))
        {
            HttpContext.Session.SetString(SessionKey,
                Input.Email);
        }

        return LocalRedirect(url);
    }

// code removed for brevity
```

The `LocalRedirect` method performs the same redirection, except it will throw an `InvalidOperationException` exception when the URL is trying to redirect to a website that is not local.

5. Another way to fix this security bug is to use the `Url.IsLocalUrl` method. Open `Areas\Identity\Pages\Account\Logout.cshtml.cs` and go to the `OnGet` method of the page method. Change the method from `OnGet` to `OnPost` for this method to be invoked on **HyperText Transfer Protocol (HTTP)** POST requests, not HTTP GET requests. Replace the `Redirect` method call with a validation check using the `IsLocalUrl` method:

```
public async Task<IActionResult> OnPost(string url =
  null)
{
    await _signInManager.SignOutAsync();
    _log.LogInformation("User logged out.");
    if (url != null)
    {
        if (Url.IsLocalUrl(url))
            return Redirect(url);
        else
            return RedirectToPage();
    }
    else
    {
```

```
        return RedirectToPage();
    }
}
// code removed for brevity
```

A call to the `Url.IsLocalUrl` method checks if the URL is local, preventing the customer running the risk of getting redirected to an arbitrary URL.

How it works...

A malicious website could imitate a legitimate website and deceive the user into using their credentials to log in, ultimately stealing usernames and passwords from victims. We use both the `LocalRedirect` and `Url.IsLocalUrl` methods, replacing the dangerous `Redirect` method to validate the URLs received as parameters. Implementing these safer functions can protect us from getting redirected to unwanted URLs.

If certain use cases require users to be redirected to an external URL, a whitelist validation technique must be applied to determine whether a URL is allowed.

7
Security Misconfiguration

An oversight in disabling security controls in any application layer, most especially in code, could leave an ASP.NET Core web application susceptible to much more varied attacks. Overlooking disabling debugging in production, inadvertently logging traces, missing necessary attributes in cookies, and HTTP security headers are just a few of the root causes of security misconfiguration. Hardening your web application for security starts with code and can also be the weak link of an app if not done correctly.

In this chapter, we're going to cover the following recipes:

- Disabling debugging features in non-development environments
- Fixing disabled security features
- Disabling unnecessary features
- Fixing information exposure through an error message
- Fixing information exposure through insecure cookies

By the end of this chapter, you will have learned how to prevent security misconfiguration by turning debugging off in code, adding security features, and stopping unwanted information leaks to prying attackers with proper application settings.

Technical requirements

This book was written and designed to use with Visual Studio Code, Git, and .NET 5.0. Code examples in recipes are presented in ASP.NET Core Razor pages. The sample solution also uses SQLite as the database engine for a more simplified setup. The complete code examples for this chapter are available at https://github.com/PacktPublishing/ASP.NET-Core-Secure-Coding-Cookbook/tree/main/Chapter07.

Disabling debugging features in non-development environments

Debugging is an essential part of a web developer's task when writing code and running tests. ASP.NET Core enables developers to have easy access to a configuration that will quickly enable or disable debugging in a particular environment with configuration files or code. However, negligence or configuration mismanagement could cause debugging to be enabled in a non-development environment such as **staging** or **production**. In this recipe, we will fix the enabled debugging feature in a non-development environment.

Getting ready

For the recipes in this chapter, we will need a sample Online Banking app.

Open the command shell and download the sample Online Banking app by cloning the ASP.NET Secure Coding Cookbook repository as follows:

```
git clone https://github.com/PacktPublishing/ASP.NET-Core-
Secure-Coding-Cookbook.git
```

Run the sample app to verify that there are no build or compile errors. In your command shell, navigate to the sample app folder at \Chapter07\debug-enabled\before\OnlineBankingApp and run the following command:

```
dotnet build
```

The dotnet build command will build our sample OnlineBankingApp project and its dependencies.

How to do it...

Let's take a look at the steps for this recipe:

1. From the starting exercise folder, launch Visual Studio Code by typing the following command:

```
code .
```

2. Open OnlineBankingApp\Startup.cs and go to the Configure startup method. The Configure method makes a call to UseDeveloperExceptionPage even if it is in a non-development environment:

```
public void Configure(IApplicationBuilder appBuilder,
    IWebHostEnvironment environment)
{
    if (environment.IsDevelopment())
    {
        appBuilder.UseDeveloperExceptionPage();
    }
    else
    {
        appBuilder.UseDeveloperExceptionPage();
        // appBuilder.UseExceptionHandler("/Error");
        appBuilder.UseHsts();
    }
    // code removed for brevity
```

UseDeveloperExceptionPage will generate an HTML page with details of SystemException. An exception can provide vital information to attackers from the stack traces and debugging information it shows, so it is not ideal to have these exposed in either *Staging* or *Production* environments.

3. We avoid the unnecessary exception details shown either in *Staging* or *Production* by removing the line of code that calls UseDeveloperExceptionPage and uncommenting the line that invokes UseExceptionHandler:

```
public void Configure(IApplicationBuilder appBuilder,
    IWebHostEnvironment environment)
{
```

```
if (environment.IsDevelopment())
{
    appBuilder.UseDeveloperExceptionPage();
}
else
{
    appBuilder.UseExceptionHandler("/Error");
    appBuilder.UseHsts();
}
```

Making a call to the `UseExceptionHandler` middleware will catch the exceptions and handle the exceptions to return a friendlier `OnlineBankingApp\Pages\Error.cshtml` page.

How it works...

Debugging is useful for ASP.NET web developers to understand what is going on with their apps. In the case of our sample Online Banking web application, misplacing the call to the `UseDeveloperExceptionPage` method in code will allow exception details to be displayed in *Staging* or *Production*.

We fix the code by placing the `UseDeveloperExceptionPage` method under the conditional check of whether the web app is running under the Development environment using the `environment.IsDevelopment` method. This prevents debugging and inspection in either *Staging* or *Production*, which in turn avoids exposing vulnerable information to hackers.

Fixing disabled security features

Adding layers of defense and protection helps an ASP.NET Core web application from getting exploited. Web application servers have built-in security features such as security headers configured to be sent as a part of the HTTP response back to the client, instructing browsers to enable the security mechanism. Not all of these security headers are turned on or added by default, so enabling it in code is left in the web developers' hands.

In this recipe, we are going to add the missing HTTP security headers to enable protection in our sample Online Banking app.

Getting ready

We will use the Online Banking app we used in the previous recipe. Using Visual Studio Code, open the sample Online Banking app folder at \Chapter07\disabled-security-features\before\OnlineBankingApp\.

You can perform the steps in this folder to fix the missing security features in this recipe.

How to do it...

Let's take a look at the steps for this recipe:

1. From the starting exercise folder, launch Visual Studio Code by typing the following command:

```
code .
```

2. Open Startup.cs and look at the Use method call in Configure. The middleware is adding the X-XSS-Protection HTTP security header but the value is set to 0:

```
app.Use(async (context, next) =>
{
    context.Response.Headers.Add("X-XSS-Protection", "0"
      );

    await next();
});
```

Setting the X-XSS-Protection response header with a value of 0 will instruct the browser to *disable its XSS filtering* and its protection against **Cross-Site Scripting (XSS)**. XSS Filters is a browser security feature that defends users from Cross-Site Scripting attacks. Fixing XSS vulnerabilities will be covered in *Chapter 8, Cross-Site Scripting*.

Other security headers such as X-Content-Type-Options and X-Frame-Options are also missing, making our sample Online Banking application lack protection against attacks.

3. To include these missing security features, we replace the old code with the following lines, which will protect our sample Online Banking web application:

```
app.Use(async (context, next) =>
{
    context.Response.Headers.Add("X-XSS-Protection",
        "1; mode=block");
    context.Response.Headers
        .Add("X-Content-Type-Options", "nosniff");
    context.Response.Headers
        .Add("X-Frame-Options", "DENY");
    context.Response.Headers.Add("Referrer-Policy",
        "no-referrer");
    await next();
});
```

Each of these HTTP response headers serves a security purpose, which will be explained in the *How it works...* section.

> **Note**
>
> While X-XSS-Protection is already deprecated, it is still a useful HTTP header to enable in your web application if you anticipate users will still be utilizing older browsers. Another alternative is to implement **Content-Security-Policy**, which we will cover in *Chapter 13, Best Practices.*

Validating the security headers

Here are the steps:

1. Navigate to **Terminal | New Terminal** in the menu or by simply pressing *Ctrl + Shift + '* in Visual Studio Code.

2. Type the following command in the terminal to build and run the sample app:

```
dotnet run
```

3. Open a browser and go to https://localhost:5001/.

4. Log in using the following credentials:

    a). Email: stanley.s.jobson@lobortis.ca

    b). Password: rUj5jtV8jrTyHnx!

5.   Once authenticated, you will be redirected to the **Home page**:

Figure 7.1 – Home page authenticated

6.   Press *F12* to open the browser's developer tools.

7.   Go to the **Network** tab and select the first HTTP traffic in the traffic list.

8.   Once a single HTTP traffic is selected, scroll through in the right pane to view the corresponding HTTP response security headers:

Figure 7.2 – Security headers

The security headers are now added as part of the HTTP response sent from our sample Online Banking web application.

How it works...

When HTTP security headers are specified as part of the response that the web server or web application sends, this instructs the web browser to enable protection from XSS, clickjacking, and other types of web application-related vulnerabilities. In the preceding code, we added the following HTTP security headers:

- `X-XSS-Protection`: The `X-XSS-Protection` security header tells browsers to enable their XSS filter when the directive is set to `1`. The XSS filter protects against XSS and stops a page from loading when XSS is detected.

- X-Content-Type-Options: The X-Content-Type-Options header, if assigned with a nosniff directive, prevents *MIME sniffing*. MIME-type sniffing is a browser behavior where it guesses what the MIME-type is of a resource of a page, but this behavior can be tricked into executing malicious content. This response header tells the browser to believe the Content-Type header's value and not attempt to guess the page's mime type implicitly.

  The absence of the Content-Type response header is usually marked as a vulnerability finding by most Dynamic Application Security Testing tools. Use X-Content-Type-Options: nosniff in conjunction with an explicitly declared Content-Type response header. The X-Content-Type-Options header is supported in all major browsers, such as Firefox, Chrome, and Edge.

- X-Frame-Options: X-Frame-Options is also an HTTP response header, which when set to DENY will tell the browser to not allow the page to be rendered or embedded in any of the following HTML elements: <iframe>, <frame>, <embed>, or <object>. Malicious websites abuse these HTML elements to masquerade as authentic by embedding or framing the legitimate websites inside. Users are tricked in to clicking on the UI on what they presume rendered in front of the browser is a legit website. This attack is called **Click-Jacking**.

Tip:

To allow one of your web pages to be framed inside your web app, which is of the same origin, assign the X-Frame-Options header with a value of SAMEORIGIN:

```
context.Response.Headers.Add("X-Frame-Options",
"SAMEORIGIN");
```

- Referrer-Policy: Lastly, to keep sensitive information in your ASP.NET Core web application URLs from getting exposed during cross-site requests, set your Referrer-Policy to no-referrer. The Referrer header shows the URL where the user's request originated, and the no-referrer value explicitly instructs the browser to remove the Referrer from the HTTP header.

Other values may be more fitting to your ASP.NET Core web application requirements. Visit the *Referrer-Policy* documentation from the *Mozilla Developer Network* for alternative values at https://developer.mozilla.org/en-US/docs/Web/HTTP/Headers/Referrer-Policy.

Disabling unnecessary features

Most ASP.NET Core web application features are useful, but some can be unnecessary or sometimes even harmful. Web developers must consider whether a web server or application functionality needs to be enabled in code. We need to remove some features to keep our ASP.NET Core web applications secure.

In this recipe, we are going to remove the `Server` HTTP header to prevent web server information disclosure.

Getting ready

We will use the Online Banking app we used in the previous recipe. Using Visual Studio Code, open the sample Online Banking app folder at `\Chapter07\unnecessary-features\before\OnlineBankingApp\`.

You can perform the steps in this folder to disable unnecessary features in this recipe.

How to do it...

Let's take a look at the steps for this recipe:

1. From the starting exercise folder, launch Visual Studio Code by typing following command:

   ```
   code .
   ```

2. Open `Program.cs` and notice the value of one of the properties of the `KestrelOptions AddServerHeader`:

   ```
   public static IHostBuilder CreateHostBuilder(string[]
     args) =>
       Host.CreateDefaultBuilder(args)
           .ConfigureWebHostDefaults(webHost =>
           {
               webHost.UseKestrel(kestrelOptions =>
               {
                   kestrelOptions.AddServerHeader = true;
                   kestrelOptions.ConfigureHttpsDefaults
                       (https =>
                       {
   ```

```
                        https.SslProtocols =
                            SslProtocols.Tls12 |
                                SslProtocols.Tls13;
                });
            });
            webHost.UseStartup<Startup>();
        });
```

The `AddServerHeader` property adds a `Server` HTTP header in the response
when this Boolean property is set to `true`. This header is not required but would give
a malicious actor information on what platform the web application is built with.

3. We remove this unnecessary HTTP header by setting the value of the
    `AddServerHeader` property to `false`:

```
public static IHostBuilder CreateHostBuilder(string[]
    args) =>
    Host.CreateDefaultBuilder(args)
        .ConfigureWebHostDefaults(webHost =>
        {
            webHost.UseKestrel(kestrelOptions =>
            {
                kestrelOptions.AddServerHeader = false;
                kestrelOptions.ConfigureHttpsDefaults
                    (https =>
                {
                    https.SslProtocols = SslProtocols.Tls12
                        | SslProtocols.Tls13;
                });
            });
            webHost.UseStartup<Startup>();
        });
```

When set to `false`, the `Server` HTTP header will no longer be sent in the
response to the client, limiting the information provided to bad actors.

> **Note**
>
> Other unwanted HTTP headers include **X-Powered-By** and **X-AspNet-Version**. Both HTTP headers divulge software information about the web host that may benefit a threat actor.
>
> If you're hosting your ASP.NET Core web application in IIS, these headers are typically present by default, and it best to remove them. To remove the X-Powered-By or the X-AspNet-Version header, follow the steps in the *customheaders* section of the IIS reference from Microsoft's official documentation: https://docs.microsoft.com/en-us/iis/configuration/system.webServer/httpProtocol/customHeaders/.

How it works...

By default, Kestrel is the web server used with our sample Online Banking application, but the Server header is available to any web server type. Some web servers have it already available in their default instance or configured through the web application's code. Using the browser's developer tools, we can see that our ASP.NET Core web app sent a Server HTTP header, giving us details that our web server is running Kestrel:

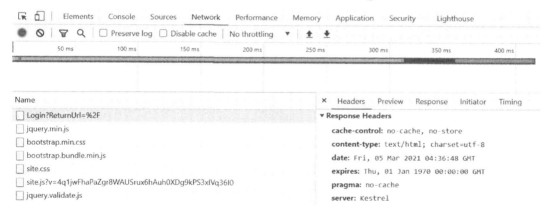

Figure 7.3 – Server HTTP header

In our recipe, we disable sending this Server header back to the browser as a response, limiting the malicious agent's information as to what type of platform the web application is running on. Knowing this detail gives the bad actor leverage on what specific exploits it could execute against the app.

Fixing information exposure through an error message

Logs can help determine events that are occurring inside an app. Application traces, debugging information, errors, warnings, and other information are also available and are written in logs. Unfortunately, sensitive data can also be carelessly logged in ASP.NET Core web applications, and inadvertent disclosure poses a risk.

In this recipe, we are going to change the misconfigured log provider properties to prevent logging information that is too sensitive to be stored in logs.

Getting ready

We will use the Online Banking app we used in the previous recipe. Using Visual Studio Code, open the sample Online Banking app folder at `\Chapter07\information-exposure1\before\OnlineBankingApp\`.

You can perform the steps in this folder to fix information exposure through an error message recipe.

How to do it...

Let's take a look at the steps for this recipe:

1. From the starting exercise folder, launch Visual Studio Code by typing the following command:

    ```
    code .
    ```

2. Open `appsettings.json` and look at the current `LogLevel` values:

    ```
    {
        "Logging": {
          "LogLevel": {
            "Default": "Trace",
            "Microsoft": "Trace",
            "Microsoft.Hosting.Lifetime": "Trace"
          }
        },
        "AllowedHosts": "*",
        "ConnectionStrings": {
    ```

```
        "OnlineBankingAppContext": "Data Source
            = OnlineBank.db"
    }
}
```

The `Trace` value specifies that our sample Online Banking web application will write trace logs into all log providers. This value is *at its minimum level*, which specifies that anything else higher will also be logged, including sensitive debugging information.

3. We fix the issue by setting these values to `Warning`, which is levels higher than `Trace`:

```
{
    "Logging": {
        "LogLevel": {
            "Default": "Warning",
            "Microsoft": "Warning",
            "Microsoft.Hosting.Lifetime": "Warning"
        }
    },
    "AllowedHosts": "*",
    "ConnectionStrings": {
        "OnlineBankingAppContext": "Data
            Source=OnlineBank.db"
    }
}
```

Assigning these categories with `Warning` property values will instruct the logger to write error logs that occur from unexpected events that don't make our sample Online Banking web application crash.

How it works

Logging in an ASP.NET Core web application is configured in the `Logging` section of `appsettings.json`. In each of the log categories (`Default`, `Microsoft`, and `Microsoft.Hosting.Lifetime`) defined in this file, their values are set to `Trace`, which is the lowest `LogLevel` with a value of `0`. This `LogLevel` is not best for a production environment, which is why we modified the values and changed them to `Warning`.

Fixing information exposure through insecure cookies

Cookies are essential in maintaining state in ASP.NET Core web applications. Sensitive cookies, such as the ones that are used for authenticated sessions should only be transmitted over HTTPS and marked as `HTTP-Only` to stop attackers from stealing information stored in these cookies.

In this recipe, we are going to configure cookie policies that will prevent our ASP.NET Core sample web application from generating persistent cookies.

Getting ready

We will use the Online Banking app we used in the previous recipe. Using Visual Studio Code, open the sample Online Banking app folder at `\Chapter07\information-exposure2\before\OnlineBankingApp\`.

You can perform the steps in this folder to fix information exposure through the persistent cookies recipe.

How to do it...

Let's take a look at the steps for this recipe:

1. From the starting exercise folder, launch Visual Studio Code by typing the following command:

```
code .
```

2. Open `Startup.cs` and look at the following sections of code under `ConfigureServices`:

```
services.AddSession(options =>
{
    options.Cookie.Name = ".OnlineBanking.Session";
    options.IdleTimeout = TimeSpan.FromSeconds(10);
    options.Cookie.HttpOnly = false;
    options.Cookie.SecurePolicy =
        CookieSecurePolicy.None;
    options.Cookie.IsEssential = true;
});
```

Setting the `SecurePolicy` property of `CookiePolicyOptions` with an enum value of `CookieSecurePolicy.None`, this configuration indicates that the session cookie in our sample app will not have a **Secure** attribute.

Also, having the `HttpOnly` property of the session cookies assigned with a `false` value makes the session cookies readable by a client-side script.

3. To prevent a malicious arbitrary JavaScript code from reading the values of our session cookies, we set the `HttpOnly` property of the session state service to `true`:

```
services.AddSession(options =>
{
    options.Cookie.Name = ".OnlineBanking.Session";
    options.IdleTimeout = TimeSpan.FromSeconds(10);
    options.Cookie.HttpOnly = true;
```

4. To also ensure that the cookie policy middleware will mark the cookies of our sample Online Banking web application with a **Secure** attribute, we assign the `SecurePolicy` property of the `CookiePolicyOptions` with `CookieSecurePolicy.Always`:

```
options.Cookie.SecurePolicy =
    CookieSecurePolicy.Always;
    options.Cookie.IsEssential = true;
});
```

Enabling the `HttpOnly` property will mark the session cookies with an `HttpOnly` attribute.

Validating the session cookie attributes

Here are the steps:

1. Navigate to **Terminal | New Terminal** in the menu or by simply pressing *Ctrl + Shift + '* in Visual Studio Code.

2. Type the following command in the terminal to build and run the sample app:

```
dotnet run
```

3. Open a browser and go to `https://localhost:5001/`.

4. Log in using the following credentials:

a). Email: `axl.l.torvalds@ut.net`

b). Password: `6GKqqtQQTii92ke!`

5. Once authenticated, you will be redirected to the **Home page**:

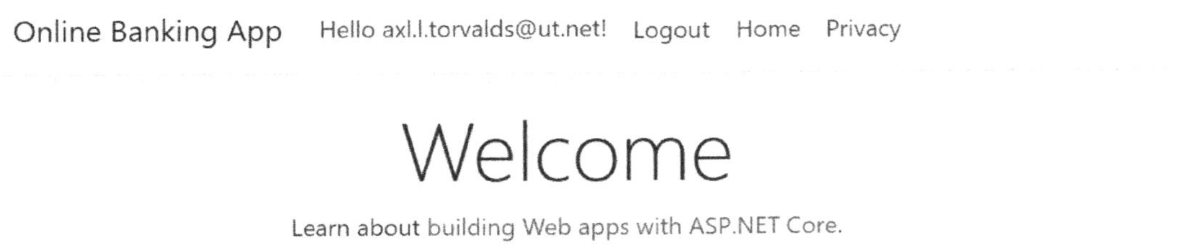

Online Banking App   Hello axl.l.torvalds@ut.net!   Logout   Home   Privacy

Welcome

Learn about building Web apps with ASP.NET Core.

Figure 7.4 – Home page authenticated

6. Press *F12* to open the browser's developer tools.

7. Expand the **Cookies** tree on the left pane of the developer tools:

Figure 7.5 – Cookies section

8. Go to the **Application** tab (the **Storage** tab in Firefox) and notice that the columns for the **HttpOnly** and **Secure** attributes are checked:

Figure 7.6 – Session cookies

This shows that the `Secure` and `HttpOnly` attributes are enabled in the cookies.

How it works

`HttpOnly` and `Secure` are two of the most important attributes in cookies yet are optional. These cookie attributes must be explicitly declared and configured as part of the cookie policy middleware. We append the `HttpOnly` attribute in session cookies by setting the `HttpOnly` property to `true`:

```
options.Cookie.HttpOnly = true;
```

Without the `HttpOnly` attribute, an arbitrary client-side script can read cookie values that potentially could contain sensitive data. No JavaScript code will be able to retrieve values from the `document.cookie` property.

> **Note**
>
> Cookies that we typically mark with an `HttpOnly` attribute contain values that may be at risk of exploitation from attacks such as **Session Hijacking** or **Cross-Site Scripting (XSS)**.

We also include the `Szecure` attribute in our application cookies by configuring the cookie policy in our middleware service pipeline:

```
options.Cookie.SecurePolicy = CookieSecurePolicy.Always;
```

`CookieSecurePolicy.Always` ensures that the cookie is only sent over **HTTPS**.

8
Cross-Site Scripting

Cross-site scripting is still one of the widespread vulnerabilities in web applications today. Also known as **XSS**, it is a security flaw that allows an attacker to insert malicious client-side code into an ASP.NET Core web page. The injected input is made possible because of the lack of sanitization and filtering, and the browser processes the unwanted arbitrary code.

An unknowing user can view a vulnerable web page in an XSS attack where the malicious script runs in the browser. Once the code executes, the attacker can potentially redirect the user to a rogue website, potentially steal its session cookies, or deface your ASP.NET Core web application.

In this chapter, we're going to cover the following recipes:

- Fixing reflected XSS
- Fixing stored/persistent XSS
- Fixing DOM XSS

By the end of this chapter, you will learn how to protect your ASP.NET Core web application from the different types of XSS by properly encoding and escaping output. You will also discover ways to escape output by using a third-party library function to mitigate cross-site scripting attacks.

Technical requirements

This book was written and designed to use with Visual Studio Code, Git, and .NET 5.0. Code examples in recipes are presented in ASP.NET Core Razor pages. The sample solution also uses SQLite as the database engine for a more simplified setup. The complete code examples for this chapter are available at `https://github.com/PacktPublishing/ASP.NET-Core-Secure-Coding-Cookbook/tree/main/Chapter08`.

Fixing reflected XSS

Reflected cross-site scripting is one type of XSS where a bad actor could inject code as part of the HTTP response. The reflected XSS is non-persistent and not stored in the database, but the attack payload is delivered back to the browser, reflecting the untrusted input.

The reflected XSS vulnerability is possible when output is not encoded and exploited when tricked users click a malicious link containing the XSS payload. In this recipe, we will fix the reflected XSS vulnerability by using the built-in encoding features of the Razor page.

Getting ready

For the recipes in this chapter, we will need the sample Online Banking app.

Open the command shell and download the sample Online Banking app by cloning the ASP.NET Secure Coding Cookbook repository as follows:

```
git clone https://github.com/PacktPublishing/ASP.NET-Core-
Secure-Coding-Cookbook.git
```

Run the sample app to verify that there are no build or compile errors. In your command shell, navigate to the sample app folder at `\Chapter08\reflected-xss\before\OnlineBankingApp` and run the following command:

```
dotnet build
```

The `dotnet build` command will build our sample `OnlineBankingApp` project and its dependencies.

Let's now see in action how reflected XSS vulnerabilities can be exploited.

Testing reflected XSS

Here are the steps:

1. Navigate to **Terminal | New Terminal** in the menu or simply press *Ctrl + Shift + '* in Visual Studio Code.

2. Type the following command in the terminal to build and run the sample app:

    ```
    dotnet run
    ```

3. Open a browser and go to `https://localhost:5001/Loans`.

4. Log in using the following credentials:

    a) Email: `stanley.s.jobson@lobortis.ca`

    b) Password: `rUj5jtV8jrTyHnx!`

5. Once authenticated, you will be redirected to the **Loans** page:

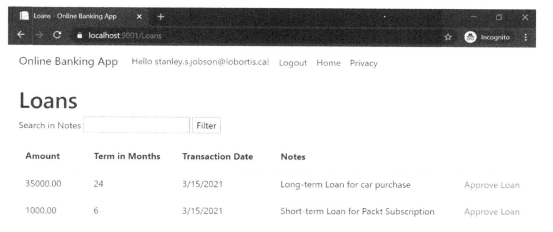

Figure 8.1 – Loans page

6. Type Packt as the keyword to search in the textbox on top of the empty table and hit the **Filter** button. Notice that the search term is displayed as a message:

Figure 8.2 – Keyword search

7. To test whether our sample Online Banking solution is vulnerable to XSS, we enter the XSS payload `<script>alert("Pwned")</script>` in the search bar and hit the **Filter** button. Examine the result of this test:

Figure 8.3 – Reflected XSS

Notice that an alert box was displayed indicating that the XSS injection was successful and proved that the **Loans** page is vulnerable to reflected XSS. Examine the URL that the test has generated. An attacker can send this URL to an unknowing user via email or social engineering tactics: `https://localhost:5001/Loans?SearchString=%3Cscript%3Ealert%28%22Pwned%22%29%3C%2Fscript%3E`.

How to do it...

Let's take a look at the steps for this recipe:

1. From the starting exercise folder, launch Visual Studio Code by typing the following command:

    ```
    code .
    ```

2. Open `Pages\Loans\Index.cshtml` and observe the markup just after the HTML table element:

    ```
    <table class="table">
        @{
            if(Model.SearchString is not null){
                <h2>Your searched for
                    @Html.Raw(@Model.SearchString) returned
                        @Model.Loan.Count results</h2>
            }
        }
    // code removed for brevity
    ```

    The loan notes search term entered is displayed on the page using `Html.Raw`, allowing the unfiltered string rendered within the `<h2>` HTML markup. A bad actor can exploit the absence of output encoding by entering malicious cross-site scripting payload attacks into the search textbox.

3. To remediate the security flaw in our code, we remove the call to the `Html.Raw` method:

    ```
    <table class="table">
        @{
            if(Model.SearchString is not null){
                <h2>Your searched for
                    @Model.SearchString returned
                        @Model.Loan.Count results</h2>
            }
        }
    ```

    `Html.Raw` should not be used to render user-controlled input. Avoid using this method.

4.   To test whether the code fix worked, repeat *steps 1-7* in the *Testing reflected XSS* section and see the result:

Figure 8.4 – Reflected XSS mitigated

Note that the reflected XSS payload no longer works.

How it works...

The **Loans** page offers a search feature to enter a keyword to locate and return the matching records. This page was vulnerable when the search term is displayed back using the Html.Raw method. Html.Raw is a method that returns an unencoded string, exposing this page to a reflected XSS attack.

We mitigate this risk and prevent exploitation by removing the call to the Html.Raw method and use the built-in Razor syntax instead to render markup for SearchString. Razor syntax that evaluates to a string type returns an escaped string that makes the SearchString output safe for rendering.

Fixing stored/persistent XSS

Stored or persistent XSS is another type of cross-site scripting vulnerability. ASP.NET Core web applications that store data can be vulnerable to this XSS attack variant. Stored XSS happens when the tainted data supplied by the attacker gets saved in a persistent store or database, eventually delivered to the users by viewing these vulnerable ASP.NET Core web pages without the app output escaping the data first. In this recipe, we will fix the stored XSS vulnerability by using encoded values when displaying data on a page.

Let's see in action how the reflected XSS vulnerability can be exploited.

Testing stored XSS

Here are the steps:

1. Navigate to **Terminal | New Terminal** in the menu or simply press *Ctrl + Shift + '* in Visual Studio Code.

2. Type the following command in the terminal to build and run the sample app:

   ```
   dotnet run
   ```

3. Open a browser and go to `https://localhost:5001/Loans`.

4. Log in using the following credentials:

   a) Email: `axl.l.torvalds@ut.net`

   b) Password: `6GKqqtQQTii92ke!`

5. Once authenticated, you will be redirected to the **Loans** page. Notice the message that gets displayed:

Figure 8.5 – Stored XSS

An alert box was displayed indicating that data on the **Loans** page is tainted, thereby making our sample Online Banking application prone to stored XSS.

Getting ready

We will use the Online Banking app we used in the previous recipe. Using Visual Studio Code, open the sample Online Banking app folder at `\Chapter08\stored-xss\before\OnlineBankingApp\`.

You can perform the steps in this folder to fix the missing security features in this recipe.

How to do it...

Let's take a look at the steps for this recipe:

1. From the starting exercise folder, launch Visual Studio Code by typing the following command:

   ```
   code .
   ```

2. Open Pages\Loans\Index.cshtml and examine the data cell that displays Note in the <td> tag:

   ```
   @foreach (var item in Model.Loan) {
       <tr>
           <td>
               @Html.DisplayFor(modelItem => item.Amount)
           </td>
           <td>
               @Html.DisplayFor(modelItem =>
                   item.PeriodInMonths)
           </td>
           <td>
               @Html.DisplayFor(modelItem =>
                   item.TransactionDate)
           </td>
           <td>
               @(new HtmlString(item.Note))
           </td>
           <td>
               <a asp-page="./Edit" asp-route-
                   id="@item.ID">Approve Loan</a> |
           </td>
       </tr>
   }
   ```

Rendered in the cell is the `Note` data from the database using the `HtmlString` class, but, by default, an instance of the `HtmlString` class is unencoded, and displaying the page's output will lead to an XSS vulnerability.

3. To fix this stored XSS security bug, we use the `Value` property of the `HtmlString` object:

```
@foreach (var item in Model.Loan) {
    <tr>
        <td>
            @Html.DisplayFor(modelItem => item.Amount)
        </td>
        <td>
            @Html.DisplayFor(modelItem =>
                item.PeriodInMonths)
        </td>
        <td>
            @Html.DisplayFor(modelItem =>
                item.TransactionDate)
        </td>
        <td>
            @(new HtmlString(item.Note).Value)
        </td>
        <td>
            <a asp-page="./Edit" asp-route-
                id="@item.ID">Approve Loan</a> |
        </td>
    </tr>
}
```

The `Value` property returns the HTML-encoded value of the `Note` field, which makes our **Loans** page safe from stored or persistent XSS attacks.

4. To test whether the code fix worked, repeat *steps 1-5* in the *Testing stored XSS* section and see the result:

Figure 8.6 – Mitigated stored XSS vulnerability

Note that the persistent XSS payload did not execute.

How it works...

Our sample Online Banking web application is seeded with loan data at `Models\ SeedData.cs`. We populate our SQLite database with one loan application:

```
Loans = new List<Loan>{
    new Loan {
        Amount = 35000.00m,
        TransactionDate = DateTime.Now,
        PeriodInMonths = 24,
        Note = "<script>alert('Pwned')</script>",
        Status = LoanStatus.Pending
    }
}
```

Notice that the `Note` property was assigned with a persistent XSS payload. This abuse case mimics the scenario where the attacker saved tainted data in the database due to a lack of validation.

As the **Loans** page is loaded, we see that the `alert` JavaScript function gets executed, and an alert box pops out. The stored XSS payload ran successfully because `item.Note` is rendered using `HtmlString`. The `HtmlString` class returns an unescaped string by default, making the persistent XSS attack possible. We fix the security problem in our code by simply utilizing the `Value` property of the `HtmlString` class, which returns the string encoded and secures our web application from stored XSS exploitation.

There's more...

Another way to mitigate the risk is to use the `HtmlEncoder` class. As we have learned in the *Output encoding using HtmlEncoder* recipe from *Chapter 1, Secure Coding Fundamentals*, the `HtmlEncoder` class has an `Encode` method that escapes the string passed in to the method's argument.

Similar to *steps 2* and *3*, you start by adding an `@inject` directive on top of the `Pages\Loans\Index.cshtml` Razor page markup to inject the `HtmlEncoder` service:

```
@inject System.Text.Encodings.Web.HtmlEncoder htmlEncoder
```

Then, a call is made to the `HtmlEncoder` service's `Encode` method, passing `item.Note`:

```
<td>
        @(htmlEncoder.Encode(item.Note))
</td>
```

The `Encode` method will escape the value of `item.Note`, thereby fixing the persistent XSS problem.

Fixing DOM XSS

The **Document Object Model (DOM)** is an object interface that represents an HTML page. This interface allows client-side scripts to manipulate, add or remove elements from the document. The client-side script used in conjunction with the JavaScript programming language can be written insecurely and opens up security vulnerabilities such as DOM-based XSS.

DOM XSS, in contrast to reflected and stored XSS, is not a server-side exploit. The weakness is in the client-side code when it attempts to modify the DOM to display data, but instead interprets the input into code due to a lack of encoding and proper escaping. In this recipe, we will fix the DOM-based XSS vulnerability by using an encoding function from a JavaScript library.

Let's now see in action how a DOM XSS vulnerability can be tested.

Testing DOM XSS

Here are the steps:

1. Navigate to **Terminal | New Terminal** in the menu or simply press *Ctrl + Shift +* ' in Visual Studio Code.

2. Type the following command in the terminal to build and run the sample app:

```
dotnet run
```

3. Open a browser and go to `https://localhost:5001/Loans`.

4. Log in using the following credentials:

    a) Email: `stanley.s.jobson@lobortis.ca`

    b) Password: `rUj5jtV8jrTyHnx!`

5. Once authenticated, you will be redirected to the **Loans** page:

Figure 8.7 – Loans page

6. Type `car` as the keyword to search in the textbox on top of the empty table and hit the **Filter** button. Notice that the search term is displayed as a message and a matching record is displayed:

Figure 8.8 – Keyword search

7. To test whether our sample Online Banking solution is vulnerable to DOM-based XSS, we enter the XSS payload, `<script>alert("Pwned")</script>`, in the search bar and hit the **Filter** button. Examine the result of this test:

Figure 8.9 – DOM XSS

Notice that an alert box was displayed, indicating that the XSS injection was successful and proving that the **Loans** page is vulnerable to DOM XSS. Examine the URL that the test has generated. A bad actor can send this URL to an unknowing user through an email or social engineering.

Getting ready

We will use the Online Banking app we used in the previous recipe. Using Visual Studio Code, open the sample Online Banking app folder at `\Chapter08\dom-xss\before\OnlineBankingApp\`.

You can perform the steps in this folder to fix the DOM XSS in this recipe.

How to do it...

Let's take a look at the steps for this recipe:

1. From the starting exercise folder, launch Visual Studio Code by typing the following command:

    ```
    code .
    ```

2. Open `Pages\Loans\Index.cshtml` and notice the JavaScript code at the lower part of the `cshtml` page within `@section Scripts`:

    ```
    @section Scripts {
        @{
            if(Model.SearchString is not null){
                <script>
                    $(document).ready(function () {
                        var param = new URLSearchParams
                            (window.location.search);
                        var searchString = param.get
                            ('SearchString');
                        var message = '<br><h2> You
                            searched for ' + searchString
                            + '</h2>';
                        $('#searchForm').append(message);
                    });
                </script>
            }
        }
    }
    ```

Dynamically appended to the page is the help knowledge-base search term retrieved from the URL's query string. Without output escaping the untrusted message string added to the page's document object model, this insecure code could lead to a DOM-based XSS.

One way of fixing this security issue in code is to use a JavaScript library that has an excellent encoding function. One of the popular JavaScript libraries is `underscore.js`.

3. To start the remediation, we open `Areas\Identity\Pages\_ValidationScriptsPartial.cshtml` and add a reference to the `underscore.js` library:

```
<environment exclude="Development">
    <script src="https://cdn.jsdelivr.net/npm/
        underscore@1.12.0/underscore-min.js"></script>
    <script src=https://ajax.aspnetcdn.com/ajax/
        jquery.validate/1.17.0/jquery.validate.min.js
// code removed for brevity
```

You can host your own copy of the `underscore.js` library or add a reference from the **Content Delivery Network (CDN)**. You specify the URL in `_ValidationScriptsPartial.cshtml` to make its functions available in the whole sample Online Banking solution.

4. We add a reference to `_ValidationScriptsPartial.cshtml` and make a call to the `_.escape` function of the `underscore.js` library:

```
@section Scripts {
    <partial name="_ValidationScriptsPartial" />
    @{
        if(Model.SearchString is not null){
            <script>
                $(document).ready(function () {
                    var param = new URLSearchParams
                        (window.location.search);
                    var searchString = param.get
                        ('SearchString');
                    var message = '<br><h2> You
                        searched for ' + _.escape
                            (searchString) + '</h2>';
```

```
                       $('#searchForm').append(message);
            });
        </script>
    }
}
```

Calling the _.escape function encodes searchString and replaces characters such as <, >, &, ', and ", which can be potentially nefarious.

5. To test whether the code fix worked, repeat *steps 1-7* in the *Testing DOM XSS* section and see the result:

Figure 8.10 – DOM XSS fixed

Notice that the alert box no longer shows and that the HTML page's DOM is not appended with a malicious <script> tag.

How it works...

Using the **jQuery Unobtrusive AJAX library**, we tried to display the searchString URL query string parameter by blindly appending the raw string from the window.location.search value. The original intention was to show the keyword used for the search. However, without the necessary and appropriate encoding of searchString, a perpetrator could craft a payload and assign it to the querystring parameter. Through this malicious link, a bad actor may trick the user into clicking it and unintentionally executing the payload.

We remediate the issue by using a third-party library called `underscore.js`. `underscore.js` has plenty of useful functions and one of them escapes strings. The `._escape` function replaces characters that could lead to DOM XSS vulnerabilities, with its HTML entity counterpart transforming `searchString` into a harmless string.

As a general rule, avoid calls to JavaScript methods such as `document.write` that can render unfiltered and unencoded data. A bad actor can exploit this vector by dynamically manipulating the DOM and executing arbitrary client-side code.

9
Insecure Deserialization

.NET has full support for **serialization** and **deserialization** of data. This language feature allows ASP.NET Core web applications to convert in-memory objects into a stream of bytes (serialize) and rebuild these byte streams back to an object (deserialize). Serialization makes the transfer, storage, and caching of data possible, as well as state persistence between systems.

In the process of deserialization, the data format can be either **JavaScript Object Notation (JSON)** or **Extensible Markup Language (XML)**, and it can also be in binary format. However, as with any input type, the data source can be untrustworthy or tampered with before it gets deserialized back into a web application as an in-memory object. This vulnerability is commonly known as **insecure deserialization**. The use of obsolete and dangerous deserializers, missing data validation, and misconfigured libraries are some of the root causes that have been identified as to why insecure deserialization attacks occur. This security flaw can be attributed to insecure code that can cause, at worst, **denial-of-service (DoS)** attacks and **remote code execution (RCE)**.

In this chapter, we're going to cover the following recipes:

- Fixing unsafe deserialization
- Fixing the use of insecure deserializers
- Fixing untrusted data deserialization

By the end of this chapter, you will have learned how to safely deserialize input using properly configured libraries, how to mitigate risks that an obsolete .NET class brings into your ASP.NET Core web application, and how to use a better deserializer alternative to securely deserialize data streams.

Technical requirements

This book was written and designed to use with Visual Studio Code, Git, and .NET 5.0. Code examples in recipes are presented in ASP.NET Core Razor pages. The sample solution also uses SQLite as the database engine for a more simplified setup. The complete code examples for this chapter are available at `https://github.com/ PacktPublishing/ASP.NET-Core-Secure-Coding-Cookbook/tree/main/ Chapter09`.

Fixing unsafe deserialization

Json.NET had always been a popular framework for processing JSON among .NET developers until .NET recently introduced its own set of serializer/deserializer classes under the `System.Text.Json` namespace. This new set of classes removes prior versions of .NET Core's dependency on the library.

Json.NET has a type-handling feature that can make your ASP.NET Core web application vulnerable to insecure deserialization if misused. The automatic type handling will allow the `Json.NET` stream deserializer to use the declared .NET type in an incoming request. Allowing your app to automatically deserialize objects based on the declared .NET type from an untrusted source can be harmful and may cause the instantiation of unexpected objects, causing arbitrary code execution in the host. In this recipe, we will fix this unsafe deserialization and prevent harmful automatic type handling.

Getting ready

For the recipes of this chapter, we will need the sample Online Banking app.

Open the command shell and download the sample Online Banking app by cloning the `ASP.NET-Core-Secure-Coding-Cookbook` repository, as follows:

```
git clone https://github.com/PacktPublishing/ASP.NET-Core-
Secure-Coding-Cookbook.git
```

Run the sample app to verify that there are no build or compile errors. In your command shell, navigate to the sample app folder at `\Chapter09\unsafe-deserialization\before\OnlineBankingApp` and run the following command:

```
dotnet build
```

The `dotnet build` command will build our sample `OnlineBankingApp` project and its dependencies.

Let's see how we can use tools to discover unsafe deserialization vulnerabilities.

Testing unsafe deserialization

To search for code vulnerabilities, we can use tools such as code analyzers or linters to perform **static application security testing** (**SAST**). This recipe will use an open source **DevSkim** VS Code extension to search for security flaws in code. We begin by installing the plugin and reviewing the result:

1. From the starting exercise folder, launch VS Code by typing the following command:

    ```
    code .
    ```

2. Open the **Extensions** view by simply pressing *Ctrl + Shift + X* or by clicking on the **Extensions** icon in the **Activity Bar** on the left-side panel of VS Code.

3. In the Search box, type in `devskim` to bring up the DevSkim extension, as shown in the following screenshot:

Figure 9.1 – DevSkim VS Code extension

4. Click **Install** to install the DevSkim VS Code extension, as shown next:

Figure 9.2 – Installation

5. Once installed, let's configure the extension settings by clicking the gear icon in the **DevSkim** view and selecting **Extension Settings**:

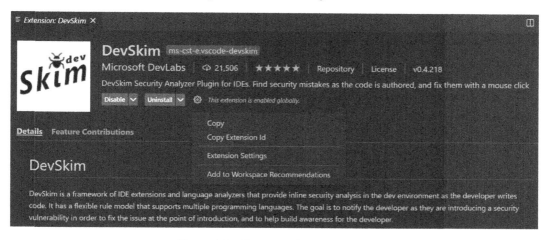

Figure 9.3 – Extension Settings option

6. Enable these **DevSkim** settings, as shown in the following screenshot:

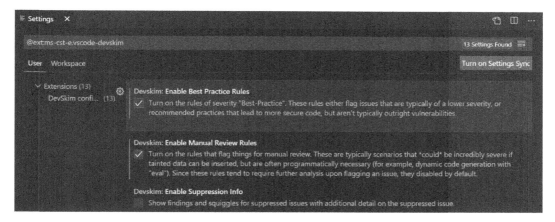

Figure 9.4 – Enabling optional settings

These two settings will enable rules that remind ASP.NET Core developers of the best practices in writing secure code:

a) **Enable Best Practice Rules**

b) **Enable Manual Review Rules**

7. Open `Pages\Loans\Upload.cshtml.cs` and examine the code underlined with a squiggly line in one of the lines of code under the `OnPostAsync` method, indicating that a secure coding rule has been triggered, as shown in the following screenshot:

```
public async Task OnPostAsync()
{
    Loan emptyLoan = null;
    var file = Path.Combine(_environment.ContentRootPath, "uploads", Upload.FileName);

    using (var fileStream = new FileStream(file, FileMode.Create))
    {
        await Upload.CopyToAsync(fileStream);
        using (var reader = new StreamReader (Upload.OpenReadStream())) {
            string fileContent = reader.ReadToEnd ();
            emptyLoan = (Loan) Newtonsoft.Json.JsonConvert.DeserializeObject(fileContent,
                new JsonSerializerSettings
                {
                    TypeNameHandling = TypeNameHandling.All
                });
        }
    }
}
```

Figure 9.5 – Warning

8. Press *Ctrl + Shift + M* to view details of the finding in the **PROBLEMS** tab or hover the mouse over the squiggly line to learn more about the security finding, as shown in the following screenshot:

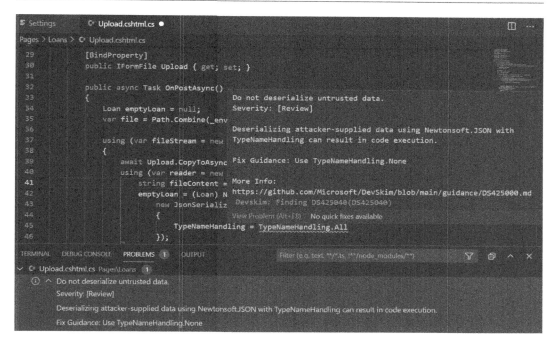

Figure 9.6 – DevSkim fix guidance

The fix guidance will suggest that you not deserialize untrusted data and instead use `TypeNameHandling.None`.

> **Note**
>
> The full-featured version of the Visual Studio **integrated development environment** (**IDE**) has built-in code analysis with security rules that match the rule that our DevSkim plugin tool has:
>
> *CA2300: Do not use insecure deserializer BinaryFormatter*
>
> *CA2301: Do not call BinaryFormatter.Deserialize without first setting BinaryFormatter.Binder*
>
> *CA2302: Ensure BinaryFormatter.Binder is set before calling BinaryFormatter. Deserialize*
>
> To learn more about the different VS Code Analysis security rules, see *Security rules* in the .NET fundamentals official documentation at `https://docs.microsoft.com/en-us/dotnet/fundamentals/code-analysis/quality-rules/security-warnings`.

How to do it...

Let's take a look at the steps for this recipe:

1. Open `Pages\Loans\Upload.cshtml.cs` and locate the vulnerable code in the `OnPostAsync` method, as pointed out by the DevSkim extension:

```
using (var reader = new StreamReader
  (Upload.OpenReadStream())) {
    string fileContent = reader.ReadToEnd ();
    emptyLoan = (Loan) Newtonsoft.Json.JsonConvert
      .DeserializeObject(fileContent,
      new JsonSerializerSettings
      {
          TypeNameHandling = TypeNameHandling.All
      });
}
```

2. Change the `TypeNameHandling` property to `TypeNameHandling.None`:

```
using (var reader = new StreamReader
  (Upload.OpenReadStream())) {
    string fileContent = reader.ReadToEnd ();
    emptyLoan = (Loan) Newtonsoft.Json.JsonConvert
      .DeserializeObject(fileContent,
        new JsonSerializerSettings
      {
          TypeNameHandling = TypeNameHandling.None
      });
}
```

Notice that in the following screenshot, the DevSkim VS Code extension no longer marks the code for review:

```
using (var fileStream = new FileStream(file, FileMode.Create))
{
    await Upload.CopyToAsync(fileStream);
    using (var reader = new StreamReader (Upload.OpenReadStream())) {
        string fileContent = reader.ReadToEnd ();
        emptyLoan = (Loan) Newtonsoft.Json.JsonConvert.DeserializeObject(fileContent,
            new JsonSerializerSettings
            {
                TypeNameHandling = TypeNameHandling.None
            });
    }
}
```

Figure 9.7 – Unsafe deserialization remediated

Changing the property no longer marks the TypeNameHandling property for security code review.

How it works...

JSON is the standard data format, and it is no surprise that ASP.NET Core web developers use a framework such as *Json.NET* that will handle the task of deserializing this data format. Most libraries have features that can help with deserialization (such as automatic type handling), but these features can cause security concerns. In this recipe, we have seen that enabling type handling with JsonSerializerSettings set to TypeNameHandling.All raises a **Do not deserialize untrusted data** security rule from our **DevSkim** tool. Assigning the TypeNameHandling property other than TypeNameHandling.None includes the .NET type name during serialization, which opens our sample Online Banking web application to insecure deserialization attacks. We fix this security flaw in the code by simply setting the TypeNameHandling property to TypeNameHandling.None, preventing automatic .NET type resolution.

> **Tips**
>
> Ensure that you are using the latest version of the serializer/deserializer libraries. Older versions may have a publicly known vulnerability that a threat actor may exploit.
>
> It is also important to log deserialization exceptions and failures. Throw exceptions when the incoming type (`Loan`) is not the expected type by using strongly typed objects.
>
> Here is a revised code snippet where we use strongly typed objects, implement proper logging (more on this in *Chapter 11, Insufficient Logging and Monitoring*), and perform exception handling (more on this in *Chapter 13, Best Practices*):
>
> ```
> try {
>     emptyLoan = (Loan) Newtonsoft.Json.JsonConvert
>       .DeserializeObject<Loan>(fileContent,
>         new JsonSerializerSettings
>         {
>     TypeNameHandling = TypeNameHandling.None
>         });
> }
> catch (JsonException je) {
>         _logger.LogError($"Unexpected error
>           deserializing data '{je.Message}'.");
>         throw new JsonException(je.Message);
> }
> ```

There's more...

Commercial SAST vendors offer an enterprise-grade solution for testing the security of your code. These solutions are either hosted on-premises or are cloud-based. They allow users and developers to run scans and generate reports listing different vulnerabilities by severity and category. The reports provide remediation and ways to fix security bugs found in your solution, and can point to the exact line of code on which an issue was discovered. SAST solutions also display **data-flow graphs** (**DFGs**) for users to understand how a vulnerability propagates from the source to the sink.

To learn more about SAST, go to the **Open Web Application Security Project (OWASP)** *Source Code Analysis Tools* documentation. This OWASP reference will provide tips on your SAST selection process to determine which solution fits your organization, and can be found at the following link: `https://owasp.org/www-community/Source_Code_Analysis_Tools`.

Fixing the use of insecure deserializers

`BinaryFormatter` is one of the types that an ASP.NET developer can use to serialize and deserialize data. Microsoft's official *BinaryFormatter Security Guide* documentation has a strict warning about the use of `BinaryFormatter` as a deserializer. `BinaryFormatter` is an insecure type to utilize because this deserializer does not check the type that it deserializes.

Getting ready

We will use the Online Banking app we used in the previous recipe. Using VS Code, open the sample `OnlineBankingApp` folder at `\Chapter09\insecure-deserializer\before\OnlineBankingApp\`.

You can perform the steps in this folder to fix the use of an insecure deserializer.

How to do it...

Let's take a look at the steps for this recipe.

1. Open `Pages\Loans\Upload.cshtml.cs` and examine the code in the `OnPostAsync` method that makes use of the dangerous `BinaryFormatter` class to deserialize `FileStream`:

```
public async Task OnPostAsync()
{
    Loan emptyLoan = null;
    var file = Path.Combine(_environment
        .ContentRootPath, "uploads", Upload.FileName);
    using (var fileStream = new FileStream(file,
        FileMode.Create))
    {
        await Upload.CopyToAsync(fileStream);
        BinaryFormatter formatter = new
            BinaryFormatter();
```

```
    fileStream.Position = 0;
    emptyLoan = (Loan) formatter.Deserialize
        (fileStream);
}
```

2. Navigate to **Terminal | New Terminal** in the menu or do this by simply pressing *Ctrl + Shift + '* in VS Code.

3. Type the following command in the terminal to build and run the sample app:

```
dotnet build
```

Notice that the build succeeded but a warning appeared:

```
warning SYSLIB0011: 'BinaryFormatter.Deserialize(Stream)' is
obsolete: 'BinaryFormatter serialization is obsolete and should
not be used.
```
```
See https://aka.ms/binaryformatter for more information.
```

More than being obsolete, `BinaryFormatter` is also unsafe. It is highly recommended to avoid this class and to use a more secure serializer/deserializer.

4. To remediate the risk, we must use a `SerializationBinder` class to validate the type that is being deserialized. We begin by adding a new file under the `Models` folder by pressing *Ctrl + N* and name it `LoanDeserializationBinder.cs`:

Figure 9.8 – LoanDeserializationBinder.cs

5. Define a `LoanDeserializationBinder` class that inherits from `SerializationBinder` and add the following code:

```
using System;
using System.Runtime.Serialization;

namespace OnlineBankingApp.Models
{
    public class LoanDeserializationBinder :
        SerializationBinder
    {
        public override Type BindToType(string
            assemblyName, string typeName)
        {
            if (typeName.Equals
                ("OnlineBankingApp.Models.Loan")){
                return typeof(Loan);
            }
            return null;
        }
    }
}
```

6. Next, we refactor the code that uses `BinaryFormatter`, assigning its `Binder` property with the instance of the `LoanDeserializationBinder` class:

```
using (var fileStream = new FileStream(file,
    FileMode.Create))
{
    await Upload.CopyToAsync(fileStream);
    BinaryFormatter formatter = new BinaryFormatter();
    formatter.Binder = new LoanDeserializationBinder();
    fileStream.Position = 0;
    emptyLoan = (Loan) formatter.Deserialize
        (fileStream);
}
```

By using the `LoanDeserializationBinder` class, we can check the type that is being deserialized, preventing our sample Online Banking web app from getting exploited.

Note

This sample Online Banking web application is able to use `BinaryFormatter` because of the settings enabled in the project file.

Inside the `OnlineBankingApp.csproj` file is a Boolean-based `EnableUnsafeBinaryFormatterSerialization` node that allows your app to use the unsafe `BinaryFormatter` class:

```
<PropertyGroup>
<TargetFramework>net5.0</TargetFramework>
<EnableUnsafeBinaryFormatterSerialization>true
</EnableUnsafeBinaryFormatterSerialization>
<UserSecretsId>4869bcd3-3dab-4dae-a167-
31816b317c8b</UserSecretsId>
</PropertyGroup>
```

It is highly advised to *avoid* enabling this setting.

How it works...

Without the `Binder` property set, `BinaryFormatter` can be harmful to our sample Online Banking web application. On its own, `BinaryFormatter` takes the incoming type as it is, with no validation. To resolve our code security problem, we define a new class that inherits from the `SerializationBinder` class and assign this to the `Binder` property of the `BinaryFormatter` instance:

```
formatter.Binder = new LoanDeserializationBinder();
```

The `LoanDeserializationBinder` class checks the type and ensures that it returns the expected `Loan` object:

```
if (typeName.Equals("OnlineBankingApp.Models.Loan")){
    return typeof(Loan);
}
```

However, while this approach reduces the risk of unwanted data deserialization, it does not entirely prevent other types of attack.

There's more...

Assessing your ASP.NET Core web application's risk profile is crucial to determine if BinaryFormatter is a fit deserializer for the job. It is recommended to avoid using this type and to lean into much safer alternatives. Depending on the data to process, secure options such as DataContractSerializer, XmlSerializer, BinaryReader, BinaryWriter—or even the classes under the System.Text.Json namespace—are far better choices.

For instance, to use the DataContractSerializer class in code, we change the namespace reference from System.Runtime.Serialization.Formatters.Binary to this:

```
using System.Runtime.Serialization;
```

We then remove BinaryFormatter to replace it with the DataContractSerializer class:

```
using (var fileStream = new FileStream(file, FileMode.Create))
{
    await Upload.CopyToAsync(fileStream);
    var safeDeserializer = new DataContractSerializer
        (typeof(OnlineBankingApp.Models.Loan));
    fileStream.Position = 0;
    emptyLoan = (OnlineBankingApp.Models.Loan)
        safeDeserializer.ReadObject(fileStream);
}
```

Using the DataContractSerializer class provides automatic type checking, making attacks such as DoS and RCE harder to execute successfully.

Fixing untrusted data deserialization

Missing type checks are not the only thing to look out for when it comes to deserialization—the data itself must be validated for its integrity.

Let's see in action how untrusted data deserialization can exploit our sample Online Banking web application.

Testing untrusted data deserialization

To test if our sample Online Banking web application is vulnerable to untrusted data deserialization, we follow these steps and use a tainted file:

1. Navigate to **Terminal | New Terminal** in the menu or do this by simply pressing *Ctrl + Shift + '* in VS Code.

2. Type the following command in the terminal to build and run the sample app:

```
dotnet run
```

3. Open a browser and go to `https://localhost:5001/Loans/Upload`.

4. Log in using the following credentials:

   a) Email: `axl.l.torvalds@ut.net`

   b) Password: `6GKqqtQQTii92ke!`

5. Once authenticated, you will be redirected to the **Upload Loan Application** page. This page will allow a loan officer to process a loan application by uploading a loan binary file:

Online Banking App   Hello axl.l.torvalds@ut.net!   Logout   Home   Privacy

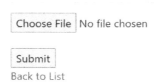

Apply for a Loan

Choose File | No file chosen

Submit
Back to List

Figure 9.9 – Upload Loan Application page

6. Start uploading a file by clicking **Choose File**, browse to the current directory, and select `file.dat`. Hit **Submit** to upload the `file.dat` file:

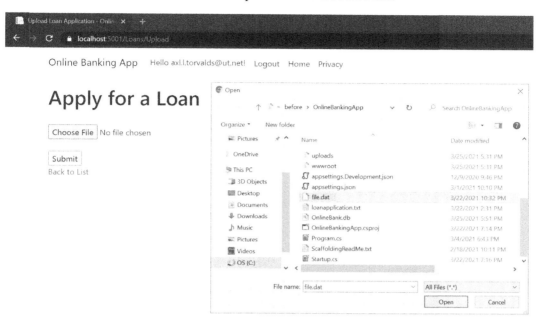

Figure 9.10 – file.dat

Let's see what happens when we upload a presumed trusted file.

7. Open the **DB Browser for SQLite (DB4S)** tool and select the `OnlineBank.db` file to view the loan record:

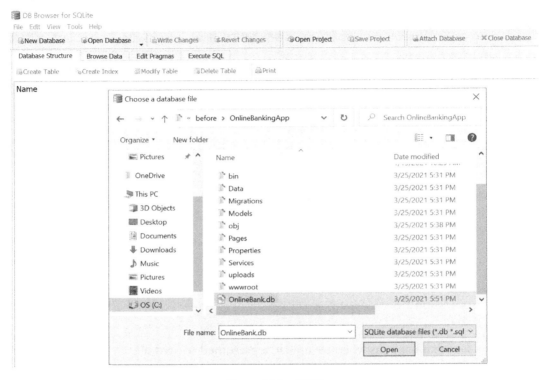

Figure 9.11 – DB4S

8. To view the records under the `Loan` table, go to the **Browse Data** tab and select **Loan** in the **Table** drop-down list, as shown in the following screenshot:

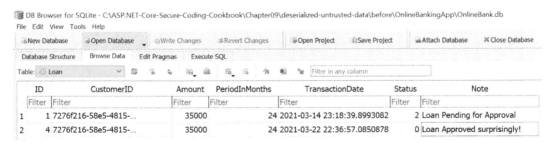

Figure 9.12 – Tampered-with loan application

Note that the **Status** setting is instantly in an approved state as the uploaded file is tampered with. This security bug exists due to a lack of data validation in code.

Getting ready

We will use the Online Banking app we used in the previous recipe. Using VS Code, open the sample `OnlineBankingApp` folder at `\Chapter09\deserialized-untrusted-data\before\OnlineBankingApp\`.

You can perform the steps in this folder to fix the untrusted data deserialization.

How to do it...

Let's take a look at the steps for this recipe:

1. Open `Pages\Loans\Upload.cshtml.cs` and examine the code in the `OnPostAsync` method. Observe that there are no data checks or validations performed that will set the loan status to its initial expected value of `LoanStatus.Pending`:

```
using (var fileStream = new FileStream(file,
  FileMode.Create))
{
    await Upload.CopyToAsync(fileStream);
    BinaryFormatter formatter = new BinaryFormatter();
    formatter.Binder = new LoanDeserializationBinder();
    fileStream.Position = 0;
    emptyLoan = (Loan)
        formatter.Deserialize(fileStream);
}
var loggedInUser = HttpContext.User;
var customerId = loggedInUser.Claims.FirstOrDefault
  (x => x.Type == ClaimTypes.NameIdentifier).Value;
    emptyLoan.CustomerID = customerId;
emptyLoan.TransactionDate = DateTime.Now;
if (await TryUpdateModelAsync<Loan>(
    emptyLoan,
    "loan",
    l => l.ID, l => l.CustomerID, l => l.Amount, l =>
        l.PeriodInMonths, l => l.TransactionDate, l =>
            l.Note))
```

```
{
    _context.Loan.Add(emptyLoan);
    await _context.SaveChangesAsync();
}
```

2. To fix this security bug, we make sure that the business rules are followed and the state of important properties such as LoanStatus is initialized:

```
var loggedInUser = HttpContext.User;
var customerId = loggedInUser.Claims.FirstOrDefault
    (x => x.Type == ClaimTypes.NameIdentifier).Value;
emptyLoan.CustomerID = customerId;
emptyLoan.TransactionDate = DateTime.Now;
emptyLoan.Status = LoanStatus.Pending;
```

With the preceding code addition, we prevent potential data tampering during deserialization.

How it works...

Data validation checks keep attackers at bay from abusing our sample Online Banking web app. When reviewing code for security flaws, we must understand the business rules behind every ASP.NET Core web page. In the preceding recipe, we performed a test and looked at the integrity of the data stored. We discovered that the file.dat file had been tampered with, and submitting the file caused the loan application to be automatically approved. Security controls were missing, and we deserialized the file blindly without any integrity checks. We fixed this issue by initializing the Loan object with initial values properly, setting the Loan.Status property to LoanStatus.Pending.

10
Using Components with Known Vulnerabilities

ASP.NET Core web developers rely on third-party commercial and open source frameworks, libraries, and packages to build web applications. This approach speeds up development time to support the rapid pace of business needs. While this saves developers a lot of time, there is a risk associated with using externally developed components. Code security in these libraries is often not guaranteed and, as with any other software, there will be security flaws. **Software composition analysis (SCA)** is necessary to find out whether your ASP.NET Core web application is using outdated and vulnerable packages.

In this chapter, we're going to cover the following recipes:

- Fixing the use of a vulnerable third-party JavaScript library
- Fixing the use of a vulnerable `NuGet` package
- Fixing the use of a library hosted from an untrusted source

By the end of this chapter, you will have learned how to use browser add-ons and command-line tools to find vulnerable versions of libraries, how to update the framework to a safer version of the `NuGet` package, how to determine what an untrusted source is, and how to take steps to remediate the risk such sources introduce in code.

Technical requirements

This book was written and designed to use with Visual Studio Code, Git, and .NET 5.0. Code examples in recipes are presented in ASP.NET Core Razor page . The sample solution also uses SQLite as the database engine for a more simplified setup. The complete code examples for this chapter are available at `https://github.com/PacktPublishing/ASP.NET-Core-Secure-Coding-Cookbook/tree/main/Chapter10`.

Fixing the use of a vulnerable third-party JavaScript library

Web development wouldn't be complete without JavaScript libraries as they help developers perform **Document Object Model (DOM)** manipulation and process **Asynchronous JavaScript And XML (AJAX)** in web pages. jQuery is one such library. However efficient the jQuery JavaScript library is, there are many **Common Vulnerabilities and Exposures (CVEs)** associated with previous versions of the jQuery library. CVEs are publicly known vulnerabilities that detail the weaknesses of particular software or components. Let's see how we can use browser extensions to discover vulnerable versions of jQuery.

Getting ready

For the recipes in this chapter, we will need a sample Online Banking app.

Open the command shell and download the sample Online Banking app by cloning the `ASP.NET-Core-Secure-Coding-Cookbook` repository, as follows:

```
git clone https://github.com/PacktPublishing/ASP.NET-Core-
Secure-Coding-Cookbook.git
```

Run the sample app to verify that there are no build or compile errors. In your command shell, navigate to the sample app folder at `\Chapter10\vulnerable-jquery1\before\OnlineBankingApp` and run the following command:

```
dotnet build
```

The `dotnet build` command will build our sample `OnlineBankingApp` project and its dependencies.

Testing outdated and vulnerable third-party libraries

To determine if your application is using a vulnerable JavaScript component, we can use a tool such as `Retire.js`. The following steps will instruct us on how to install `Retire.js` and use it to test outdated and vulnerable third-party libraries in our sample Online Banking web application:

1. Using your preferred browser, install the `Retire.js` browser extension. The steps to install `Retire.js` are more or less the same for most browsers.

   a) With Chrome, type the following in the address bar to open the **Chrome Web Store**:

   ```
   https://chrome.google.com/webstore/category/
   extensions?hl=en-US&authuser=1
   ```

   b) Once the **Chrome Web Store** loads, you will see a search bar on the left side of the page. Type `Retire.js` and hit *Enter*:

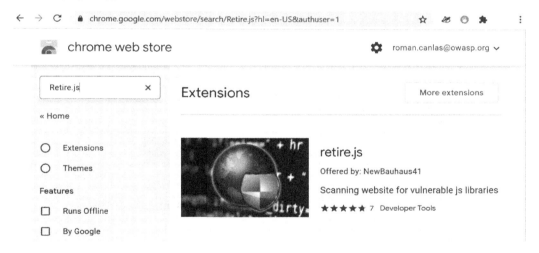

Figure 10.1 – Retire.js in Chrome Web Store

c) Select `retire.js` from the search result. You will now be redirected to the `Retire.js` extensions page where you can install the extension. Click the **Add to Chrome** button to begin the installation:

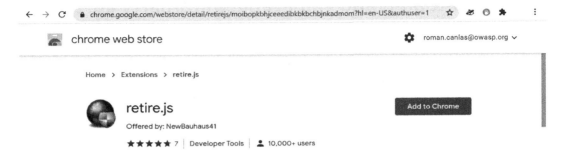

Figure 10.2 – Retire.js extensions page

d) Once installed, you will see a message pop out that will inform you **retire.js has been added to Chrome**:

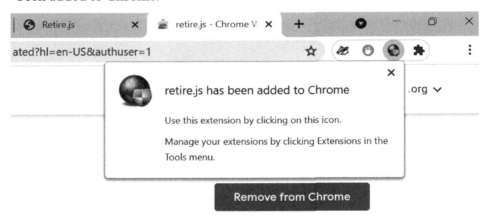

Figure 10.3 – Retire.js successful installation

2. From the starting exercise folder, launch VS Code by typing the following command:

```
code .
```

3. Navigate to **Terminal | New Terminal** in the menu or do this by simply pressing *Ctrl + Shift + '* in VS Code.

4.   Type the following command in the terminal to build and run the sample app:

```
dotnet run
```

5.   Open a browser and go to `https://localhost:5001/Loans`.

6.   Log in using the following credentials:

   a) Email: `stanley.s.jobson@lobortis.ca`

   b) Password: `rUj5jtV8jrTyHnx!`

7.   Once authenticated, you will be redirected to the **Loans** page.

8.   Notice that the `retire.js` plugin is loaded in the toolbar and is marked with *a red exclamation point*. Clicking it will show you details of the warning:

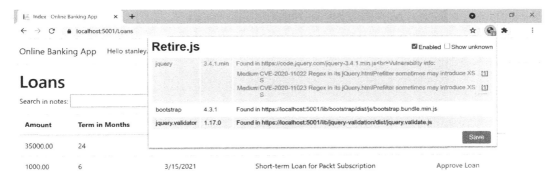

Figure 10.4 – Retire.js in action

9.   The `retire.js` plugin will display a pop-up window that shows the CVE information. Our Online Banking solution is using `jQuery version 3.4.1`, which is known to have a vulnerability with a **Medium** severity.

In this recipe, we will fix the vulnerable third-party component by using the latest version of the library.

How to do it...

Let's take a look at the steps for this recipe:

1.   From the starting exercise folder, launch VS Code by typing the following command:

```
code .
```

2. Open `Pages\Shared\_Layout.cshtml` and notice the script tag referencing an external `jquery-3.4.1.min.js` JavaScript file:

```
<script src="https://code.jquery.com/jquery-3.4.1.min.js"
integrity="sha256-CSXorXvZcTkaix6Yvo6HppcZGetbYMGWSFlBw8H
fCJo=" crossorigin="anonymous"></script>
```

This jQuery version is vulnerable to **cross-site scripting** (**XSS**).

3. To remediate this security risk, we update the jQuery script reference to the latest version of jQuery as recommended by the jQuery team, which is to upgrade to version 3.5.0 (or use the latest version).

4. In your browser, go to `https://code.jquery.com/jquery/`.

5. Scroll down until you find the latest version of **jQuery Core** (as of this writing, it is **jQuery Core 3.6.0**):

jQuery Core - All 3.x Versions

- jQuery Core 3.6.0 - <u>uncompressed</u>, <u>minified</u>, <u>slim</u>, <u>slim minified</u>

- jQuery Core 3.5.1 - <u>uncompressed</u>, <u>minified</u>, <u>slim</u>, <u>slim minified</u>

- jQuery Core 3.5.0 - <u>uncompressed</u>, <u>minified</u>, <u>slim</u>, <u>slim minified</u>

Figure 10.5 – jQuery CDN references

6. Click the **minified** link to display the **Code Integration** pop-up window for the minified version of jQuery 3.6.0, and then click the **Copy to Clipboard** icon to copy the whole script tag reference to the jQuery CDN.

7. Once we have the CDN script reference to the latest version of jQuery, we update our `_Layout.html` file by replacing the whole vulnerable script element:

```
<script src="https://code.jquery.com/
jquery-3.6.0.min.js" integrity="sha256-/
xUj+3OJU5yExlq6GSYGSHk7tPXikynS7ogEvDej/m4="
crossorigin="anonymous"></script>
```

8. To test if the code fix worked, repeat *Steps 3-9* in the *Testing outdated and vulnerable third-party libraries* section and see the result:

Figure 10.6 – No vulnerability found

Notice that the Retire.js plugin no longer shows that the page is vulnerable.

How it works...

Retire.js is a useful free open source browser add-on that scans your web pages for vulnerable JavaScript libraries. Retire.js executes a passive scan of resources loaded in the page and identifies vulnerable JavaScript libraries based on **Uniform Resource Locators** (**URLs**), filenames, file content, or hashes.

We install this browser add-on to identify that our **Loans** page is vulnerable to XSS based on CVE-2020-11022. We remediate the risk of XSS exploitation by updating the jQuery library to the latest version.

There's more...

Let's discover and fix another vulnerability using the Retire.js browser plugin:

1. Open the sample OnlineBankingApp folder at \Chapter10\jquery2\ before\OnlineBankingApp\.

2. Navigate to **Terminal | New Terminal** in the menu or do this by simply pressing *Ctrl* + *Shift* + *'* in VS Code.

3. Type the following command in the terminal to build and run the sample app:

    ```
    dotnet run
    ```

4. Open a browser and go to https://localhost:5001/Loans.

5. Log in using the following credentials:

    a) Email: `ax1.1.torvalds@ut.net`

    b) Password: `6GKqqtQQTii92ke!`

6. Once authenticated, you will be redirected to the **Loans** page.

7. Notice that the `Retire.js` browser add-on's icon has an exclamation in the toolbar.

8. Click the `Retire.js` icon and the extension will display a pop-up window that shows the vulnerability information:

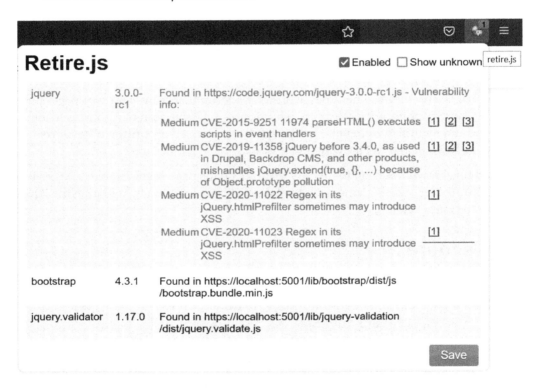

Figure 10.7 – Scan result

The add-on indicates that there are at least four CVEs that are of **Medium** severity found in the jQuery library.

9. Click one of the hyperlinks beside each CVE to see details of the vulnerabilities. One of the items in the list shows that the page has a vulnerable jQuery version based on `CVE-2015-9251`, `CVE-2019-11358`, `CVE-2020-11022`, and `CVE-2020-11023`, all of which are XSS vulnerabilities.

> **Tip**
>
> Your application may or may not be directly affected by the CVE. For instance, 2019-11358 affects Drupal and Backdrop **content management systems (CMSes)**. However, it is still a good idea to remediate the risk even if your ASP. NET Core web application is not directly affected.

10. You can hit the **Save** button to save the information into a page. A window will appear, asking if you want to view it in a browser:

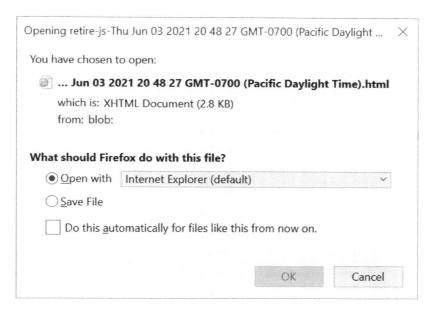

Figure 10.8 – Saving as a file

11. The rendered page displays the same information as what is shown in the browser add-on:

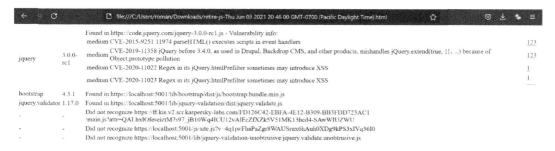

Figure 10.9 – Saved report

To fix this security issue, we also need to upgrade to the latest version of jQuery by updating the CDN reference.

12. Open `Pages\Shared\_Layout.cshtml` and notice the `script` tag referencing an external `jquery-3.0.0-rc1.js` JavaScript file:

```
<script src="https://code.jquery.com/
jquery-3.0.0-rc1.js"></script>
```

13. Repeat *Steps 4-6* in the *How to do it...* section of this recipe.

14. Replace the reference to `jquery-3.0.0-rc1.js` with the content from the clipboard:

```
<script src="https://code.jquery.com/
jquery-3.6.0.min.js" integrity="sha256-/
xUj+3OJU5yExlq6GSYGSHk7tPXikynS7ogEvDej/m4="
crossorigin="anonymous"></script>
```

```
<script src="~/lib/bootstrap/dist/js/
bootstrap.bundle.min.js"></script>
```

```
<script src="~/js/site.js" asp-append-version="true"></
script>
```

After rebuilding the project and loading the page again while the extension is enabled, the add-on will display that there are no vulnerabilities found:

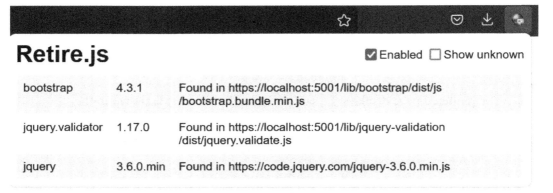

Figure 10.10 – No vulnerabilities found

> **Note**
> As with any software, a browser extension can also have vulnerabilities. Be cautious when using browser add-ons and keep abreast of their latest versions and updates.

See also

You can build your own software composition and library/package analysis tools that retrieve CVE information by utilizing the **National Institute of Standards and Technology's (NIST's) National Vulnerability Database (NVD)** data feeds and **application programming interfaces (APIs)**.

The NVD holds a collection of data of all publicly known vulnerabilities. The documentation for their APIs can be found at this link: `https://nvd.nist.gov/vuln/data-feeds#APIS`.

Fixing the use of a vulnerable NuGet package

Libraries and components can be installed and consumed from a package manager such as NuGet. VS Code has native support, which eases the installation process for ASP.NET Core web developers. With this, it quickly *introduces* the risk of installing and using a vulnerable NuGet package.

Getting ready

We will use the Online Banking app we used in the previous recipe. Using VS Code, open the sample OnlineBankingApp folder at \Chapter10\vulnerable-package\before\OnlineBankingApp\.

Let's see how we can use tools to discover vulnerable NuGet packages in our app.

Testing vulnerable NuGet packages

To determine if your application is using a vulnerable NuGet package, we can use another tool such as **Dotnet Retire**. To begin, we first install the dotnet retire vulnerability scanner in our sample Online Banking app:

1. From the starting exercise folder, launch VS Code by typing the following command:

```
code .
```

2. Navigate to **Terminal | New Terminal** in the menu or do this by simply pressing *Ctrl + Shift + '* in VS Code.

3. Type the following command in the terminal to install dotnet-retire:

```
dotnet tool install -g dotnet-retire
```

Upon successful installation, you will see the following message:

```
You can invoke the tool using the following command:
dotnet-retire
Tool 'dotnet-retire' (version '5.0.0') was successfully
installed.
```

4. Next, execute the tool by typing the following command:

```
dotnet-retire
```

Notice the result of the scan:

```
info: RetireNet.Packages.Tool.Services.RetireLogger[0]
      Scan starting
info: RetireNet.Packages.Tool.Services.RetireLogger[0]
      Analyzing 'OnlineBankingApp'
fail: RetireNet.Packages.Tool.Services.RetireLogger[0]
      Found use of 1 vulnerable libs in 2 dependency
      paths.
      * Microsoft Security Advisory 4021279:
      Vulnerabilities in.NET Core, ASP.NET Core Could
      Allow Elevation of Privilege in
      System.Net.Http/4.3.1
      https://github.com/dotnet/corefx/issues/19535
info: RetireNet.Packages.Tool.Services.RetireLogger[0]
      Scan complete.
```

The scan results indicate that there is one vulnerable library, which is `version 4.3.1` of the `System.Net.Http` package.

You can perform the steps in this folder to fix the vulnerable NuGet package.

How to do it...

Let's take a look at the steps for this recipe.

1. From the starting exercise folder, launch VS Code by typing the following command:

```
code .
```

2. Open `OnlineBankingApp.csproj`. Notice that one of the packages referenced is the vulnerable version of `System.Net.Http`:

```
<PackageReference Include="Microsoft.Extensions.Logging.
Debug" Version="5.0.0" />
<PackageReference Include="Microsoft.VisualStudio.Web.
CodeGeneration.Design" Version="5.0.1" />
<PackageReference Include="SendGrid" Version="9.22.0" />
<PackageReference Include="System.Net.Http"
Version="4.3.1" />
<PackageReference Include="System.Text.Encodings.Web"
Version="5.0.1" />
```

To fix this security flaw, we upgrade the NuGet package to the latest version.

3. Navigate to **Terminal | New Terminal** in the menu or do this by simply pressing *Ctrl* + *Shift* + *'* in VS Code.

4. Type the following command in the terminal to install the latest version of the `System.Net.Http` package:

```
dotnet add package System.Net.Http
```

5. Upon successful installation, you will see that the version is updated in `OnlineBankingApp.csproj`:

```
<PackageReference Include="Microsoft.Extensions.Logging.
Debug" Version="5.0.0" />
<PackageReference Include="Microsoft.VisualStudio.Web.
CodeGeneration.Design" Version="5.0.1" />
<PackageReference Include="SendGrid" Version="9.22.0" />
<PackageReference Include="System.Net.Http"
Version="4.3.4" />
<PackageReference Include="System.Text.Encodings.Web"
Version="5.0.1" />
```

6. Omitting `--version` or `-v` in the `dotnet add package` command will install the latest NuGet package.

7. To test if the code fix worked, repeat *Step 4* in the *Testing vulnerable NuGet packages* section and see the result:

```
info: RetireNet.Packages.Tool.Services.RetireLogger[0]
      Scan starting
```

```
info: RetireNet.Packages.Tool.Services.RetireLogger[0]
      Analyzing 'OnlineBankingApp'
info: RetireNet.Packages.Tool.Services.RetireLogger[0]
      Found no usages of vulnerable libs!
info: RetireNet.Packages.Tool.Services.RetireLogger[0]
      Scan complete.
```

Observe the result. The `dotnet retire` tool did not find any vulnerable packages.

How it works...

`dotnet retire` is a command-line tool that helps developers understand the ASP.NET Core application's dependencies. These dependencies often have vulnerabilities that we should all be aware of, so it is necessary to execute security scans.

Security scans from `dotnet retire` search for referenced vulnerable NuGet libraries to prevent our sample Online Banking web app from getting exploited with publicly known vulnerabilities.

Fixing the use of a library hosted from an untrusted source

The sources of the libraries and components we use must be from a *secure* and *trusted* source. The hosts of these libraries, which are most of the time hosted in CDNs, can also be attacked and abused.

Getting ready

We will use the Online Banking app we used in the previous recipe. Using VS Code, open the sample `OnlineBankingApp` folder at `\Chapter10\untrusted-source\before\OnlineBankingApp\`.

You can perform the steps in this folder to fix the use of a package hosted from an untrusted source.

How to do it...

Let's take a look at the steps for this recipe:

1. From the starting exercise folder, launch VS Code by typing the following command:

    ```
    code .
    ```

2. Open Pages\Loans\Index.cshtml and examine the script reference below the markup:

    ```
    <script src="http://code.jquery.com/
    jquery-3.6.0.min.js" integrity="sha256-/
    xUj+3OJU5yExlq6GSYGSHk7tPXikynS7ogEvDej/m4="
    crossorigin="anonymous"></script>
    ```
    ```
    <script src="~/lib/bootstrap/dist/js
    /bootstrap.bundle.min.js"></script>
    ```
    ```
    <script src="~/js/site.js" asp-append-version="true"></
    script>
    ```

    Notice that while the jQuery version is the latest version, the protocol is **HyperText Transfer Protocol (HTTP)**.

3. Simply change the protocol from http to https:

    ```
    <script src="https://code.jquery.com/
    jquery-3.6.0.min.js" integrity="sha256-/
    xUj+3OJU5yExlq6GSYGSHk7tPXikynS7ogEvDej/m4="
    crossorigin="anonymous"></script>
    ```
    ```
    <script src="~/lib/bootstrap/dist/js
    /bootstrap.bundle.min.js"></script>
    ```
    ```
    <script src="~/js/site.js" asp-append-version="true"></
    script>
    ```

Changing the protocol from http to https ensures that the reference to the JavaScript library in CDN is secure and will not be prone to weaknesses brought in by insecure transport.

> **Tip**
> Aside from hosts that serve resources over insecure HTTP, we must also be aware of utilizing JavaScript libraries that are hosted in shady and lesser-known domains.

How it works...

ASP.NET Core web developers must ensure that a library is coming from a proper source, and in our case, we are utilizing the official CDN from `code.jquery.com`, which is trusted. Developers must also add a reference to the jQuery library (or any JavaScript library) through secure links with **HTTP Secure (HTTPS)**:

```
https://code.jquery.com/jquery-3.6.0.min.js
```

There's more...

There is also a risk of hosts and CDNs getting compromised, so to verify the integrity of a resource, developers must use the **Subresource Integrity (SRI)** security feature. SRI in browsers provides integrity checks of resources our ASP.NET Core web application fetches. It allows developers to pass a hash generated from the original and untampered resource it expects against the hash of the resource that the web app is trying to fetch from the host:

```
<script src="https://code.jquery.com/jquery-3.6.0.min.js"
integrity="sha256-/xUj+3OJU5yEx1q6GSYGSHk7tPXikynS7ogEvDej
/m4=" crossorigin="anonymous"></script>
```

Most CDNs provide you the hash, but you can generate your own using command-line tools or do this from an online tool such as the **SRI Hash Generator** (https://www.srihash.org/).

To learn more about the details of SRI, read the **Mozilla Developer Network (MDN)** documentation on SRI, found at https://developer.mozilla.org/en-US/docs/Web/Security/Subresource_Integrity.

11
Insufficient Logging and Monitoring

Attacks on ASP.NET Core web applications can happen at any given moment in time. Developers must empower their security teams to reconstruct an incident by generating adequate logs from web applications. Logging the right information will help determine an event's details and identify critical data for auditing purposes. The downside of failing to log key security information prevents security teams from producing proper analysis or reports. Too much logging, however, can lead to sensitive data exposure. Applying a necessary and immediate response to act on such security events is only possible through active monitoring. Developers must enable monitoring in the logs that our ASP.NET Core web applications generate for a more real-time defense.

In this chapter, we're going to cover the following recipes:

- Fixing insufficient logging of exceptions
- Fixing insufficient logging of **database** (**DB**) transactions
- Fixing excessive information logging
- Fixing a lack of security monitoring

By the end of this chapter, you will have learned how to correctly add proper exception logging in our sample Online Banking app, how to log a critical DB transaction, how to prevent logging too much data or information, and how to enable security monitoring.

Technical requirements

This book was written and designed to use with **Visual Studio Code** (**VS Code**), Git, and .NET Core 5.0. The code examples in the recipes are presented mostly in ASP.NET Core Razor Pages. The sample solution also uses SQLite as the DB engine for a more simplified setup. The complete code examples for this chapter are available at `https://github.com/PacktPublishing/ASP.NET-Core-Secure-Coding-Cookbook/tree/main/Chapter11`.

Fixing insufficient logging of exceptions

Security-related events such as user authentication or enabling and disabling of **two-factor authentication** (**2FA**)—when this occurs—must be recorded and kept track of. These events are essential for auditing in order to understand the sequence of events when a security incident happens.

In this recipe, we will fix the insufficient logging of security-related exceptions by utilizing ASP.NET Core's built-in logging provider.

Getting ready

For the recipes of this chapter, we will need a sample Online Banking app.

Open the command shell and download the sample Online Banking app by cloning the `ASP.NET-Core-Secure-Coding-Cookbook` repository, as follows:

```
git clone https://github.com/PacktPublishing/ASP.NET-Core-Secure-Coding-Cookbook.git
```

Run the sample app to verify that there are no build or compile errors. In your command shell, navigate to the sample app folder at `\Chapter11\insufficient-logging-exception\before\OnlineBankingApp` and run the following command:

```
dotnet build
```

The `dotnet build` command will build our sample `OnlineBankingApp` project and its dependencies.

How to do it...

Let's take a look at the steps for this recipe:

1. From the starting exercise folder, launch VS Code by typing the following command:

```
code .
```

2. Open `Areas\Identity\Pages\Account\Manage\Disable2fa.cshtml.cs` and notice the code under `OnGet`:

```
public async Task<IActionResult> OnGet()
{
    var customer = await
        _customerManager.GetUserAsync(User);
    if (customer== null)
    {
    return NotFound($"Unable to load customer with
        ID '{_ customerManager.GetUserId(User)}'.");
    }


    if (!await _customerManager
        .GetTwoFactorEnabledAsync(customer))
    {
        throw new InvalidOperationException($"Cannot
            disable 2FA for customer with ID
                '{_customerManager.GetUserId(User)}'
                    as it's not currently enabled.");
    }


    return Page();
}
```

3. Also, notice the code under the `OnPostAsync` method:

```csharp
public async Task<IActionResult> OnPostAsync()
{
    var customer = await
        _customerManager.GetUserAsync(User);
    if (customer == null)
    {
        return NotFound($"Unable to load customer with
            ID '{_customerManager.GetUserId(User)}'.");
    }

    var disable2faResult = await
        _customerManager.SetTwoFactorEnabledAsync
            (customer, false);
    if (!disable2faResult.Succeeded)
    {
        throw new InvalidOperationException
        ($"Unexpected error occurred disabling 2FA for
            customer with ID '{_customerManager
                .GetUserId (User)}'.");
    }

    _logger.LogInformation("Customer with ID
        '{UserId}' has disabled 2fa.",
            _customerManager.GetUserId(User));
    StatusMessage = "2fa has been disabled. You can
        reenable 2fa when you setup an authenticator
            app";
    return
        RedirectToPage("./TwoFactorAuthentication");
}
```

Both methods have a line of code where an `InvalidOperationException` exception is thrown. The exception indicates that an attempt to disable 2FA was made but failed. These events should be considered anomalies and logged. These events can be considered anomalies, and each should be logged.

4. To fix a lack of event logging, we refactor the OnGet method and add logging when the InvalidOperationException exception is thrown:

```
public async Task<IActionResult> OnGet()
{
    var customer = await
        _customerManager.GetUserAsync(User);
    if (customer == null)
    {
        return NotFound($"Unable to load customer with
            ID '{_customerManager.GetUserId(User)}'.");
    }

    if (!await
        _customerManager.GetTwoFactorEnabledAsync
            (user))
    {
        _logger.LogError($"Cannot disable 2FA for
            customer with ID '{_customerManager
                .GetUserId(User)}' as it's not
                    currently enabled.");
        throw new InvalidOperationException($"Cannot
            disable 2FA for customer with ID
                '{_customerManager.GetUserId(User)}'
                    as it's not currently enabled.");
    }

    return Page();
}
```

5. We also refactor the `OnPostAsync` method, as shown here:

```
public async Task<IActionResult> OnPostAsync()
{
    var customer = await
        _customerManager.GetUserAsync(User);
    if (customer == null)
    {
        return NotFound($"Unable to load customer with
            ID '{_customerManager.GetUserId(User)}'.");
    }

    var disable2faResult = await
        _customerManager.SetTwoFactorEnabledAsync
            (customer, false);
    if (!disable2faResult.Succeeded)
    {
        _logger.LogError($"Unexpected error occurred
            disabling 2FA for customer with ID
                '{_customerManager.GetUserId
                    (User)}'.");
        throw new InvalidOperationException
            ($"Unexpected error occurred disabling 2FA
                for customer with ID'{_customerManager
                    .GetUserId(User)}'.");
    }

    _logger.LogInformation("Customer with ID
        '{UserId}' has disabled 2fa.",
            _customerManager.GetUserId(User));
    StatusMessage = "2fa has been disabled. You can
        reenable 2fa when you setup an authenticator
            app";
    return
        RedirectToPage("./TwoFactorAuthentication");
}
```

We used the `_logger` object from the **dependency injection** (**DI**) to call the `LogError` method, which writes an error log in the current logging provider.

How it works...

We have preconfigured our sample Online Banking app to add Windows event logging by calling the `ConfigureLogging` method. The `ConfigureLogging` method will create an `ILogger` object for the Windows `EventLog` provider. We set the `SourceName` property of the `ILogger` object to `OnlineBankingApp` to identify the logs generated by our sample Online Banking application:

```
public static IHostBuilder CreateHostBuilder(string[] args) =>
    Host.CreateDefaultBuilder(args)
        .ConfigureLogging(logging =>
        {
            logging.AddEventLog(eventLogSettings =>
            {
                eventLogSettings.SourceName =
                    "OnlineBankingApp";
            });
        })
```

We also have configured informational logging by adding an entry in the `Logging` section of the `appsettings.json` file. This will create an `OnlineBankingApp` category with its log level set to `Information`:

```
{
    "Logging": {
        "EventLog": {
            "LogLevel": {
                "Default": "Warning",
                "OnlineBankingApp": "Information"
            }
        },
```

With these settings in place, we can now use the Windows `EventLog` provider for our logging. The instance of the `ILogger` object, `_logger`, is already made available through DI. We now simply make a call to the `ILogger` object's `LogError` method in the lines of code where a critical exception occurred.

> **Note**
> It is important to note that the location and how the logs are stored are essential criteria. The configuration or the code shouldn't place the logs in the same location as the web server. We must implement proper access control to prevent unauthorized viewing of logs. There are open source and enterprise security solutions that provide tools to view, collect, and store logs securely.

Fixing insufficient logging of DB transactions

Basic DB transactions such as creating, reading, and deleting records are essential to have audit trails, especially when an error occurs as a DB function is performed.

In this recipe, we will fix the insufficient logging of a failed DB transaction, when a related exception is thrown.

How to do it...

Let's take a look at the steps for this recipe:

1. From the starting exercise folder, launch VS Code by typing the following command:

    ```
    code .
    ```

2. Open Pages\Backups\Edit.cshtml.cs and notice a lack of DB operation logging in the OnPostAsync method:

    ```
    public async Task<IActionResult> OnPostAsync()
    {
        if (!ModelState.IsValid){
            return Page();
        }

        _context.Attach(Backup).State =
            EntityState.Modified;

        try{
            await _context.SaveChangesAsync();
        }
    ```

```
        catch (DbUpdateException){
            if (!BackupExists(Backup.ID)){
                return NotFound();
            }
            else{
                throw;
            }
        }
        return RedirectToPage("./Index");
    }
```

However, DB operations such as performing a backup and updating its related records should be logged.

3. To fix the missing logging of high-value DB transactions, let's add a logger using the ILogger interface through DI. Begin by defining a _logger member of type ILogger:

```
public class EditModel : PageModel
{
    private readonly OnlineBankingApp.Data
        .OnlineBankingAppContext _context;
    private readonly ILogger<EditModel> _logger;
// code removed for brevity
```

4. Next, inject the ILogger member into the EditModel constructor:

```
public EditModel(OnlineBankingApp.Data
    .OnlineBankingAppContext context,
        ILogger<EditModel> logger)
{
    _logger = logger;
    _context = context;
}
```

5. In the try-catch block, add the following lines of code:

```
try{
    await _context.SaveChangesAsync();
}
```

```
catch (DbUpdateException ex){
    if (!BackupExists(Backup.ID)){
        _logger.LogError("Backup not found");
        return NotFound();
    }
    else{
        _logger.LogError($"An error occurred in
            backing up the DB { ex.Message } ");
        throw;
    }
}
```

Adding these lines of code will write an error log in the `EventLog` logging provider using the same logging settings that were explained in the preceding recipe.

How it works...

During a sensitive DB operation such as a DB backup, an unexpected error can occur. Such exceptions may cause a faulty system or—worse—an attack in our sample Online Banking app. We mitigate the risk of losing data integrity by keeping track of these DB operations and knowing when an event happened. We make a call to the `LogError` function to write a log into the Windows event log:

```
if (!BackupExists(Backup.ID)){
    _logger.LogError("Backup not found");
    return NotFound();
}
else{
    _logger.LogError($"An error occurred in backing up the
        DB { ex.Message } ");
    throw;
}
```

As a best practice, we provide an appropriate error log message for specific exceptions (`DbUpdateException`) that we anticipate and, at the most, log only the `Message` property of the generic exception, avoiding revealing sensitive information in the logs that we create (more about best practices on exception handling in *Chapter 13, Best Practices*).

Fixing excessive information logging

As we learned in *Chapter 4*, *Sensitive Data Exposure*, ensuring you prevent the exposure of personal details is the key to keeping your application secure, and the same goes for logging information. While logs are helpful, there is also a risk involved in logging excessive data. Perpetrators will find ways to get useful information, and the log store is one source they will try to discover.

In this recipe, we will fix the excessive logging of information such as usernames and passwords.

How to do it...

Let's take a look at the steps for this recipe:

1. From the starting exercise folder, launch VS Code by typing the following command:

   ```
   code .
   ```

2. Open `Areas\Identity\Pages\Account\Login.cshtml.cs` and locate the lines of code that send too much sensitive information into the logs:

   ```
   if (ModelState.IsValid)
   {
       // This doesn't count login failures towards
       account lockout
       // To enable password failures to trigger
       account lockout, set lockoutOnFailure: true
       var signInResult = await
           _signInManager.PasswordSignInAsync
               (Input.Email, Input.Password,
                   Input.RememberMe, lockoutOnFailure
                       : false);
   if (signInResult.Succeeded)
       {
           _logger.LogInformation($"Customer with
               email { Input.Email } and password
                   { Input.Password } logged in");
   ```

3. To fix the issue, we replace the line with a proper log entry:

```
if (ModelState.IsValid)
{
    // This doesn't count login failures towards
    account lockout
    // To enable password failures to trigger account
    lockout, set lockoutOnFailure: true
    var signInResult = await
        _signInManager.PasswordSignInAsync
            (Input.Email, Input.Password,
                Input.RememberMe, lockoutOnFailure:
                    false);
    if (signInResult.Succeeded)
    {
        _logger.LogInformation("User logged in.");

        if (string.IsNullOrEmpty(HttpContext
            .Session.GetString(SessionKeyName)))
        {
        HttpContext.Session.SetString
            (SessionKeyName, Input.Email);
        }
```

Refactoring the code to remove sensitive information such as usernames and passwords prevents an incident where a perpetrator can get hold of the log store and use the information gathered to exploit our sample Online Banking app.

How it works...

We can view the logs generated by our sample Online Banking app by opening the Windows **Event Viewer** via the Run command. Here are the steps to do this:

1. Type *Windows + R*, and once the **Run** window shows up, as shown in the following screenshot, type eventvwr.msc:

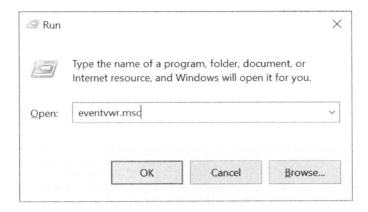

Figure 11.1 – Run command

2.   In **Event Viewer (Local)**, expand **Windows Logs**, then **Application**. Look for the logs where the **Source** name is equivalent to `OnlineBankingApp`:

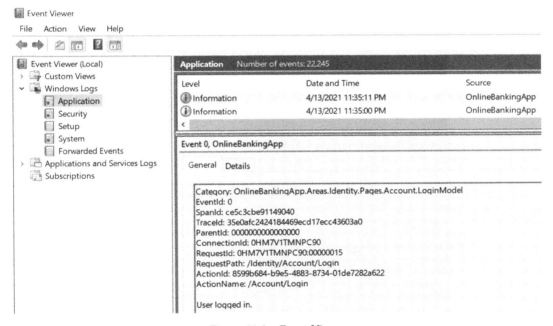

Figure 11.2 – Event Viewer

The informational logs you see in **Event Viewer** are the records generated by the `LogInformation` method call in the preceding recipe. We have modified the code to prevent explici.t logging of sensitive information such as a user's credentials. We use a generic informational message to remediate the issue of exposing details we would not want anyone to misuse.

Fixing a lack of security monitoring

Monitoring allows us to actively observe events that occur in our ASP.NET Core web applications. Missing out on incidents as they happen in real time can lead to an attacker causing more damage as each minute goes by. Developers must enable monitoring in their ASP.NET Core web applications to have early preventive detection.

In this recipe, we will fix a lack of security monitoring in our sample Online Banking web app by implementing **Azure Application Insights**.

How to do it...

Let's take a look at the steps for this recipe:

1. From the starting exercise folder, launch VS Code by typing the following command:

    ```
    code .
    ```

2. Navigate to **Terminal | New Terminal** in the menu or do this by simply pressing *Ctrl + Shift + '* in VS Code.

3. Install the *Application Insights* **software development kit** (**SDK**) by running the following command in the VS Code terminal:

    ```
    dotnet add package Microsoft.ApplicationInsights.
    AspNetCore
    ```

4. Open `Startup.cs` and make a call to the `AddApplicationInsightsTelemetry` method under `ConfigureServices`:

    ```
    public void ConfigureServices(IserviceCollection
        services)
    {
        services.AddApplicationInsightsTelemetry();
    // code removed for brevity
    ```

    The `AddApplicationInsightsTelemetry` method, as the name implies, will add an Insights telemetry collection to our sample Online Banking app.

5. Open the `appsettings.json` file to add the instrumentation key:

```
{
    "ApplicationInsights": {
      "InstrumentationKey": "My-Instrumentation-Key"
    },
    "Logging": {
      "EventLog": {
        "LogLevel": {
          "Default": "Warning",
          "OnlineBankingApp": "Information"
        }
      },
```

> **Note**
>
> To generate an instrumentation key, follow the *Create an Application Insights resource* instructions in the Microsoft official online documentation for Azure Monitor, found at `https://docs.microsoft.com/en-us/ azure/azure-monitor/app/create-new-resource`.

6. Type the following command in the terminal to build and run the sample app:

```
dotnet run
```

7. Open a browser and go to `https://localhost:5001/:`.

    Incoming requests will now be collected by the Application Insights SDK, including the `ILogger` logs with `Medium`, `Error`, and `Critical` severity.

How it works...

We implement telemetry collection by integrating our sample Online Banking web application with *Azure Application Insights*. Application Insights collects more than performance metrics and logs generated by our `ILogger` provider—it also performs analysis and application security detection. This cloud-based service sends alerts and notifications in the event of a security issue such as an unsecured form, insecure **Uniform Resource Locator (URL)** access, and shady user activity.

There's more...

The preceding steps for the recipe are there to enable the telemetry collection from the server side. Here are the steps to enable monitoring from the client side:

1. Open `Pages\_ViewImports.cshtml` and inject th'e `JavaScriptSnippet` service from the Application Insights SDK:

```
@using OnlineBankingApp
@namespace OnlineBankingApp.Pages
@addTagHelper *, Microsoft.AspNetCore.Mvc.TagHelpers
@inject Microsoft.ApplicationInsights.AspNetCore.
JavaScriptSnippet JavaScriptSnippet
```

2. Open `Pages\Shared\_Layout.cshtml` and insert the JavaScript snippet in the head section, with a call to the `Html.Raw` helper method:

```
. . .
        <link rel="stylesheet" href="~/lib/bootstrap/
            dist/css/bootstrap.min.css" />
        <link rel="stylesheet" href="~/css/site.css" />
        @Html.Raw(JavaScriptSnippet.FullScript)
    </head>
```

By placing the JavaScript in the `_Layout.cshtml` file, we enable client-side monitoring on all pages that use the layout template of our sample Online Banking web app.

12
Miscellaneous Vulnerabilities

The **OWASP Top 10** is the de facto standard for lists used by security professionals to learn about the most common web application vulnerabilities. It is one of the flagship projects by the **Open Web Application Security Project** (**OWASP**) organization. As you may have noticed, chapters *2-11* of this book covered each of the 2017 OWASP Top 10 security risks. This report changes every 3 to 4 years, depending on the information collected by security experts in OWASP. New or old risks may be introduced or removed from this collection, but this document is not a complete list, and there are other vulnerabilities that are not covered. This chapter will talk about a few more of the existing risks, some of which are no longer a part of the OWASP Top 10 but are still critical to know.

In this chapter, we're going to cover the following recipes:

- Fixing the disabled anti-Cross-Site Request Forgery protection
- Preventing Server-Side Request Forgery
- Preventing log injection
- Preventing HTTP response splitting
- Preventing clickjacking
- Fixing insufficient randomness

In this chapter, you will learn how to use ASP.NET Core's protection features against **Cross-Site Request Forgery (CSRF)**. You will also understand how **Server-Side Request Forgery (SSRF)** can be introduced in your code and ways to prevent it from happening. Additionally, you will discover how **response splitting** can occur and how to use one of the fundamentals of secure coding, validation, for added protection. Next, you will implement the `frame-ancestor` **Content Security Policy (CSP)**, sent as an HTTP response from your ASP.NET Core web application, to stop clickjacking attacks. Furthermore, you will practice a basic sanitization technique to stop attackers from injecting and forging your logs. Lastly, you will learn how to generate a cryptographically secure and random number to protect your hashed passwords from being deciphered.

Technical requirements

This book was written and designed for use with Visual Studio Code, Git, .NET 5.0. Code examples in recipes are presented in ASP.NET Core Razor pages. The sample solution will also use SQLite as the database engine for a more simplified setup. The complete code examples for this chapter are available at `https://github.com/PacktPublishing/ASP.NET-Core-Secure-Coding-Cookbook/tree/main/Chapter12`.

Fixing the disabled anti-Cross-Site Request Forgery protection

There is an inherent trust between the browser and web server that adversaries can often abuse. Users of web applications, typically issued with an authenticated session by the ASP.NET Core web application, are tricked by perpetrators into performing an unintentional action by simply visiting or interacting with a malicious website. This method of attack abuses the already established authenticated state of the user by making the browser send a specially crafted request from a malicious website. This **Cross-Site Request Forgery (CSRF)** vulnerability prompts us to review our code and enable request validation, which we will learn about in this recipe.

Getting ready

For the recipes in this chapter, we will need a sample Online Banking app.

Open the command shell and download the sample Online Banking app by cloning the ASP.NET Secure Coding Cookbook repository, as follows:

```
git clone https://github.com/PacktPublishing/ASP.NET-Core-
Secure-Coding-Cookbook.git
```

Run the sample app to verify that there are no build or compile errors. In your command shell, navigate to the sample app folder at `\Chapter12\cross-site-request-forgery\before\OnlineBankingApp` and run the following command:

```
dotnet build
```

The `dotnet build` command will build our sample `OnlineBankingApp` project and its dependencies.

In this recipe, we will fix the Razor pages where the CSRF protection is disabled.

How to do it...

Let's take a look at the steps for this recipe:

1. From the starting exercise folder, launch Visual Studio Code by typing the following command:

   ```
   code .
   ```

2. Open `Startup.cs` and locate the code in `ConfigureServices` that configures the filter to skip the anti-forgery token validation process:

   ```
   services.AddRazorPages(options =>
   {
       options.Conventions.AuthorizeAreaFolder("Identity,
           "/Account/Manage");
       options.Conventions.AuthorizeAreaPage("Identity",
           "/Account/Logout");
   })
   .AddRazorPagesOptions(options =>
   {
       options.Conventions.ConfigureFilter(new
           IgnoreAntiforgeryTokenAttribute());
   });
   ```

   Passing an instance of `IgnoreAntiforgeryTokenAttribute` to the `ConfigureFilter` method adds the attribute globally to our sample Online Banking web application.

3. Change the type of token attribute that you pass into the `ConfigureFilter` method and replace it with `AutoValidateAntiforgeryTokenAttribute`:

```
.AddRazorPagesOptions(options =>
{
    options.Conventions.ConfigureFilter(new
        AutoValidateAntiforgeryTokenAttribute());
});
```

`AutoValidateAntiforgeryTokenAttribute` will require request verification using the anti-forgery tokens it receives from unsafe HTTP verbs such as HTTP POST.

4. Next, open `Pages\Loans\Create.cshtml.cs` and find the `IgnoreAntiforgeryToken` attribute, which annotates the `OnlineBankingApp.Pages.Loans.CreateModel` view model:

```
using OnlineBankingApp.Models;
using System.Security.Claims;


namespace OnlineBankingApp.Pages.Loans
{
    [IgnoreAntiforgeryToken(Order = 1001)]
    public class CreateModel : PageModel
    {
        private readonly OnlineBankingApp.Data
            .OnlineBankingAppContext _context;
// code removed for brevity
```

While we have re-enabled the request verification globally in `Startup.cs`, we can still disable the CSRF protection on a per-view model using `IgnoreAntiforgeryToken`.

5. Replace this attribute from `PageModel` with `AutoValidateAntiforgeryToken` to explicitly enable anti-forgery tokens to be sent to unsafe HTTP requests:

```
using OnlineBankingApp.Models;
using System.Security.Claims;

namespace OnlineBankingApp.Pages.Loans
{
    [AutoValidateAntiforgeryToken]
    public class CreateModel : PageModel
    {
        private readonly OnlineBankingApp.Data
            .OnlineBankingAppContext _context;
// code removed for brevity
```

> **Note**
>
> Since we have enabled `AutoValidateAntiforgeryToken` globally from `Startup.cs`, it is good to know that we can use this attribute at the action level.

How it works...

When dealing with cross-site requests, the common mistake is to disable the validation of anti-forgery tokens to make this request possible across a different domain. In our sample Online Banking web app, we have disabled this globally within `AddRazorPagesOptions`, which configures the Razor views, and by setting the filter with `IgnoreAntiforgeryTokenAttribute`, thus removing the request validation from every page:

```
.AddRazorPagesOptions(options =>
{
    options.Conventions
        .ConfigureFilter(new
            IgnoreAntiforgeryTokenAttribute());
});
```

Similarly, you can disable this at the class level by annotating the class with `IgnoreAntiforgeryToken`. An `Order` with a number of `1001` is specified along with this attribute to determine the sequence of the filter's execution:

```
[IgnoreAntiforgeryToken(Order = 1001)]
```

Each approach poses a huge risk, so anti-forgery tokens must be generated and the request validated by the web server to prevent CSRF and verify its authenticity. Due to this, we have used `AutoValidateAntiforgeryTokenAttribute` to configure the filter instead:

```
.AddRazorPagesOptions(options =>
{
    options.Conventions
        .ConfigureFilter(new
            AutoValidateAntiforgeryTokenAttribute());
});
```

Another way of doing this is at the class level, where you can annotate the class with `AutoValidateAntiforgeryToken` on top of the class definition:

```
[AutoValidateAntiforgeryToken]
public class CreateModel : PageModel
```

The preceding code enables the validation of anti-forgery tokens for unsafe HTTP methods, which are HTTP verbs other than `GET`, `OPTIONS`, `HEAD`, and `TRACE`.

There's more...

The **Synchronizer Token Pattern** (**STP**) is a secure coding and development pattern where tokens are sent as part of the request to the web server, proving that it is genuine. The web server then validates the token to confirm its authenticity. Manually creating your tokens is possible with a **Globally Unique Identifier** (**GUID**), but it is advisable to rely on the built-in tokens generated by .NET Framework.

Anti-forgery tokens are also generated from HTML elements in the form of hidden fields. Generating these tokens alone is not a complete solution to stop CSRF vulnerabilities in your code. Request validation from the server side must also be enabled.

JavaScript-based applications can make an AJAX call to send HTTP requests with these anti-forgery tokens. The client-side script will explicitly look for the `__RequestVerificationToken` hidden form field and retrieve its value. Here is an example of what `__RequestVerificationToken` looks like when rendered into the HTML page:

```
<input name="__RequestVerificationToken"
type="hidden" value="CfDJ8NZYeppsy75Pga3ZTfYs_
GOXLIV7qV8nWInxNkWX2KTNH5O6U08mXz8qZYB3UPum5QFFO0zm
ElIyE8her6r0wf85eobep6SYfJCP6UBDeTe9Jpao8cEgdiUYK
yY5IWfQX4MhzYupGn5uciC74mbfQ0U" />
```

If your request validation fails, it might be that the form tag helper's `asp-antiforgery` value is set to `false`. Always be on the lookout for this tag and either set it to `true` or remove the `asp-antiforgery` attribute, making the `__RequestVerificationToken` hidden form field render automatically by default:

```
<form method="post" asp-antiforgery="true" >
```

Another way to generate tokens in your Razor pages is to use the `AntiForgeryToken` HTML helper method. Place the following code inside your markup:

```
@Html.AntiForgeryToken()
```

The `AntiForgeryToken` HTML helper will create the `__RequestVerificationToken` hidden form field with the encrypted value.

Preventing Server-Side Request Forgery

ASP.NET Core web applications are composed of different layers and components to make it a whole working system. Most of the time, it requires a backend service that will either process or provide data to the base web application. These disparate services interconnect to form a cohesive and functioning web application. This is either done in the form of a web service or a REST-based API hosted internally or externally from the system, and our code then calls the operations of these APIs and web services (or microservices).

However, without proper filtering or being able to validate the data that's been sent to these services, the host could start executing unexpected actions. This vulnerability is otherwise known as **Server-Side Request Forgery** (**SSRF**), with adversaries exploiting the lack of validation or sanitization available.

Getting ready

Run the sample app to verify that there are no build or compile errors. In your command shell, navigate to the sample app folder at `\Chapter12\server-side-request-forgery \before\OnlineBankingApp` and run the following command:

```
dotnet build
```

The `dotnet build` command will build our sample `OnlineBankingApp` project and its dependencies.

We also need to install an older version of MongoDB (version 3.4). Follow the *Install MongoDB* instructions at `https://docs.mongodb.com/v3.4/installation`.

Once installed, ensure that the `mongod` service executable runs with the `--rest` switch. This will enable MongoDB's REST API. See the following example:

```
C:\Program Files\MongoDB\Server\3.4\bin\mongod.exe" --rest
--service --config="C:\Program Files\MongoDB\Server\3.4\mongod.
cfg"
```

Populate MongoDB with data by running the following command:

```
db.createCollection('Payees')
```

Also, run the following command:

```
db.Payees.insertMany([{'Name':'Mint Mobile','Address':'P.O.
Box 15124 Albany, NY 12212-5124','PhoneNo':'1(800)
683-7392','AccountNo':'8244-1044','Description':'Business
Line'},{'Name':'Private Internet Access VPN','Address':'5555
DTC Parkway, Suite 360. Greenwood Village, CO
80111','PhoneNo':'(720) 277-9121','AccountNo':'6510-
2236','Description':'VPN Personal Subscription'}])
```

The first MongoDB command, `db.createCollection`, creates our `Payees` collection, which we will use in our sample Online Banking app. `db.Payees.insertMany` adds data to our `Payees` collection.

Now, we are ready to complete this recipe.

How to do it...

Let's take a look at the steps for this recipe:

1. From the starting exercise folder, launch Visual Studio Code by typing the following command:

```
code .
```

2. Open \Pages\Payees\Index.cshtml.cs and go to the OnGetAsync method, where a call to PayeeService is executed:

```
public async Task OnGetAsync()
{
    var mongouri = Request.Query["mongouri"];
    mongouri = string.IsNullOrWhiteSpace(mongouri)
            ? "http://localhost:28017/test/Payees/"
            : Request.Query["mongouri"];

    Roots = await _payeeService.GetPayeesAsync
        (mongouri);
}
```

Notice that the code accepts input from the mongouri query string parameter. mongouri is the URL to the MongoDB REST interface where a list of payees is retrieved. This can be potentially exploited by an attacker and be used to send an arbitrary URL or abuse to the MongoDB instance using its available REST API operations. This requires no access control or checks.

3. To remediate the vulnerable code, we can add a validation using regular expressions to make sure that the URL is in a format that we expect. We will begin by adding a reference to the Regex class namespace; that is, System.Text.RegularExpression:

```
using System.Text.RegularExpressions;
```

4. Next, create a new method and name it `IsValidMongoRestUri` using the following code:

```
private bool IsValidMongoRestUri(string mongouri)
{
    string pattern = @"^http://localhost:28017/
        test/Payees/\\?$";
    Regex regex = new Regex(pattern, RegexOptions
        .IgnoreCase);
    return regex.IsMatch(mongouri);
}
```

5. Add a reference to the `System.Http.Net` namespace.

6. Invoke the `IsValidMongoRestUri` method to validate the `mongouri` string that was passed via the query string:

```
public async Task OnGetAsync()
{
    var mongouri = Request.Query["mongouri"];

    if (string.IsNullOrWhiteSpace(mongouri))
    {
        mongouri =
            "http://localhost:28017/test/Payees/";
    }
    else
    {
        if(!IsValidMongoRestUri(mongouri))
        {
            throw new HttpRequestException("Invalid
                Request");
        }
    }
    Roots = await _payeeService.GetPayeesAsync
        (mongouri);
}
```

The preceding code will also throw an `HttpRequestException` when `mongouri` is in an unexpected format.

How it works...

When we blindly allow a `querystring` parameter to be controlled, this vector of attack gives a bad actor an avenue to exploit our sample Online Banking web application. We use the `mongouri` query string to retrieve the REST API endpoint. Since validation is missing, a malicious user can pass along a URI that could potentially execute an unwanted action. For instance, we can assign this value to the `mongouri` parameter, and the MongoDB REST API will execute this operation:

```
mongouri=http://localhost:28017/admin/$cmd/?
    filter_eval=function()
    {ifdb.version().charAt(0)=='3'){sleep(2000)}}&limit=1';
```

Breaking down the value of `mongouri`, this contains a series of continuous MongoDB statements and functions that will cause a 2-second suspension of the JavaScript execution context if the first character of the MongoDB version (which is 3 in this case) equates to true. If we were to print this in a pretty format, here is what these continuous statements and function would look like:

```
filter_eval=function(){
    if(db.version().charAt(0)=='3'){
        sleep(2000)
        }
    }
```

To prevent this unwanted execution of an arbitrary command, we can use regular expressions to validate that the URL is correct according to the format that we expected, stopping anyone from using MongoDB's db command through its HTTP interface. We created a boolean method called `IsValidMongoRestUri` that checks if the `mongouri` value it receives matches the URL we expect:

```
private bool IsValidMongoRestUri(string mongouri)
{
    string pattern = @"^http://localhost:28017/test/
    Payees/\\?$";
    Regex regex = new Regex(pattern,
        RegexOptions.IgnoreCase);
    return regex.IsMatch(mongouri);
}
```

One of the fundamentals of secure coding being used, in this case, is proper input validation to prevent SSRF.

There's more...

In addition to your URI validation, you can either use the `Uri.CheckHostName` or `IPAddress.TryParse` method. `Uri.CheckHostName` helps us check if the DNS or domain is valid, while `IPAddress.TryParse` verifies whether the IP address is valid.

Preventing log injection

In *Chapter 11, Insufficient Logging and Monitoring*, we learned about the importance of logging. Logging provides us with the necessary visibility to find out about a series of important events in our ASP.NET Core web application. However, hackers can also exploit logging if the user-controlled log information we create is not validated. Having malicious inputs in our log entries can also exploit the vulnerabilities of a log viewer, if one exists.

For instance, a web-based log viewer might have a cross-site script vulnerability, and viewing the log entries with an XSS payload, along with the data, can exploit this weakness. In this recipe, we will prevent the log injection vulnerability in our code by implementing input sanitization.

Getting ready

Run the sample app to verify that there are no build or compile errors. In your command shell, navigate to the sample app folder at `\Chapter12\log-injection\before\ OnlineBankingApp` and run the following command:

```
dotnet build
```

The `dotnet build` command will build our sample `OnlineBankingApp` project and its dependencies.

How to do it...

Let's take a look at the steps for this recipe:

1. From the starting exercise folder, launch Visual Studio Code by typing the following command:

    ```
    code .
    ```

2. Open `Pages\Loans\Create.cshtml.cs` and locate the code in `OnPostAsync`, where it logs a warning when the app is unable to submit a loan:

```
if (await TryUpdateModelAsync<Loan>(
    emptyLoan,
    "loan",
    l => l.ID, l => l.CustomerID, l => l.Amount, l =>
        l.PeriodInMonths, l => l.TransactionDate,
            l => l.Note))
{
    _context.Loan.Add(emptyLoan);
    await _context.SaveChangesAsync();
}
else {
    _logger.LogWarning("Problem creating loan:" +
        emptyLoan.CustomerID + ";" + emptyLoan.Amount
            + ";" + emptyLoan.PeriodInMonths + ";"+
                emptyLoan.Note);
}
```

Creating a log entry without sanitizing the input could expose our sample Online Banking web app to log injection.

3. Applying what we have learned from the basics of secure coding from *Chapter 1, Secure Coding Fundamentals*, we can use methods such as `String.Replace` or `Regex.Replace` to replace malicious characters from the input. We will begin by validating whether `Note` is not empty or null before we sanitize the input:

```
else {
    if (!String.IsNullOrEmpty(emptyLoan.Note)) {
        emptyLoan.Note = Regex.Replace(value, @"^[a
            zA-Z0-9 ]+$", string.Empty);
    }

    _logger.LogWarning("Problem creating loan:" +
        emptyLoan.CustomerID + ";"
            + emptyLoan.Amount + ";"
            + emptyLoan.PeriodInMonths + ";"
```

```
        + emptyLoan.Note);
}
```

By using the `Regex.Replace` method, we can use pattern matching to replace potentially dangerous characters from the logs.

How it works...

In our sample Online Banking web application, we have a loans application page where we can submit a loan application. On this page, we can enter information such as the loan amount, loan period, and an optional note, which is provided as free form text.

If there's an issue in saving the loan submission, we can log the information that was entered, including the unvalidated `Note` data:

```
_logger.LogWarning("Problem creating loan:" + emptyLoan
    .CustomerID + ";"
        + emptyLoan.Amount + ";"
        + emptyLoan.PeriodInMonths + ";"
        + emptyLoan.Note);
```

While it is good to create a log entry for this bank transaction to understand why it failed to save, the note can be an entry point for log injection. We can prevent log injection by sanitizing the `Note` field using the `Replace.Regex` method:

```
if (!String.IsNullOrEmpty(emptyLoan.Note))
{
    emptyLoan.Note = Regex.Replace(value, @"^[a-zA-Z0-9
        ]+$", string.Empty);
}
```

We can verify if `Note` is null or empty before making a call to the `Regex.Replace` method. We can use the *^[a-zA-Z0-9]+$* regular expression pattern here, which specifies that alphanumeric characters and spaces are only allowed as valid input for `Note`.

There's more...

If parts of a log entry are user-controlled and not validated or sanitized, an attacker can exploit this weakness by feeding logs with forged and false information. Adversaries can inject non-sensical information into our logs and leave a lot of noise behind, preventing an effective security incident analysis. This vulnerability is known as **log forging**. The code presented in this recipe should also be able to mitigate this security flaw.

Preventing HTTP response splitting

HTTP response splitting or **CRLF injection** is another injection vulnerability where the attacker can send an unfiltered HTTP request that includes a carriage return and line feed characters. Allowing a carriage return (*%0d*, in URL encoded form) and line feed (*%0a*, also in URL encoded form) in the request introduces a *split* in the HTTP response headers, thus changing the behavior of the ASP.NET Core web application. This HTTP response header modification can lead to the exploitation of many other vulnerabilities, such as open redirection or cross-site scripting, to name a couple.

In this recipe, we will prevent HTTP response splitting in our code by adding a validation check to the \n and \r characters.

Getting ready

Run the sample app to verify that there are no build or compile errors. In your command shell, navigate to the sample app folder at \Chapter12\crlf-injection\before\ OnlineBankingApp and run the following command:

```
dotnet build
```

The dotnet build command will build our sample OnlineBankingApp project and its dependencies.

How to do it...

Let's take a look at the steps for this recipe:

1. From the starting exercise folder, launch Visual Studio Code by typing the following command:

    ```
    code .
    ```

2. Open Areas\Identity\Pages\Account\Login.cshtml.cs and locate the lines of code where a parameter can be potentially injected with a carriage return and a line feed character.

3. Notice the highlighted code in the OnGetAsync method:

    ```
    public async Task OnGetAsync(string returnUrl = null)
    {
        if (!string.IsNullOrEmpty(ErrorMessage))
        {
    ```

```
            ModelState.AddModelError(string.Empty,
                ErrorMessage);
    }


    returnUrl ??= Url.Content("~/");
//code removed for brevity
```

4. Also, notice the highlighted code in the OnPostAsync method:

```
public async Task<IActionResult> OnPostAsync(string
    returnUrl = null)
{

    returnUrl ??= Url.Content("~/");


    ExternalLogins = (await
        _signInManager.GetExternalAuthentication
            SchemesAsync()).ToList();
//code removed for brevity
```

In both these methods, returnUrl is the argument that we will need to validate.

5. To remediate the potential security flaw, we will add a new method called
    SplitExist. The helper is a boolean method called SplitExist that takes
    a string as input and validates each of the characters to check for any CRLF
    injection attempts:

```
private bool SplitExist(string input)
{
    return input.FirstOrDefault(c => c == 0x13 ||
        c == 0x10) != 0
        ? true
        : false;
}
```

6. Use the SplitExist method to validate returnUrl. Refactor the code in
    OnGetAsync, as follows:

```
public async Task OnGetAsync(string returnUrl = null)
{
    if (!string.IsNullOrEmpty(ErrorMessage))
    {
```

```
        ModelState.AddModelError(string.Empty,
            ErrorMessage);
    }


    if (!string.IsNullOrEmpty(returnUrl))
    {
        if(SplitExist(returnUrl))
        {
            throw new
                InvalidOperationException(string
                    .Format("Invalid character in the
                        return URL"));
        }
    }
    else
    {
        returnUrl = Url.Content("~/");
    }
```

7. Also, refactor the code in OnPostAsync, as follows:

```
public async Task<IActionResult> OnPostAsync(string
returnUrl = null)
{
    if (!string.IsNullOrEmpty(returnUrl))
    {
        if(SplitExist(returnUrl))
        {
            throw new InvalidOperationException
                (string.Format("Invalid character
                    in the return url"));
        }
    }
    else
    {
        returnUrl = Url.Content("~/");
```

```
        }
```

```
        ExternalLogins = (await _signInManager
            .GetExternalAuthenticationSchemes
                Async()).ToList();
```

If the `returnUrl` parameter is not null, a call to the `SplitExist` method occurs to check if the string has either a **carriage return** or a **line feed** character.

How it works...

If an HTTP response splitting vulnerability exists, it is due to a lack of or improper validation for the possible entry points and inputs. In this recipe, we pointed out that `returnUrl` is a potential target, so we added a new method called `SplitExist` that checks for the carriage return and line feed characters in the string:

```
private bool SplitExist(string input)
{
    return input.FirstOrDefault(c => c == 0x13 ||
        c == 0x10) != 0
        ? true
        : false;
}
```

This method goes through the `returnUrl` string character by character and verifies that any of its characters are neither `0x13`, which is the ASCII equivalent of a carriage return character, nor `0x10`, which is the ASCII equivalent of a line feed.

> **Note**
>
> This vulnerability used to exist within the framework itself from a prior version of ASP.NET Core (ASP.NET Core version 5, Release Candidate 1) but was resolved in the succeeding version.

There's more...

The validation approach in this recipe may no longer be necessary to implement, considering that the ASP.NET Core team has already implemented their own character validation.

As an example, while the sample Online Banking application is in a running state, try to open up a browser and go to `https://localhost:5001/Identity/Account/Login?ReturnUrl=%2FAccount%0D%0ALocation%3A%20 http%3A%2F%2Fwww.packtpub.com`.

Notice the exception shown on the page:

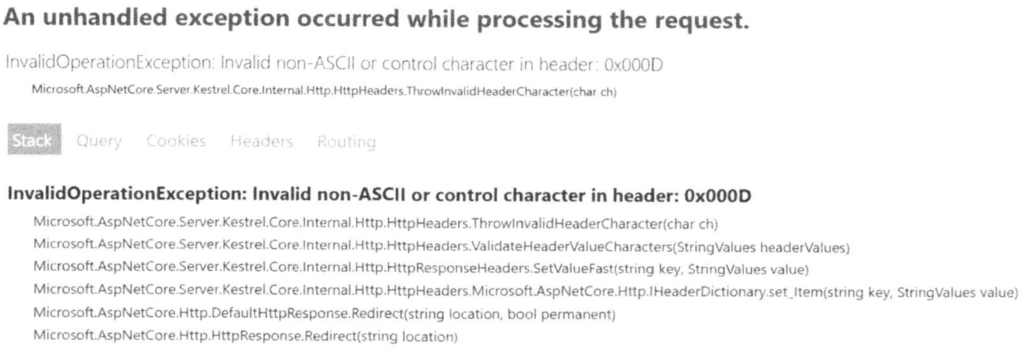

An unhandled exception occurred while processing the request.

InvalidOperationException: Invalid non-ASCII or control character in header: 0x000D

    Microsoft.AspNetCore.Server.Kestrel.Core.Internal.Http.HttpHeaders.ThrowInvalidHeaderCharacter(char ch)

Stack Query Cookies Headers Routing

InvalidOperationException: Invalid non-ASCII or control character in header: 0x000D

    Microsoft.AspNetCore.Server.Kestrel.Core.Internal.Http.HttpHeaders.ThrowInvalidHeaderCharacter(char ch)
    Microsoft.AspNetCore.Server.Kestrel.Core.Internal.Http.HttpHeaders.ValidateHeaderValueCharacters(StringValues headerValues)
    Microsoft.AspNetCore.Server.Kestrel.Core.Internal.Http.HttpResponseHeaders.SetValueFast(string key, StringValues value)
    Microsoft.AspNetCore.Server.Kestrel.Core.Internal.Http.HttpHeaders.Microsoft.AspNetCore.Http.IHeaderDictionary.set_Item(string key, StringValues value)
    Microsoft.AspNetCore.Http.DefaultHttpResponse.Redirect(string location, bool permanent)
    Microsoft.AspNetCore.Http.HttpResponse.Redirect(string location)

Figure 12.1 – InvalidOperationException

The web app threw an **InvalidOperationException** because the ASP.NET framework detects the existence of the carriage return and line feed character in the URL. If the request was successful, it will split the HTTP request, adding a `location` HTTP header and redirecting the user to `www.packtpub.com`:

```
HTTP/2 302 Found
cache-control: no-cache, no-store
date: Tue, 11 May 2021 17:18:39 GMT
pragma: no-cache
content-type: text/html; charset=utf-8
location: http://www.packtpub.com
server: Kestrel
x-xss-protection: 1; mode=block
x-content-type-options: nosniff
```

Although there is a check in place, the ASP.NET Core framework is an ever-growing and changing platform. A vulnerability may or may not be introduced in code in the future.

Preventing clickjacking

Clickjacking occurs when your web application allows itself to render inside a nefarious website (typically through IFrames), thus altering the whole UI. The user is then presented with a different-looking page, tricking them into executing an unbeknownst action on your web application by having the user think that they are interacting with the deceiving page, while they are actually entering information and clicking buttons on your web application instead.

To protect your ASP.NET Core web application from falling victim to clickjacking exploitation, you can implement a CSP that will stop an IFrame from a malicious website from rendering your web app.

Getting ready

We will be using the Online Banking app we used in the previous recipe here. Run the sample app to verify that there are no build or compile errors. In your command shell, navigate to the sample app folder at `\Chapter12\clickjacking\before\OnlineBankingApp` and run the following command:

```
dotnet build
```

The `dotnet build` command will build our sample `OnlineBankingApp` project and its dependencies.

Clickjacking proof of concept (PoC)

To understand the threat of clickjacking, follow and observe these steps:

1. Open `wwwroot\iframe-demo.html` and notice that our sample Online Banking web app has been placed inside an IFrame:

```
<!DOCTYPE html>
<html>
<body>
<h1>iframe Demo</h1>
<iframe src="https://localhost:5001/Identity/Account
/Login?ReturnUrl=%2F" title="iFrame Demo">
</iframe>
</body>
</html>
```

2. Navigate to **Terminal | New Terminal** in the menu or by simply pressing *Ctrl + Shift + '* in Visual Studio Code.

3. Type the following command in the Terminal to build and run the sample app:

```
dotnet run
```

This step is necessary for us to view the sample Online Banking web app in the IFrame.

4. Open `wwwroot\iframe-demo.html` in a browser and observe that our sample Online Banking web app is rendered inside the IFrame:

iframe Demo

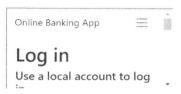

Figure 12.2 – Online Banking web app inside an IFrame

Imagine an adversary making its web page more deceiving than our **proof of concept (PoC)**. This could lead you to clicking or executing unwanted transactions in our sample Online Banking web app.

> **Note**
>
> The clickjacking vulnerability is made possible by mistakenly suppressing the `X-Frame-Options: sameorigin` HTTP response header, which is sent with every response by default:
>
> ```
> services.AddAntiforgery(options =>{
>     options.SuppressXFrameOptionsHeader = true;
> });
> ```

How to do it...

Using Visual Studio Code, open the sample Online Banking app folder at `\Chapter12\click-jacking\before\OnlineBankingApp\`.

Perform the following steps in this folder to add a content security policy that will prevent your web application from being rendered inside an IFrame:

1. From the starting exercise folder, launch Visual Studio Code by typing the following command:

```
code .
```

2. Open `Startup.cs` and look at the `Use` method call in `Configure`. The middleware is adding the necessary security headers, as we learned in *Chapter 7, Security Misconfiguration*:

```
app.Use(async (context, next) =>
{
    context.Response.Headers.Add("X-XSS-
        Protection",  "1; mode=block");
        context.Response.Headers.Add
            ("X-Content-Type-Options", "nosniff");

    await next();
});
```

Notice that there are no HTTP response headers preventing the web application from getting rendered inside an IFrame.

3. To include a content security policy HTTP header, we can add a new line:

```
app.Use(async (context, next) =>
{
    context.Response.Headers.Add("X-XSS-
        Protection",  "1; mode=block");
    context.Response.Headers.Add("X-Content-Type-
        Options", "nosniff");
    context.Response.Headers.Add("X-Frame-Options",
        "DENY");
```

```
context.Response.Headers.Add("Content-Security-
    Policy", " frame-ancestors 'none'");

await next();
});
```

These HTTP response headers serve a security purpose and will be explained in the following section.

4. Remove the following lines of code, which suppress the X-Frame-Options: sameorigin header:

```
services.AddAntiforgery(options =>
{
    options.SuppressXFrameOptionsHeader = true;
});
```

5. Alternatively, you can assign SuppressXFrameOptionHeader with a value of false:

```
services.AddAntiforgery(options =>
{
    options.SuppressXFrameOptionsHeader = false;
});
```

This will un-suppress the X-Frame-Options header and will make it available as part of the HTTP response.

Validating the CSP HTTP header

Follow these steps:

1. Navigate to **Terminal** | **New Terminal** in the menu or simply press *Ctrl* + *Shift* + ' in Visual Studio Code.

2. Type the following command in the Terminal to build and run the sample app:

```
dotnet run
```

3. Open a browser and go to https://localhost:5001/.

4. Log in using the following credentials:

    a). Email: stanley.s.jobson@lobortis.ca

    b). Password: rUj5jtV8jrTyHnx!

5. Once authenticated, you will be redirected to the Online Banking app's **Home page:**

Figure 12.3 – Home page authenticated

6. Press *F12* to open the browser's developer tools.

7. Go to the **Network** tab and select the first piece of HTTP traffic in the traffic list.

8. Once you've selected a form of HTTP traffic, scroll through the right-hand pane to view the corresponding HTTP response security headers:

Figure 12.4 – CSP HTTP response header

The Content Security Policy HTTP security header has now been added as part of the HTTP response being sent from our sample Online Banking web application, thus protecting it from clickjacking attacks.

9. Repeat the steps provided in the *Clickjacking proof of concept (PoC)* section of this recipe and notice that our sample Online Banking web app is no longer rendered inside the IFrame:

iframe Demo

Figure 12.5 – Framing denied

Adding the CSP for `frame-ancestors` and re-enabling the **X-Frame-Options** HTTP header stops our sample Online Banking web app from being framed.

How it works...

Security headers such as **Content Security Policy** and **X-Frame-Options** help protect our ASP.NET Core web applications from being exposed to a wide variety of vulnerabilities, including clickjacking. This vulnerability propagates if we enable or disable such services.

There are also valid reasons to consider why you would want to have your web application rendered in an IFrame. Some integration with Content Management Systems requires framing, so the best way to get around this is to specify the whitelisted hosts in the CSP:

```
Content-Security-Policy: frame-ancestors 'self' https://www.
packpub.com
```

The `self` value indicates that we are allowing our sample Online Banking web app to be rendered inside an IFrame from our own origin (excluding subdomains). The value of `https://www.packpub.com` specifies that we are allowing the Packt website to have our web app placed inside its IFrame.

Fixing insufficient randomness

Pseudo-random numbers may suffice for less than critical operations, but these numbers are not genuinely random. Computers use mathematical formulas to produce these pseudo-random numbers, but they are not random enough to be used in cryptographic operations such as salt creation. The predictability and deterministic nature of the data that's produced by these random methods and function generators increases the chance of a password hash being cracked, thus causing hash collision attacks.

Getting ready

Using Visual Studio Code, open the sample Online Banking app folder at `\Chapter13\insufficient-randomness\before\OnlineBankingApp`.

How to do it...

Let's take a look at the steps for this recipe:

1. Type the following command in the Terminal to build the sample app to confirm there are no compilation errors:

    ```
    dotnet build
    ```

2. Open the `\Chapter13\insufficient-randomness\before\OnlineBankingApp\Areas\Identity\PasswordHasher.cs` file and notice the `CreateSalt` method:

    ```
    private byte[] CreateSalt()
    {
        var buffer = new byte[SaltBytes];
        Random rnd = new Random();
        rnd.NextBytes(buffer);
        return buffer;
    }
    ```

3. The `CreateSalt` method generates a salt using the `Random` class and makes a call to `NextBytes` to fill in the buffer, which is an array of bytes. While the `NextBytes` method does a decent job of generating a random sequence of numbers and bytes, it is not strong enough for the purposes of our salt generation.

4. We can refactor our code to use `RNGCryptoServiceProvider` to generate a cryptographically secure and random number instead, replacing the `Random` class we used previously:

    ```
    private byte[] CreateSalt()
    {
        var buffer = new byte[SaltBytes];
        var rng = new RNGCryptoServiceProvider();
    ```

```
        rng.GetBytes(buffer);
        rng.Dispose();
        return buffer;
    }
```

The `GetBytes` method loads a cryptographically strong array of random bytes.

How it works...

A salt is a piece of random data that's included with sensitive information (such as passwords) before it's fed into a hashing method or function and saved in a persistent store. Salt offers additional protection as this piece of arbitrary data makes keys or passwords less predictable.

We can use the `RNGCryptoServiceProvider` class to generate random numbers to protect our hashed passwords from being deciphered:

```
    var rng = new RNGCryptoServiceProvider();
    rng.GetBytes(buffer);
```

> **Note**
>
> There is a performance difference when generating a random array of bytes with `RNGCryptoServiceProvider` compared to the **Pseudo-Random Number Generator (PRNG)** class, such as `Random`, but `RNGCryptoServiceProvider` provides more randomness quality and is cryptographically better.

Here is the rest of the code, which makes a call to the `CreateSalt` method. There is a `GetHash` method that expects a hash as a second parameter, along with the password to be hashed. If the salt is `null`, it will make a call to the `CreateSalt` method to generate a salt:

```
private string GetHash(string password, byte[] salt)
{
    var saltBytes = salt ?? CreateSalt();
    var argon2 = new Argon2id(Encoding.UTF8
        .GetBytes(password))
```

```
    {
        Salt = saltBytes,
        DegreeOfParallelism = Threads,
        Iterations = Iterations,
        MemorySize = Memory
    };
```

The value of `saltBytes` is used to configure the `Argon2id` class constructor's `Salt` property to hash the password.

13
Best Practices

Overall, the security of your ASP.NET Core web application typically relies on the steps a developer takes to implement security measures and write secure code. In the previous chapters and recipes of this book, we've learned what insecure code would look like, the risks such weaknesses introduce, and, most importantly, how to mitigate these security issues. But beyond the basics of secure coding are proven methods of writing code that are efficient for security. This is because they enable the necessary defensive or protective mechanisms available in the .NET framework, all of which we will examine in this chapter.

In this final chapter, we're going to cover the following recipes:

- Proper exception handling
- Using security-related cookie attributes
- Using a Content Security Policy
- Fixing leftover debug code

By the end of this chapter, you will have learned how to handle errors and exception safely, use attributes in cookies that will help protect your application from various security threats, apply a **Content Security Policy** (**CSP**) to create trust boundaries in the resources that you use in your ASP.NET Core web application, and, finally, learn how to write debugging code properly.

Technical requirements

This book was written and designed to be used with Visual Studio Code, Git, and .NET 5.0. The code examples in these recipes will be presented in ASP.NET Core Razor pages. The sample solution also uses SQLite as the database engine for a more simplified setup. The complete code examples for this chapter are available at `https://github.com/PacktPublishing/ASP.NET-Core-Secure-Coding-Cookbook/tree/main/Chapter13`.

Getting ready

For the recipes in this chapter, we will need a sample Online Banking app.

Open the command shell and download the sample Online Banking app by cloning the ASP.NET Secure Coding Cookbook repository, as follows:

```
git clone https://github.com/PacktPublishing/ASP.NET-Core-
Secure-Coding-Cookbook.git
```

Run the sample app to verify that there are no build or compile errors. In your command shell, navigate to the sample app folder at `\Chapter13\exception-handling\before\OnlineBankingApp` and run the following command:

```
dotnet build
```

The `dotnet build` command will build our sample `OnlineBankingApp` project and its dependencies.

Proper exception handling

The practice of handling errors and exceptions is part of clean and efficient coding. This technique is added in development to make our code more readable and maintainable. But more often than not, a bug arises in code due to improper error handling. This statement is also true not just with ordinary bugs. but with security bugs too. Mishandled exceptions occur because of the incorrect ways of catching these anomalies, which induces unwanted exploitation.

In this recipe, we will fix the improper handling of exceptions and prevent our sample Online Banking web app from swallowing exceptions.

Getting ready

Using Visual Studio Code, open the sample Online Banking app folder at `\Chapter13\exception-handling\before\OnlineBankingApp\`.

How to do it...

Let's take a look at the steps for this recipe:

1. From the starting exercise folder, launch Visual Studio Code by typing the following command:

```
code .
```

2. Open `Services\KnowledgebaseService.cs` and observe the `try-catch` block in the `Search` method:

```
using (XmlReader reader = XmlReader.Create(file,
    settings))
{
    try {
        XDocument xmlDoc = XDocument.Load(reader);
        // code removed for brevity
            return searchResult;
    }
    catch (Exception){
        return searchResult;
    }
}
```

Notice that the `try-catch` block is only catching a single and generic exception. The catch block also ignores the exception that may occur in our sample Online Banking web application by *swallowing* the exception.

As a best practice, we need to be specific with our exception handling. So, let's refactor our code by specifying a type of `Exception` type that is likely to occur, closest to what the block of code is trying to execute.

3. To apply the best practice in exception handling, we must add new catch blocks and rethrow the exception by instantiating its corresponding `FileFormatException` and `XmlException` types:

```
using (XmlReader reader = XmlReader.Create(file,
    settings))
{
    try {
        XDocument xmlDoc = XDocument.Load(reader);
```

```
            // code removed for brevity
        return searchResult;
    }
    catch (XmlException ex){
        _logger.LogCritical(String.Format("Reader
            error: {0}", ex.Message));
        throw new XmlException(ex.Message);
    }
    catch (Exception ex){
        _logger.LogCritical(String.Format("Reader
            error: {0}", ex.Message));
        throw new XmlException(ex.Message);
    }
}
```

> **Note**
> Throwing a new instance of either `Exception` or `XmlException` will
> make us lose the original details of the exception, which includes the stack
> trace information. The downside of this approach is that it will be harder
> to debug an application if an issue arises in production. The risk of leaking
> sensitive information from the stack trace, however, will be minimized.

How it works...

Ignoring exceptions and not catching them is bad practice and a habit that ASP.NET Core
web developers should avoid. Neglecting error conditions is an avenue for a bad actor to
take advantage of and cause malicious behavior from being seen or flagged. Ensure that
you rethrow the exceptions with fewer details to prevent information leakage. We can
do this by catching the specific exception and just gathering the exception's `Message`
property, so that we can pass it into the new instance we create with the rethrow:

```
catch (XmlException ex) {
    throw new XmlException(ex.Message);
}
```

We should anticipate that an `XmlException` type may occur since we are processing
XML files. We can add a new catch statement for this specific exception type. Using a
single catch for the generic `Exception` type is not useful if we have specific ways of
handling the exception for each type.

There's more...

Unhandled exceptions are also handled by the web server. For our sample Online Banking web application, the Kestrel web server handles the exceptions that are thrown by the app and sends an HTTP 500 Internal Error status code response before the rest of the HTTP headers are sent. Kestrel closes the connection afterward. This event could lead to the stack trace from the exception details being exposed if the trace was sent as part of the response. Following the steps in this recipe will prevent the exception details from being leaked.

Using security-related cookie attributes

Cookies are an essential part of web application development. It is a means to maintain a state in a stateless HTTP protocol and carry the most vital information that's used in security-like tokens and session data. As we learned in the *Fixing information exposure through insecure cookies* recipe of *Chapter 7, Security Misconfiguration*, the cookie attributes that we enable or disable a cookie's protection from abuse. In that recipe, we learned how the Secure and HTTP Only attributes make our cookies limited, in that they can either be sent only through secure transport, persist in the browser, or prevent arbitrary client-side scripts from reading their sensitive values.

In this recipe, we are going to learn how to use another security-related cookie attribute, **SameSite**. SameSite is a relatively new cookie attribute (at the time of writing) and is utilized to limit third-party websites from accessing a cookie marked with the context of a first party.

Getting ready

We will be using the Online Banking app we used in the previous recipe. Using Visual Studio Code, open the sample Online Banking app folder at \Chapter13\secure-cookie-policy\before\OnlineBankingApp\.

How to do it...

Let's take a look at the steps for this recipe:

1. From the starting exercise folder, launch Visual Studio Code by typing the following command:

```
code .
```

2. Open `Startup.cs` and begin adding a cookie policy globally to the middleware by adding a reference to the `Microsoft.AspNetCore.CookiePolicy` namespace:

```
using Microsoft.AspNetCore.Mvc;
using Microsoft.AspNetCore.CookiePolicy;
```

3. Next, we must add the following lines of code under the `ConfigureServices` method:

```
public void ConfigureServices(IserviceCollection
    services)
{
    services.Configure<CookiePolicyOptions>(options =>
    {
        options.MinimumSameSitePolicy =
            SameSiteMode.Strict;
        options.Secure = Environment.IsDevelopment()
            ? CookieSecurePolicy.None :
                CookieSecurePolicy.Always;
        options.HttpOnly = HttpOnlyPolicy.Always;
    });
// truncated
```

The preceding example adds the necessary security-related cookie attributes for the cookies that are generated by our sample Online Banking web app, with the addition of `MinimumSameSitePolicy`, which controls the behavior of the `SameSite` attribute of the cookies for our sample Online Banking web app. The `MinimumSameSitePolicy` property of the cookie policy's options is assigned with the `SameSiteMode.Strict` value, marking the `SameSite` cookie attribute with a `Strict` value.

4. To implement the same secure cookie policy with the Anti-CSRF token stored in the cookie, assign the `SecurePolicy` property to the `CookieSecurePolicy.Always` enum value:

```
services.AddAntiforgery(options =>
{
    options.SuppressXFrameOptionsHeader = false;
    options.Cookie.SecurePolicy =
        CookieSecurePolicy.Always;
});
```

5. Although the global cookie policy that's set via ConfigureServices will make your Anti-CSRF tokens in the cookie be marked with a SameSite attribute, you can also explicitly indicate this property to SameSiteMode.Strict. This means that the Anti-CSRF cookie will only be sent to the server if it is within same-site requests:

```
services.AddAntiforgery(options =>
{
    options.SuppressXFrameOptionsHeader = false;
    options.Cookie.SecurePolicy =
        CookieSecurePolicy.Always;
    options.Cookie.SameSite = SameSiteMode.Strict;
});
```

6. If session state cookies from the session middleware are a concern, you can limit the session state cookies to the first-party context by assigning the same SameSite property with SameSiteMode.Strict:

```
services.AddSession(options =>
{
    options.Cookie.Name = ".OnlineBanking.Session";
    options.Cookie.SameSite = SameSiteMode.Strict;
    options.Cookie.SecurePolicy =
        CookieSecurePolicy.Always;
    options.IdleTimeout = TimeSpan.FromSeconds(10);
});
```

7. Execute the cookie policy middleware by making a call to the UseCookiePolicy method in Configure:

```
app.UseRouting();

app.UseCookiePolicy();
app.UseAuthentication();
```

UseCookiePolicy, when invoked, applies the global cookie policy we have defined in ConfigureServices.

How it works...

Setting the `SameSite` cookie attribute to `Strict` limits the context as to when the cookies are sent as part of a request. As the name implies, cookies are only strictly sent within same-site and first-party requests, thus preventing third-party websites or web applications from sending the cookie when initiating the requests. This can be configured with the Session and Antiforgery service options:

```
options.Cookie.SameSite = SameSiteMode.Strict;
```

This can be done in the global cookie policy options as well:

```
options.MinimumSameSitePolicy = SameSiteMode.Strict;
```

There are a couple of things to note regarding some of the nuances of the SameSite attribute:

- Using the SameSite attribute requires the **Secure** attribute. Modern browsers will *automatically reject* the cookie if the SameSite attribute is not accompanied by a Secure attribute.

- Modern browsers, *by default*, will set your cookie's SameSite attribute to Lax if you don't explicitly specify a value. Lax allows the cookie to be sent in requests when a user follows a link.

Limiting your cookies to first-party requests also prevents your ASP.NET Core web application from cross-site attacks and vulnerabilities such as **Cross-Site Request Forgery (CSRF)**.

> **Note**
>
> A fair warning: If your ASP.NET Core web application integrates with third-party websites extensively, and these sites need to use your cookies, users might experience some malfunctioning because of the restrictive nature of the **Strict** SameSite attribute.
>
> Depending on the risk level of your web app, you may want to lower the restriction to `SameSiteMode.Lax`.

Using a Content Security Policy

Central to the web security ecosystem is the software we use daily to interact with our ASP.NET Core web application – the modern browser. Browsers have built-in security mechanisms to protect its users from attacks, making the overall user experience safe from web-based vulnerabilities. Additionally, how we write our code in our web apps is crucial to instructing the browser on how to enable these security features.

In the *Fixing disabled security features* recipe of *Chapter 7, Security Misconfiguration*, we learned that we can send special HTTP response headers to trigger the security features and tell the browser how to behave. We can tell the browser which hosts are safe to pull resources from and where it is safe to execute the scripts. These whitelisting rules can be defined using a **CSP**.

In this recipe, we will learn how to implement a basic CSP so that we can whitelist where the browser will retrieve our web resources.

Getting ready

We will be using the Online Banking app we used in the previous recipe. Using Visual Studio Code, open the sample Online Banking app folder at \Chapter13\content-security-policy\before\OnlineBankingApp\.

How to do it...

Let's take a look at the steps for this recipe:

1. From the starting exercise folder, launch Visual Studio Code by typing the following command:

    ```
    code .
    ```

2. Open Startup.cs and look at the Use method call in Configure. The middleware adds the HTTP security headers that we learned about in *Chapter 7, Security Misconfiguration*, in the *Fixing disabled security features* recipe:

    ```
    app.Use(async (context, next) =>
    {
        context.Response.Headers.Add("X-XSS-Protection",
            "1; mode=block");
        context.Response.Headers.Add("X-Content-Type-
            Options", "nosniff");
        context.Response.Headers.Add("X-Frame-Options",
            "DENY");
        await next();
    });
    app.UseHttpsRedirection();
    app.UseStaticFiles();
    ```

3. Let's add an additional layer of defense by adding a CSP to the collection of HTTP response headers:

```
app.Use(async (context, next) =>
{
    context.Response.Headers.Add("X-XSS-Protection",
        "1; mode=block");
    context.Response.Headers.Add("X-Content-Type-
        Options", "nosniff");
    context.Response.Headers.Add("X-Frame-Options",
        "DENY");

    string scriptSrc = "script-src 'self'
        https://code.jquery.com;";
    string styleSrc = "style-src 'self' 'unsafe-inline';";
    string imgSrc = "img-src 'self'
        https://www.packtpub.com/;";
    string objSrc = "object-src 'none'";
    string defaultSrc = "default-src 'self';";
    string csp = $"{defaultSrc}{scriptSrc}{styleSrc}
        {imgSrc}{objSrc}";

    context.Response.Headers.Add($"Content-Security-
        Policy", csp);
    await next();
});
```

Here, we have defined string variables to hold each of the most common CSP headers and their source locations. Then, we added them to the HTTP response headers collection as a `Content-Security-Policy` HTTP header.

Validating the Content Security Policy HTTP headers

Follow these steps to verify that the CSP is now being sent as part of the HTTP response:

1. Navigate to **Terminal | New Terminal** from the menu or simply press *Ctrl + Shift + '* in Visual Studio Code.

2. Type the following command in the Terminal to build and run the sample app:

```
dotnet run
```

3. Open a browser and go to `https://localhost:5001/`.

4. Log in using the following credentials:

   a) Email: `stanley.s.jobson@lobortis.ca`

   b) Password: `rUj5jtV8jrTyHnx!`

5. Once authenticated, you will be redirected to the home page:

Figure 13.1 – Home page authenticated

6. Press *F12* to open the browser's developer tools.

7. Go to the **Network** tab and select the first piece of HTTP traffic in the traffic list.

8. Once you have selected a form of HTTP traffic, scroll through the right-hand pane to view the corresponding HTTP response security headers:

Figure 13.2 – Content Security Policy

By doing this, the security headers will be added as part of the HTTP response that's sent by our sample Online Banking web application.

How it works...

Each of the string variables corresponds to a CSP header.

`scriptSrc` defines a list of trusted source locations to load JavaScript from. The `self` value pertains to our sample Online Banking web app itself and the host (`https://code.jquery.com`) where we downloaded the jQuery library:

```
string scriptSrc = "script-src 'self' https://code.jquery.
com;";
```

`styleSrc` defines a list of trusted source locations for loading stylesheets. We are using `self` here to indicate that it is acceptable to load stylesheets local to our web app, but we are also using `unsafe-inline` to allow the use of inline `<style>` elements. It is generally not safe to use `unsafe-inline`, but since there is no user-controlled input that can influence the stylesheet of our sample Online Banking web app, I have approved its use, as shown here:

```
string styleSrc = "style-src 'self' 'unsafe-inline';";
```

> **Note**
>
> We can't say that **CSS injection** will not occur. Future versions of the sample web app may allow user-controlled data to manage the stylesheet properties.
>
> For more information on CSS injection, visit the *Testing for CSS injection* section of the *OWASP Web Security Testing Guide* (*WSTG*):
>
> `https://owasp.org/www-project-web-security-testing-guide/stable/4-Web_Application_Security_Testing/11-Client-side_Testing/05-Testing_for_CSS_Injection.html`.

Next, we must define the acceptable values for the `img-src` CSP header. We can add the `https://www.packtpub.com/` host as a trusted source for our images:

```
string imgSrc = "img-src 'self' https://www.packtpub.com/;";
```

To have a safe CSP, `object-src` needs to be set to `none`. This CSP header will list the acceptable sources for plugins and was kept for legacy applets, which is an obsolete technology. Not placing this header indicates a high severity for being unsafe by **Google's CSP Validator** (more information about this tool can be found in the *There's more…* section of this recipe):

```
string objSrc = "object-src 'none'";
```

Finally, the `default-src` CSP header is the fallback for all other CSP headers that weren't defined.

```
string defaultSrc = "default-src 'self';";
string csp = $"{defaultSrc}{scriptSrc}{styleSrc}
    {imgSrc}{objSrc}";
context.Response.Headers.Add($"Content-Security-Policy", csp);
```

The preceding code also concatenates the CSP headers using string interpolation and adds them to the HTTP response headers collection.

There's more...

You must include a *nonce* as the source for `script-src` or `style-src` if you need to place inline scripts and styles in your Razor pages. This cryptographic string *must be unique in every request*, to ensure that a malicious actor does not inject the inline scripts or styles that are executed and rendered through an XSS vulnerability in your ASP.NET Core web application. To enable this security feature quickly and to relieve the task of generating an unguessable nonce, use the `NWebsec TagHelpers for ASP.NET Core` by performing the following steps:

1. Install the necessary package:

    ```
    dotnet add package NWebsec.AspNetCore.Mvc.TagHelpers
    ```

2. Import the `NWebSec` tag helpers into `_ViewImports.cshtml`:

    ```
    @addTagHelper *, Microsoft.AspNetCore.Mvc.TagHelpers
    @addTagHelper *, NWebsec.AspNetCore.Mvc.TagHelpers
    ```

    Then, utilize the `nws-csp-add-nonce` helper within your `script` or `style` tags:

    ```
    @model IndexModel
    @{
        ViewData["Title"] = "Home page";
    }
    <style nws-csp-add-nonce="true"></style>
    <script nws-csp-add-nonce="true">
        console.log('nonce added');
    ```

```
</script>
this in turn will render the following markup
<style nonce="QqTsxf7Oqqu0GOLPa36y21IV"></style>
<script nonce="HlbkIsOBsmI66GXwH5635KBk">
    console.log('nonce added');
</script>
```

Furthermore, the CSP header we used in this recipe is not comprehensive. To learn more about other CSP headers, read the *CSP* documentation on the *Mozilla Developer Network (MDN)* website: `https://developer.mozilla.org/en-US/docs/Web/HTTP/Headers/Content-Security-Policy`.

There are tools online that you can use to generate your own CSP. The Report URI CSP Generator allows you to simply tick the CSP headers you want to include in your CSP and fill in the textboxes with acceptable hosts, as shown here:

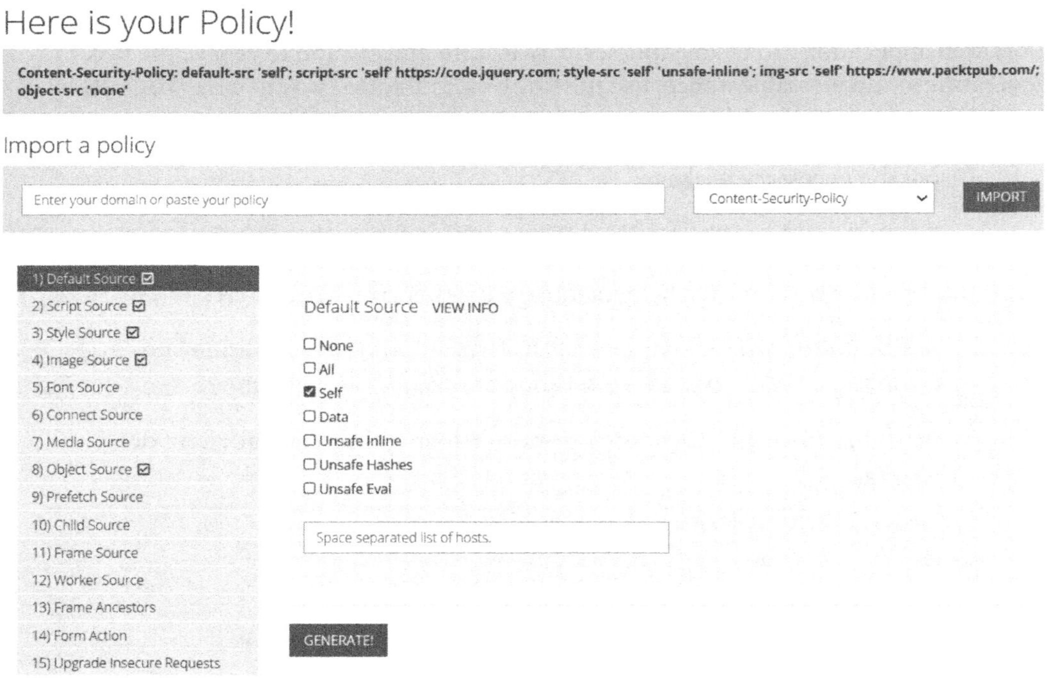

Figure 13.3 – Report URI CSP Generator

Here is the link to the online tool: `https://report-uri.com/home/generate`.

Another excellent tool you can use to validate the safety of the generated CSP is Google's CSP validator, available at `https://csp-evaluator.withgoogle.com/`:

CSP Evaluator

CSP Evaluator allows developers and security experts to check if a Content Security Policy (CSP) serves as a strong mitigation against cross-site scripting attacks. It assists with the process of reviewing CSP policies, which is usually a manual task, and helps identify subtle CSP bypasses which undermine the value of a policy. CSP Evaluator checks are based on a large-scale study and are aimed to help developers to harden their CSP and improve the security of their applications. This tool (also available as a Chrome extension) is provided only for the convenience of developers and Google provides no guarantees or warranties for this tool.

Content Security Policy

Sample unsafe policy   Sample safe policy

```
default-src 'self';script-src 'self' https://code.jquery.com;style-src 'self' 'unsafe-inline';img-src 'self'
    https://www.packtpub.com/;object-src 'none'|
```

CSP Version 3   ⌄   @

CHECK CSP

Evaluated CSP as seen by a browser supporting CSP Version 3   expand/collapse all

✓ default-src   ⌄
ⓘ script-src   ⌄
✓ style-src   ⌄
✓ img-src   ⌄
✓ object-src   ⌄

Figure 13.4 – Google's CSP Validator

The CSP Validator was developed by *Lukas Weichselbaum*, one of Google's Staff Information Security Engineers. With this tool, you can verify the policy you've placed in the box against different versions of CSP, and verify whether your CSP has a strong defense against **Cross-Site Scripting** (**XSS**).

Fixing leftover debug code

Debugging and testing your code is part of an overall cycle of building an ASP.NET Core web application. The .NET platform offers a wide array of libraries and components for debugging, including diagnostics and tracing effectively. However, it is a bad practice for developers to leave debugging code as-is and neglect to remove it from the repository or add conditional checks, thus leading to unnecessary code being deployed in production.

In this recipe, we will learn how to ensure that environment validation is applied to verify whether the necessary debugging methods are called.

Getting ready

We will be using the Online Banking app we used in the previous recipe. Using Visual Studio Code, open the sample Online Banking app folder at `\Chapter13\leftover-debug-code\before\OnlineBankingApp\`.

How to do it...

Let's take a look at the steps for this recipe:

1. From the starting exercise folder, launch Visual Studio Code by typing the following command:

    ```
    code .
    ```

2. Open `Startup.cs` and, at `Configure`, notice the call to the following function:

    ```
    app.UseStatusCodePages(
       "text/plain", "Status code page, status code: {0}");
    ```

    `UseStatusCodePages` is a piece of middleware that provides `status code` as a response. This is useful for determining what status code was returned by our sample Online Banking app, but these status codes are not useful to our users.

3. In the same `Startup.cs` file, notice the call to the following statement:

    ```
    services.AddDatabaseDeveloperPageExceptionFilter();
    ```

    `AddDatabaseDeveloperPageExceptionFilter` is an exception filter that provides exception details related to database operations. This method is useful for debugging and finding resolutions to DB-related issues. However, it must not be called in a production environment.

4. To prevent these debugging methods from being executed in production, add a check that will verify whether the current context is running in a development environment before making these calls:

    ```
    if (Environment.IsDevelopment())
    {
        services.AddDatabaseDeveloperPageExceptionFilter();
    }
    ```

5. `UseStatusCodePages` is also placed in a code block that will only be invoked when the environment is in development due to the `IsDevelopment()` method:

```
if (env.IsDevelopment())
{
    app.UseDeveloperExceptionPage();
    app.UseStatusCodePages(
        "text/plain", "Status code page, status code:
            {0}");
}
else
{
    app.UseExceptionHandler("/Error");
    app.UseHsts();
}
```

This prevents our sample Online Banking web application from divulging sensitive information when an unexpected error occurs.

How it works...

The `IsDevelopment` method checks whether the code is running under the context of a development environment. This method is a useful test before we execute debugging methods such as `UseStatusCodePages` and `AddDatabaseDeveloperPageExceptionFilter`.

`AddDatabaseDeveloperPageExceptionFilter` could potentially expose sensitive information when invoked by a database error. Performing secure code reviews regularly and executing static application security testing as part of the development cycle can help detect these problems early.

There's more...

Secure software development is a broad subject and writing secure code is just a subset of this practice. Every ASP.NET Core web developer must ensure that the basic tenets of security (*Confidentiality*, *Integrity*, and *Availability*) are applied in code. Write code with these security requirements in mind.

While this chapter discussed how to fix security issues and bugs, the techniques we've learned about here can be used to proactively review code and search for vulnerabilities early in the process. Detecting security problems in code beforehand and having that *Shift Left* culture helps developers further reduce risk, resulting in a more attack-resilient ASP. NET Core web application at the end of each cycle.

Packt.com

Subscribe to our online digital library for full access to over 7,000 books and videos, as well as industry leading tools to help you plan your personal development and advance your career. For more information, please visit our website.

Why subscribe?

- Spend less time learning and more time coding with practical eBooks and Videos from over 4,000 industry professionals

- Improve your learning with Skill Plans built especially for you

- Get a free eBook or video every month

- Fully searchable for easy access to vital information

- Copy and paste, print, and bookmark content

Did you know that Packt offers eBook versions of every book published, with PDF and ePub files available? You can upgrade to the eBook version at packt.com and as a print book customer, you are entitled to a discount on the eBook copy. Get in touch with us at customercare@packtpub.com for more details.

At www.packt.com, you can also read a collection of free technical articles, sign up for a range of free newsletters, and receive exclusive discounts and offers on Packt books and eBooks.

Other Books You May Enjoy

If you enjoyed this book, you may be interested in these other books by Packt:

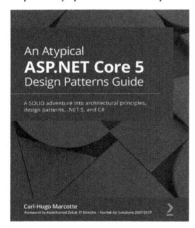

An Atypical ASP.NET Core 5 Design Patterns Guide

Carl-Hugo Marcotte

ISBN: 978-1-78934-609-1

- Apply the SOLID principles for building flexible and maintainable software
- Get to grips with .NET 5 dependency injection
- Work with GoF design patterns such as strategy, decorator, and composite
- Explore the MVC patterns for designing web APIs and web applications using Razor
- Discover layering techniques and tenets of clean architecture
- Become familiar with CQRS and vertical slice architecture as an alternative to layering
- Understand microservices, what they are, and what they are not
- Build ASP.NET UI from server-side to client-side Blazor

ASP.NET Core 5 and Angular - Fourth Edition

Valerio De Sanctis

ISBN: 978-1-80056-033-8

- Implement a web API interface with ASP.NET Core and consume it with Angular using RxJS observables

- Set up an SQL database server using a local instance or a cloud data store

- Perform C# and TypeScript debugging using Visual Studio 2019

- Create TDD and BDD unit tests using xUnit, Jasmine, and Karma

- Perform DBMS structured logging using third-party providers such as SeriLog

- Deploy web apps to Windows and Linux web servers, or Azure App Service, using IIS, Kestrel, and nginx

Packt is searching for authors like you

If you're interested in becoming an author for Packt, please visit authors.
packtpub.com and apply today. We have worked with thousands of developers and
tech professionals, just like you, to help them share their insight with the global tech
community. You can make a general application, apply for a specific hot topic that we are
recruiting an author for, or submit your own idea.

Share Your Thoughts

Now you've finished *ASP.NET Core 5 Secure Coding Cookbook*, we'd love to hear your
thoughts! Scan the QR code below to go straight to the Amazon review page for this book
and share your feedback or leave a review on the site that you purchased it from.

https://packt.link/r/180107156X

Your review is important to us and the tech community and will help us make sure we're
delivering excellent quality content.

Index

Made in the USA
Coppell, TX
04 October 2021